Postcard History Series

Federalsburg

in Vintage Postcards

POSTCARD HISTORY SERIES

Federalsburg

IN VINTAGE POSTCARDS

Federalsburg Historical Society, Inc.

ARCADIA
PUBLISHING

ISBN 978-0-7385-1574-8

Published by Arcadia Publishing
Charleston SC, Chicago IL, Portsmouth NH, San Francisco CA

Printed in the United States of America

Library of Congress Catalog Card Number: 2003109647

For all general information contact Arcadia Publishing at:
Telephone 843-853-2070
Fax 843-853-0044
E-mail sales@arcadiapublishing.com
For customer service and orders:
Toll-Free 1-888-313-2665

Visit us on the Internet at www.arcadiapublishing.com

Contents

Acknowledgments		6
Introduction		7
1.	Street Scenes and Residences	9
2.	Business and Industry	47
3.	The Railroad and The River	69
4.	Schools and Churches	93
5.	Postcards of Interest	109
Bibliography		126

Acknowledgments

The Federalsburg Historical Society was formed in February of 2002. Our mission statement reads, "The Federalsburg Historical Society, Inc. is a non-profit, community-based organization dedicated to preserving and presenting to the public the history of the people, places, and events of the town of Federalsburg on the Eastern Shore of Maryland. Working in conjunction with the Caroline County Historical Society, Inc., we promote and celebrate our unique heritage through historical research, education and events." We hope that the information contained within these pages will provide the reader with a better understanding of Federalsburg, a town whose motto is "Pride in the past, faith in the future."

We sincerely wish to thank the following individuals who lent to the Federalsburg Historical Society part of their postcard collection for the purpose of compiling this book: Francis A. "Sonny" Callahan, Robert S. Detweiler, Scott Freeman, R. Allan Gorsuch, William F. Gray Jr., Mary Holt, Charles S. Long, Archie Palamaras, Danny Phillips, Jeff Porter, Carlene Schmick, and Jeanne H. Trice. We thank the many people who provided information through countless telephone conversations. We wish to thank the Caroline County Public Library and their website, which has issues of the *Denton Journal* newspaper online from 1880 to 1965. This was an invaluable source of information. We wish to thank the mayor and council and the town of Federalsburg for their interest and support of this project.

Finally, we wish to thank those members who dedicated time to the material gathering, proofing, and construction of this book, especially Wendy Garner, Steve Matthews, Danny Phillips, John Phillips, Carlene Schmick, and Sam Smith.

INTRODUCTION

The town of Federalsburg is rich in history, although the actual date of its founding and reason for the name is not clearly known. Local historians agree that the town was founded in 1791 by Isaac Nichols on a tract of land called "Rawley" to the east of the Northwest Fork of the Nanticoke River. This waterway has long been called the Marshyhope Creek. The first village settled along this area was known as Marshyhope and later as Northwest Fork Bridge. Eventually the town was named Federalsburg (Federalsburgh.) One myth is that the town was named for the dominant influence of the Federalist Party in the latter part of the 18th century and that the title attached to the village. However, records show that Federalsburg was referred to in the land records of Caroline before 1787 and therefore before the Federalist Party was formed. We may never know the exact cause for the name but it has lasted for well over 200 years.

By the mid-1850s, there were two streets, Main and Bridge Streets, that served as the principal highways. Early businesses included general stores, a smith and carriage shop, and the village hotel and industries included grist and lumber mills, tanyards, and shipbuilding. The town has been surrounded by rich farmlands, and in the latter part of the 19th and early 20th centuries, canneries provided a profitable industry. The railroad was built through the village in 1867–1868, which helped to move produce and other goods to Baltimore and Philadelphia. During the 1900s, there were dairies, bakeries, banks, a printing office, photographers, ice plants, ice cream makers, and many other establishments.

Until 1880, Main Street was the dividing line between Caroline and Dorchester Counties, which created a problem for those residents on the Dorchester side who had to go to Cambridge to pay their taxes and whose children had to attend a different school outside of town. A petition was sent to the legislature, and the boundary line was changed in 1880 to allow the town to be entirely in Caroline County. A sum of $614 was paid to Dorchester County by the transferred taxpayers to alleviate this concern.

The history of the town would not be complete without the mentioning of the periodic flooding of the Marshyhope. From time to time, the creek has overflowed its banks, causing much misery and damage of property. The largest and most destructive flood known occurred in 1935 when the water level on Main Street was measured as high as 12 feet. The railroad bridge and numerous dams washed out around the town. People were rescued from their porch roofs or second floors by rowboat. Other less disastrous floods occurred both before and after until in the mid–1960s when the channel of the creek was diverted by the U.S. Soil Conservation Service.

Much of the history of the town has been lost through the passage of time, but fortunately, from time to time, postcards were made of some of the scenes of interest. We present these to you in the hope that they will bring back memories for some and help later generations to understand what life was like in the past.

One

Street Scenes and Residences

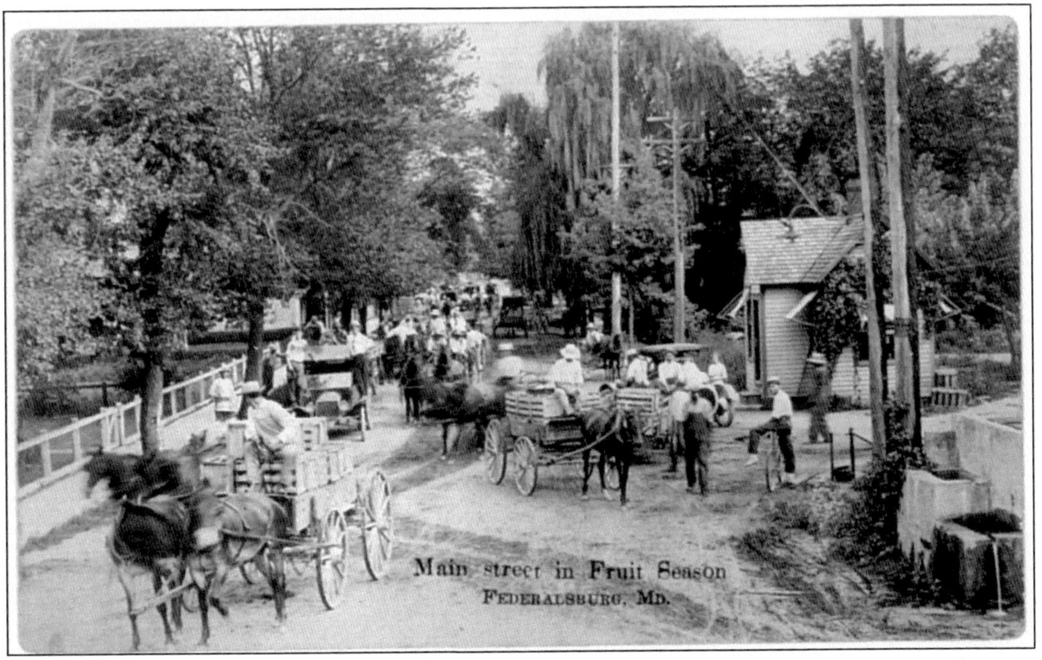

South Main Street from the Railroad Looking North. Farmers brought their strawberries, packed in crates, to the "Auction Block," where they were auctioned off to the highest bidder by auctioneers Leonard Covey and Calvert Todd. Strawberries were the big cash crop in the spring and the schools ran on "strawberry schedule" so that the boys and girls could pick strawberries in the mornings. (From the Laurence G. Claggett collection.)

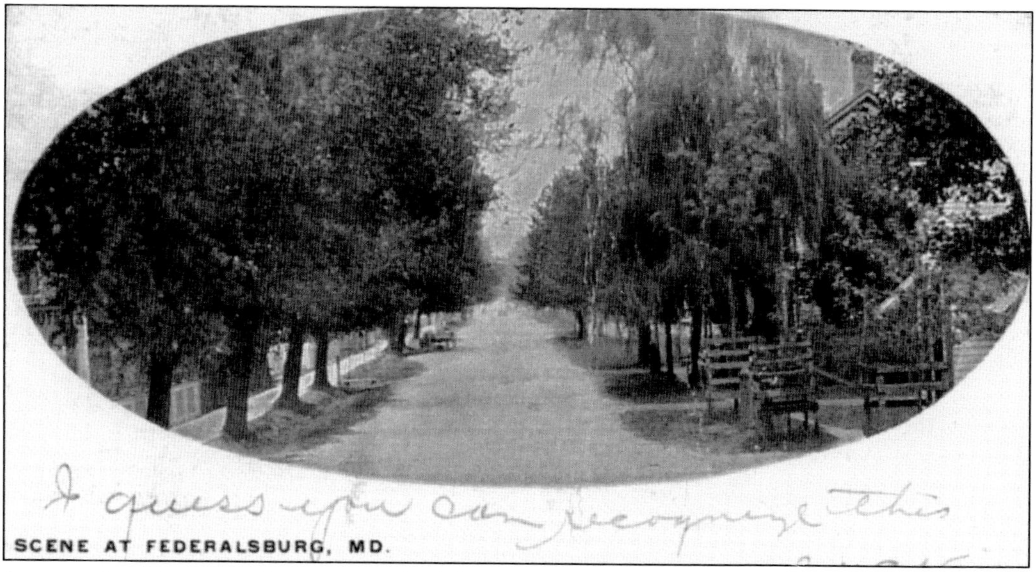

South Main Street. This is a view looking from the train station towards town around 1904. At that time, Main Street went from the station to the "Point" (the intersection between Main Street, Bloomingdale Avenue, and Old Denton Road), about three-fourths of a mile. A cement sidewalk was laid beside it without a break except at street crossings. Many of the streets in town limits were hard, white shell roads. About three miles inside the town and about four miles outside the limits had been laid by 1904. These roads were built at a cost around $1,000 per mile. One-half of the entire expense of all the shell roads leading into the town was met by subscription, raised by the cooperation of the citizens in town and the surrounding country. (From the Laurence G. Claggett collection.)

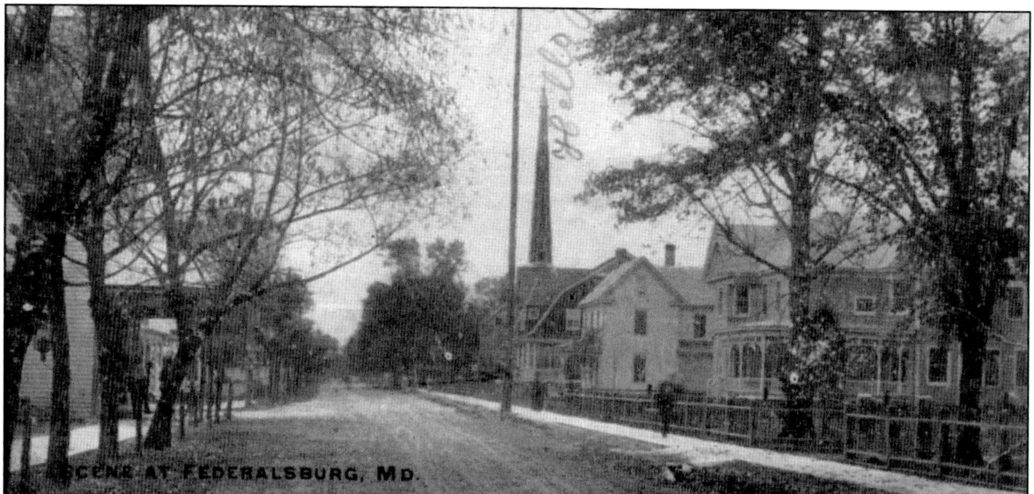

Looking South on Main Street around 1904. On the left was the store of Orlando Patton, dealer in fine groceries, fruits, meats, flour, dry goods, notions, boots, shoes, queensware, and a complete line of gents' furnishings, according to an 1904 advertisement. The building was at the corner of Main and Bridge (Central Avenue) Streets. On the right would be Senator E.E. Goslin's lawn and the home of Mrs. Julia Wright, and later the residence of A.H. Covey. (From the Archie Palamaras collection.)

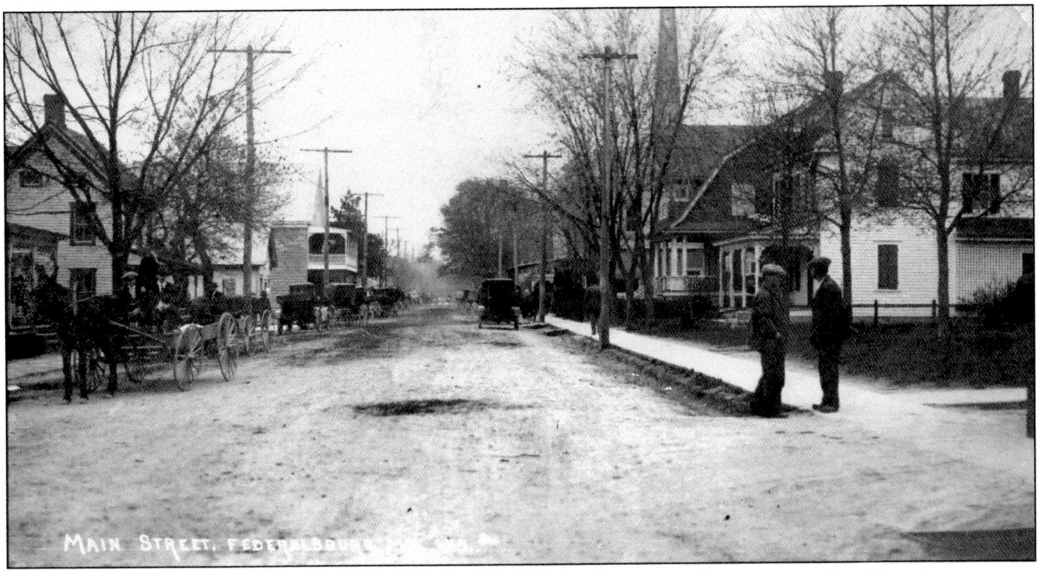

South Main Street. This picture is looking south from the intersection of Bridge Street, now known as Central Avenue. The house on the right has been the Town Office and is now the office of Powell Realtors. The building on the left with the upstairs porch was the John W. Hurlock hardware store, and later the Jones Brothers Hardware and Morean's Hardware. This building is now being renovated by Joe and Donna Glime and will open as The Hub, an antiques mall. (From the Danny Phillips collection.)

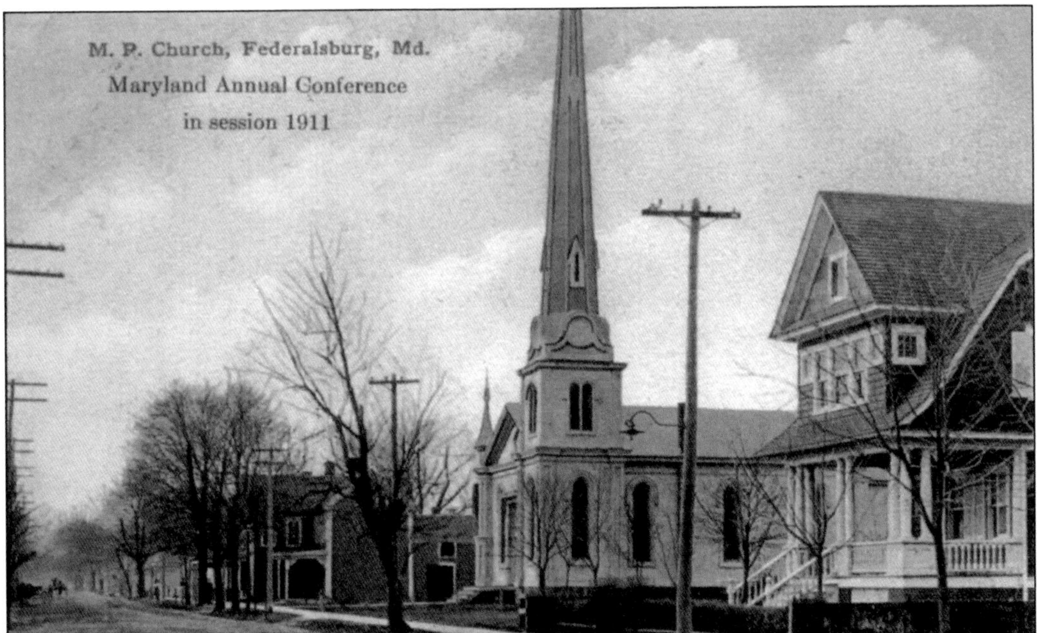

South Main Street. This is a closer view of the M.P. Church (Christ United Methodist Church) with its beautiful steeple. You can see that Maple Avenue, which today runs beside the church, has not been cut through yet. (From the Danny Phillips collection.)

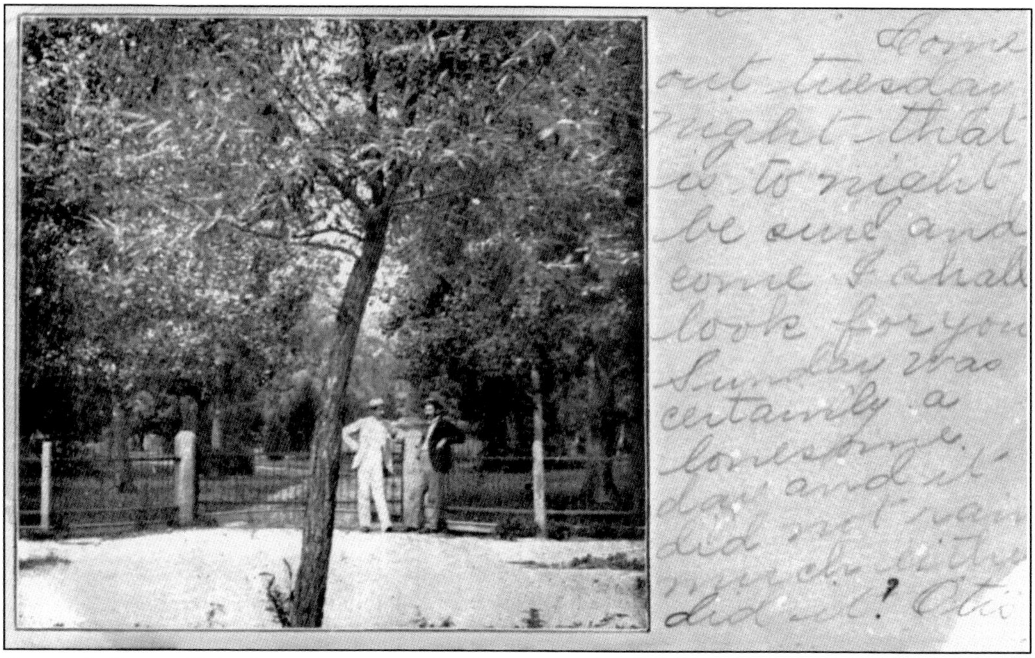

Goslin's Lawn. This view of a property bordering South Main Street was part of a 150-acre tract belonging to Sen. Edward E. Goslin, which included his residence, the old family home, and a beautiful lawn. He was president of the First National Bank, built the first tomato canning factory in town, and was a prominent dealer in cord-wood, among other interests. He was a member of the Nanticoke Lodge of Masons, Number 172 and had been a past master. He had never married. In 1890, he entered public life as a member of the House of Delegates. He withdrew from public office after the 1904 session until 1909 when he was elected to the State Senate. Goslin died unexpectedly in 1914, at the age of 58. He was considered one of the leading public men on the Eastern Shore for his time. (Top postcard from the Charles S. Long collection; bottom postcard from the Danny Phillips collection.)

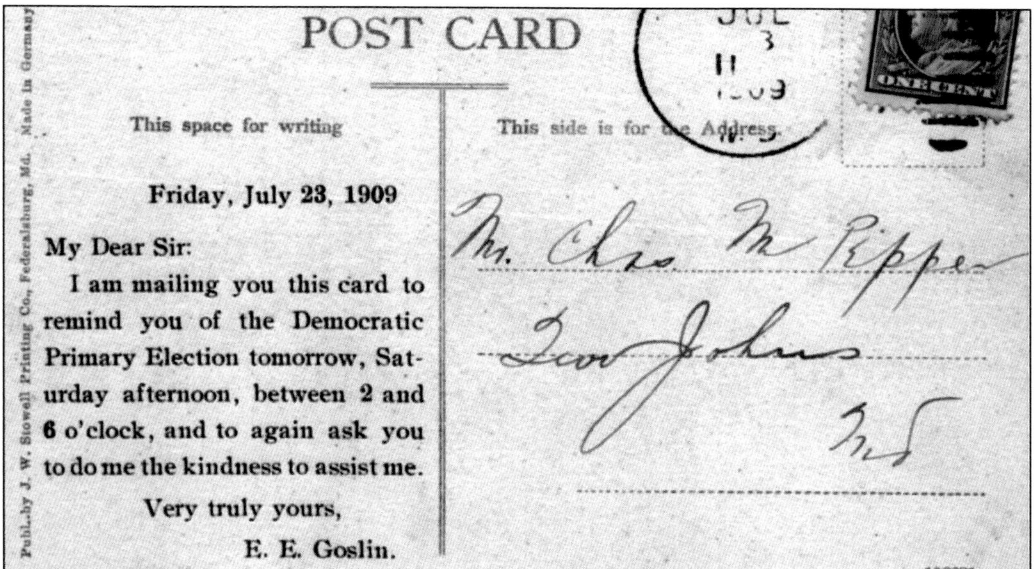

POST CARD

This space for writing

Friday, July 23, 1909

My Dear Sir:

I am mailing you this card to remind you of the Democratic Primary Election tomorrow, Saturday afternoon, between 2 and 6 o'clock, and to again ask you to do me the kindness to assist me.

Very truly yours,

E. E. Goslin.

This side is for the Address.

Publ. by J. W. Stowell Printing Co., Federalsburg, Md. Made in Germany

198621

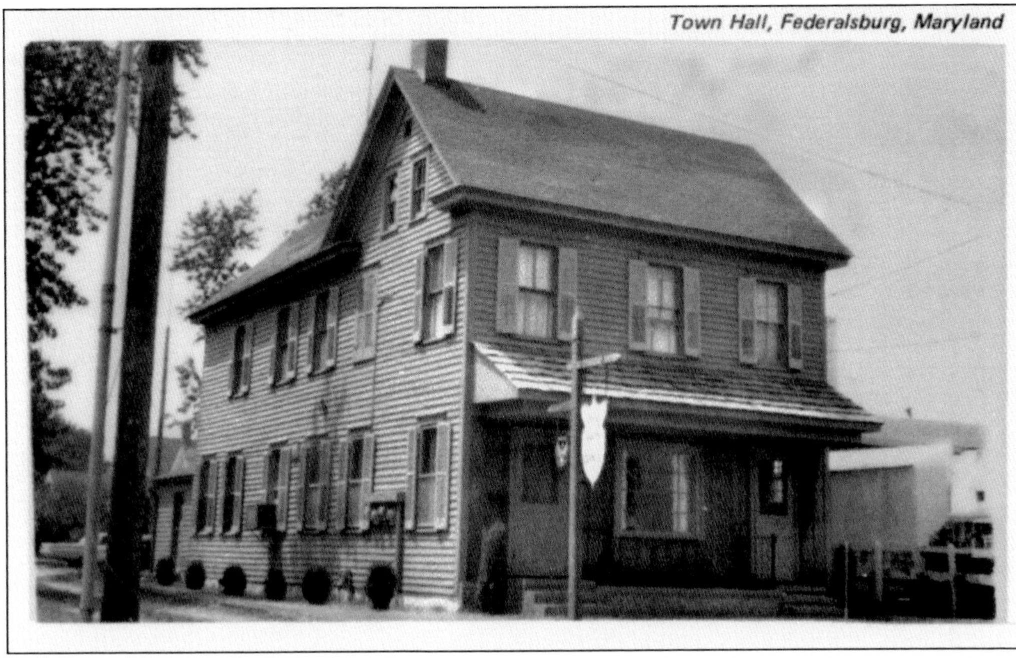

Old Town Hall. This house on South Main Street had been damaged by a fire and was remodeled by Torbert Williamson for use as the town hall. In 1978, the Federal Theatre on North Main Street was remodeled and became the town office and senior center. This house now serves as the office of Powell Realtors. (From the Danny Phillips collection.)

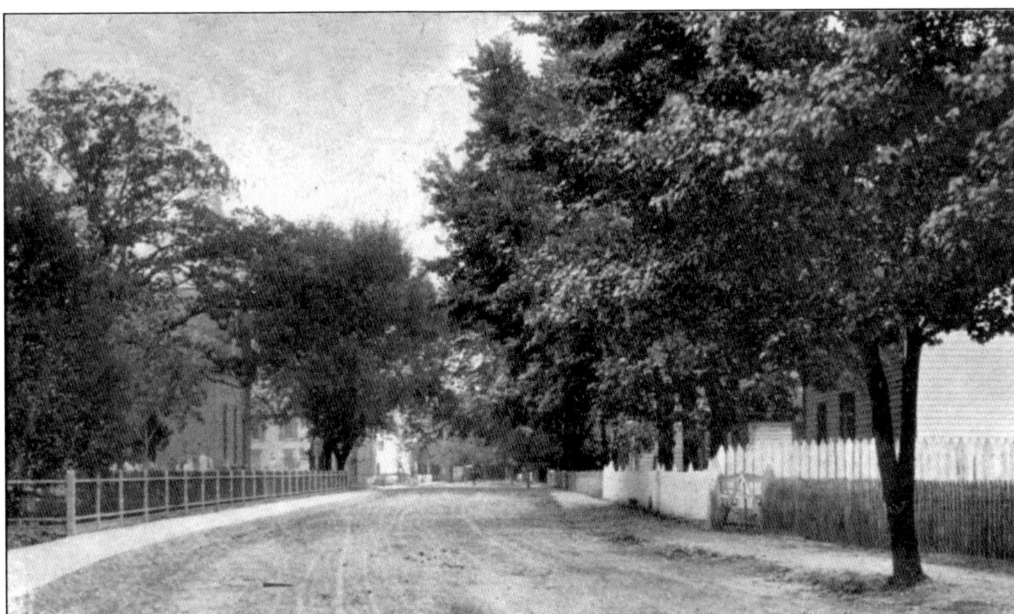

North Main Street around 1904. The left-side view is of Union M.E. Church, now Union United Methodist Church, and its cemetery. The fence around the cemetery has been replaced by a brick wall and the wooden church has been bricked. The postcard was mailed on July 30, 1906. (From the Jeff Porter collection.)

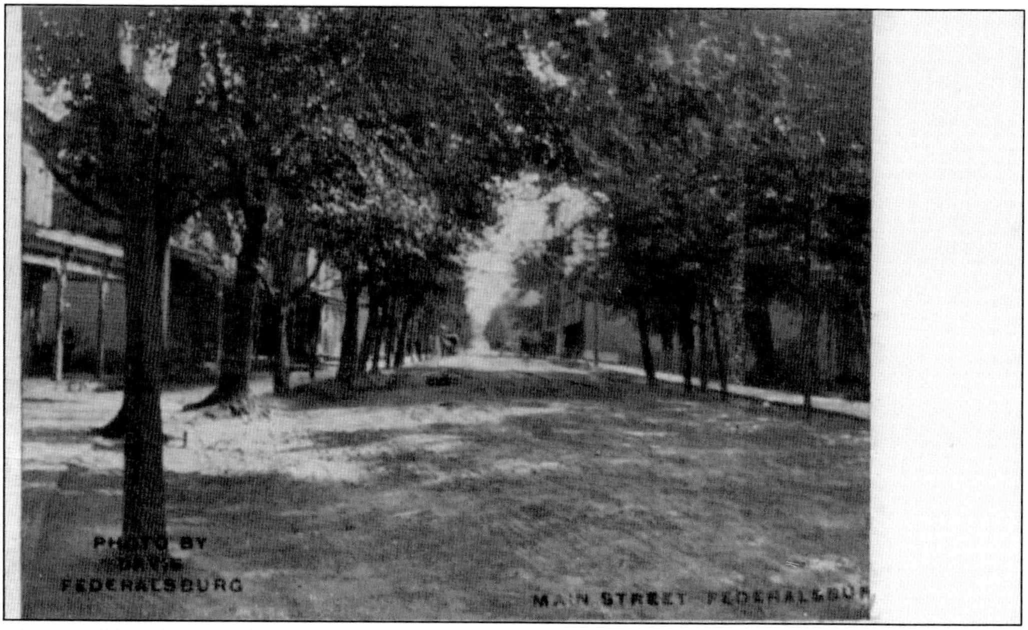

North Main Street. The road is not yet paved and the trees are growing along the edge of the street. (From the Danny Phillips collection.)

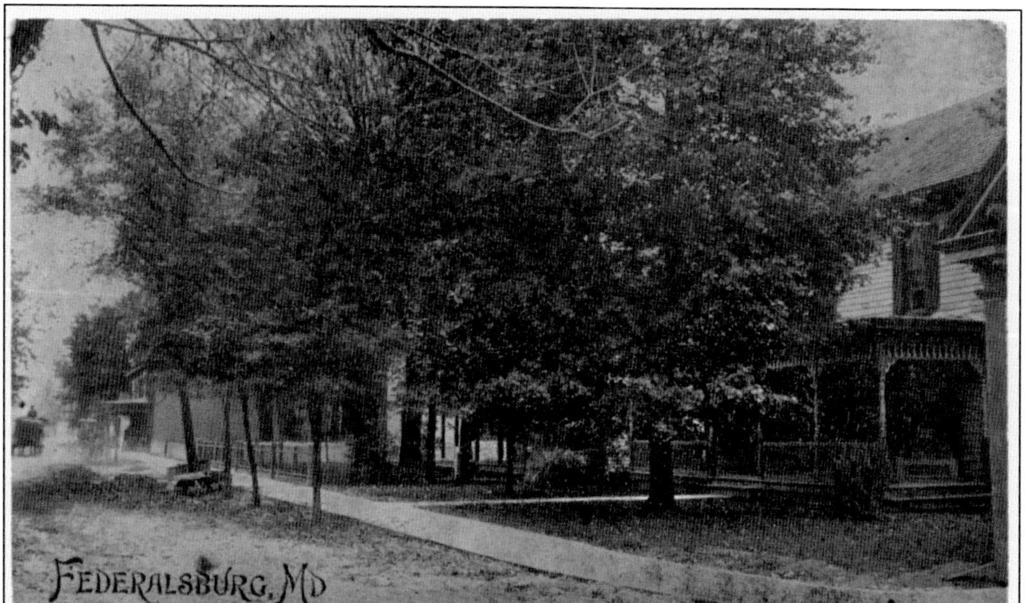

North Main Street. This is an early view with sidewalks but the roads are not yet paved. Front porches were popular as were front-yard fences. (From the Archie Palamaras collection.)

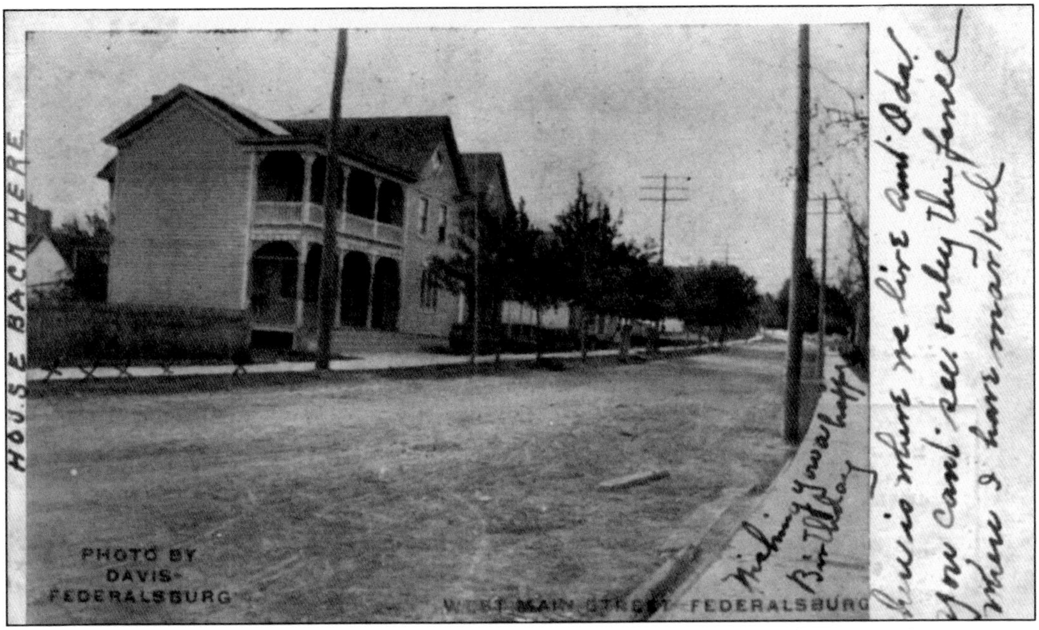

North Main Street Around 1904. This establishment was known as the Davis Photo House. Mr. William H. Davis established an enterprise as a photographer around 1895. Along with the photo business, there was a framing department with a line of mouldings for made-to-order work. Several photographs from this house captured prizes for best work submitted. The photo on this postcard, as well as others in this book, were taken by Davis Photo House. This house has since been converted to apartments. (From the Danny Phillips collection.)

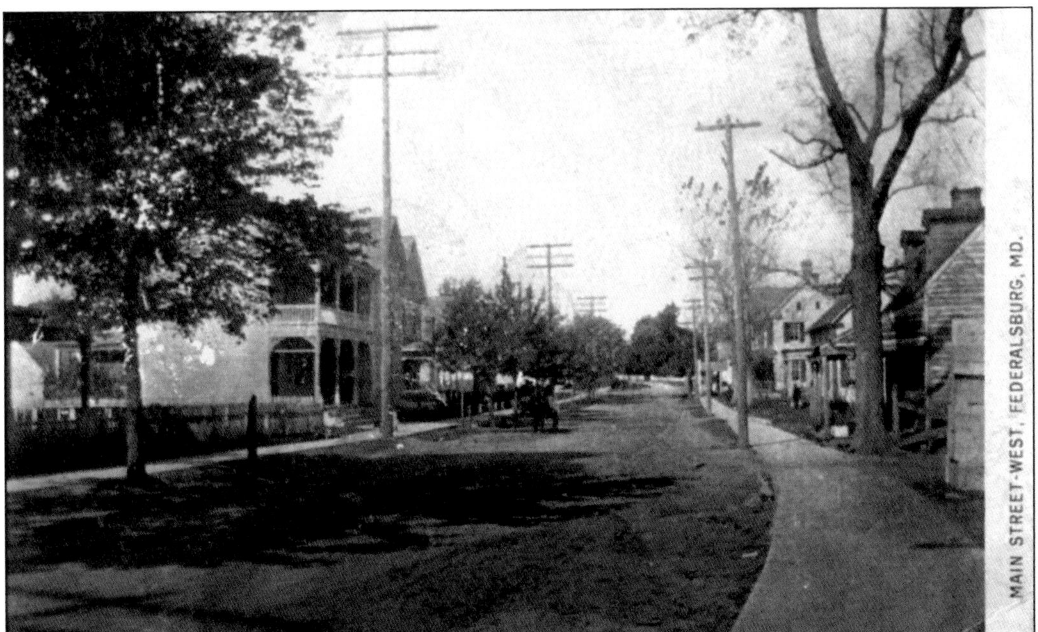

North Main Street. This Davis photo is a similar view as above but includes the scene on both sides of the street. The postmark was dated 1908. (From the Jeanne H. Trice collection.)

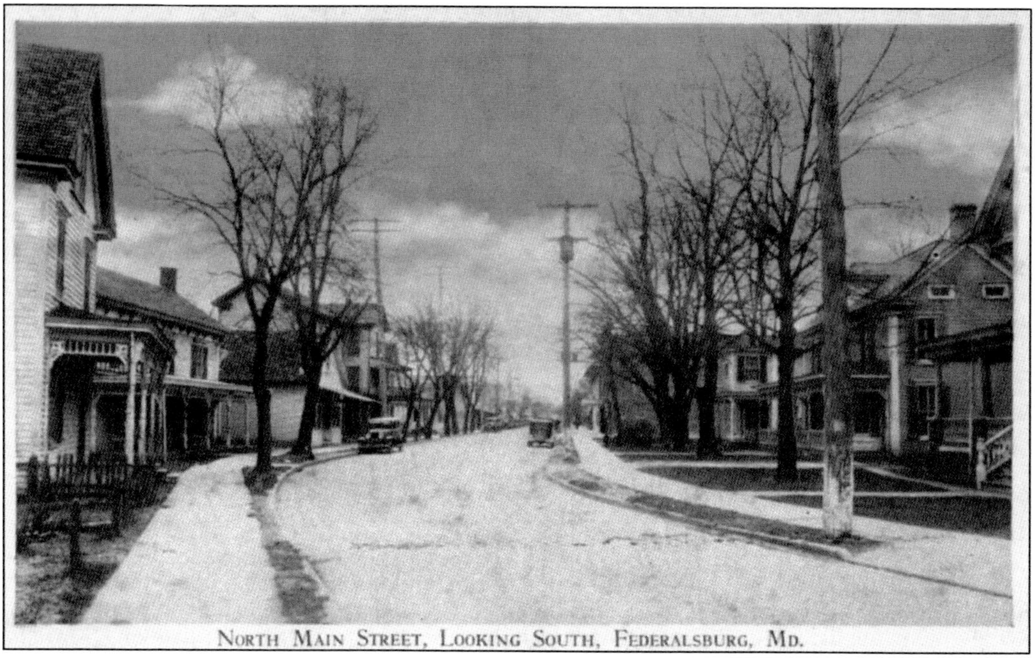

NORTH MAIN STREET. The first house on the left is still at this location but without the front porch. The second house on the left was moved to West Central Avenue. The main streets are paved with oyster shells and have curbing. (From the Danny Phillips collection.)

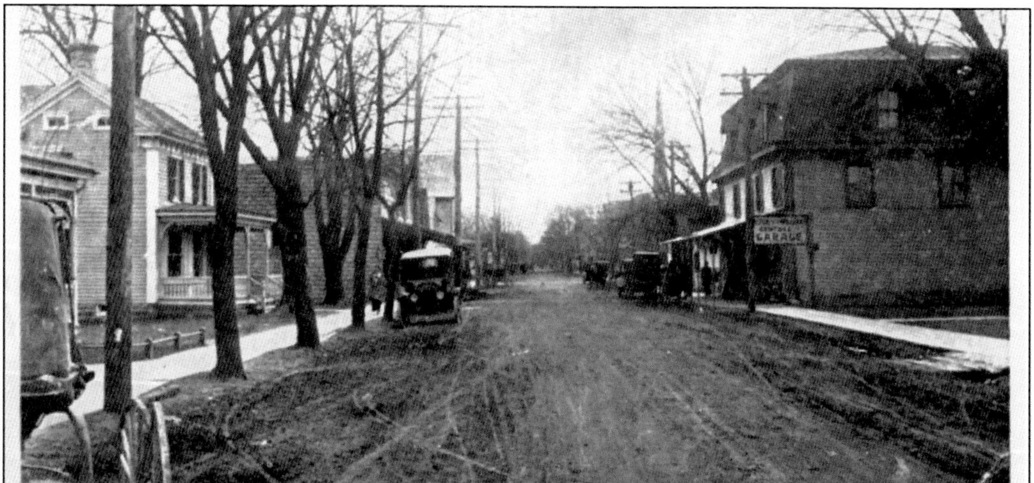

NORTH MAIN STREET. The postcard says "Main Street looking north," but should read "North Main Street looking south." The building on the right was known as "The Block," which was built around 1867 as a store and once served as the town hall. Many businesses and activities took place here, including general merchandising, a tailoring shop, the town's earliest printing office, a drug store, the post office, an ice cream "saloon," and a hardware store. It also housed the first theater of the town, known as the Music Hall. The building was moved to make room for the Masonic Temple, then razed in 1931 to make way for a modern theater, known as the Federal Theatre. (From the Francis A. "Sonny" Callahan collection.)

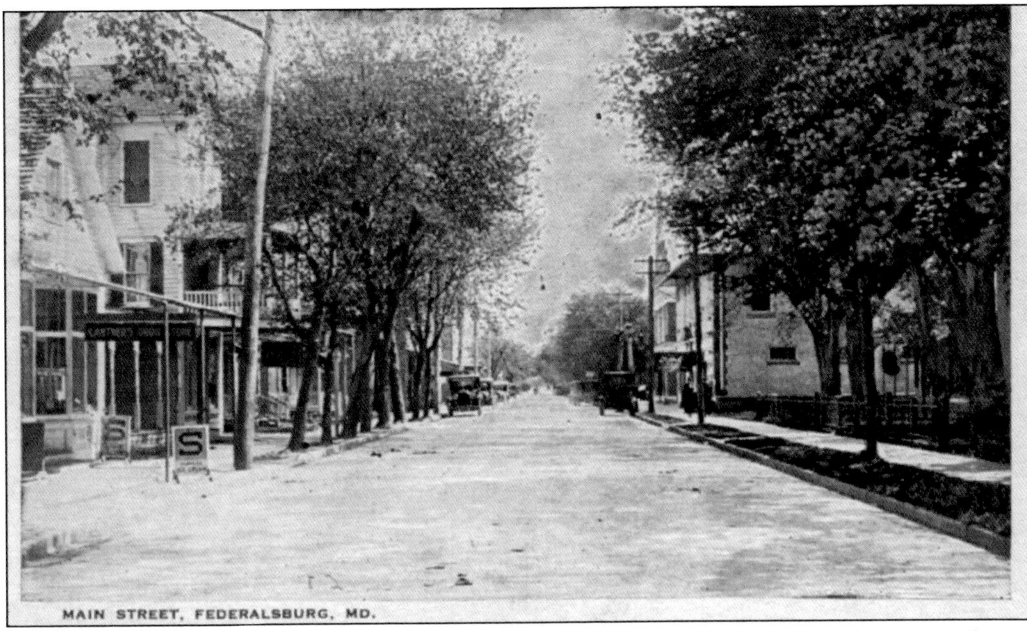

NORTH MAIN STREET. Looking south, the buildings on the right are the Masonic Temple and Long and Short, Inc. On the left was the first location of Cantner's Drug Store, which is still in business today in town. (From the Danny Phillips collection.)

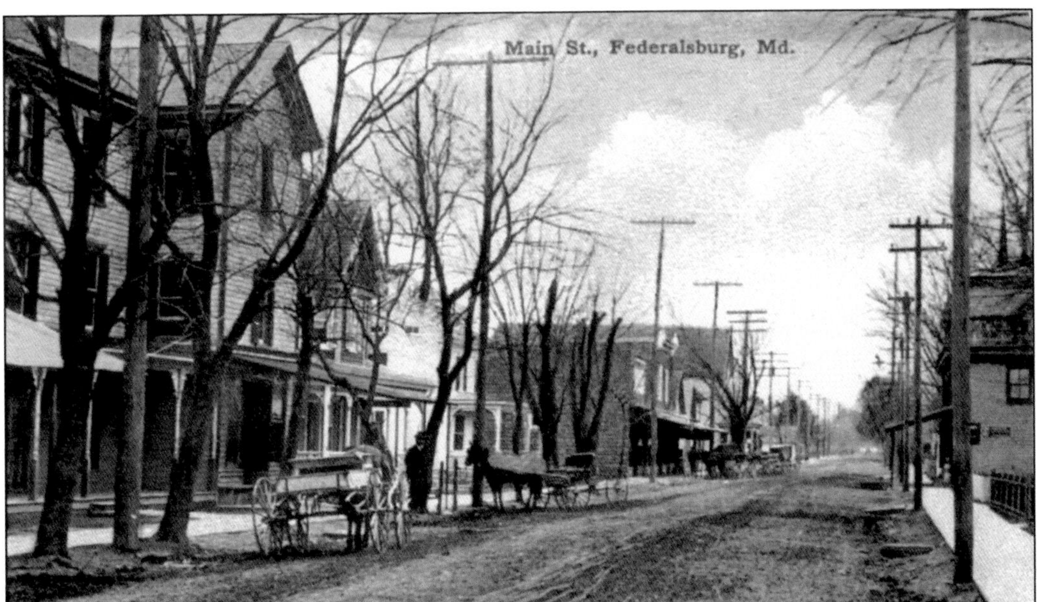

NORTH MAIN STREET. Looking south, the building on the left is now in use as an apartment house on the second and third floors and Millman's Barber Shop and Satellite Depot/D&M Electronics on the first floor. The first floor has been used for other retail businesses, including Wm. Richardson Jeweler from 1953 to 1993. At one time, the building also served as the town office. (From the Danny Phillips collection.)

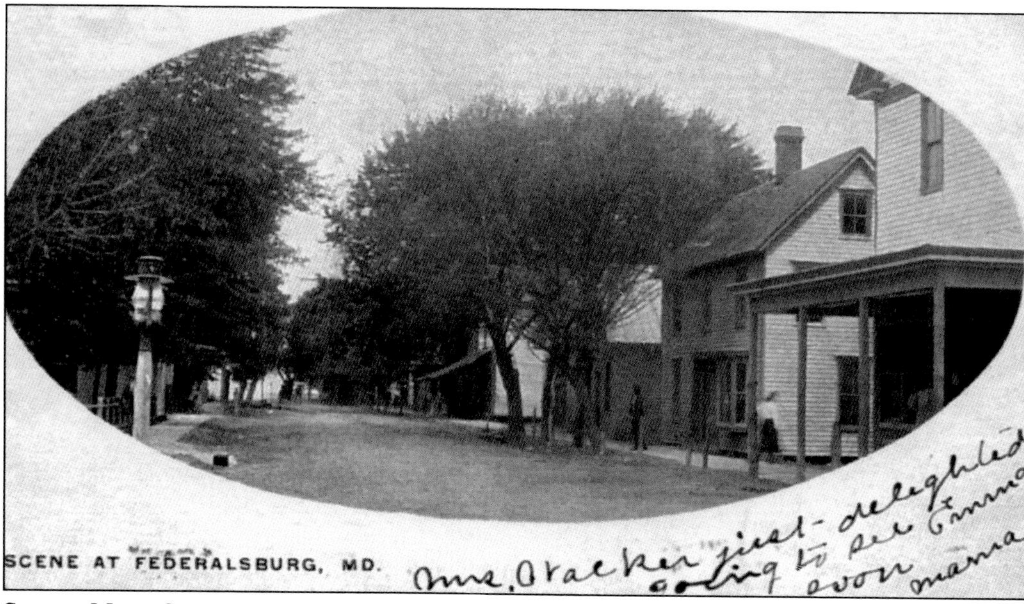

SOUTH MAIN STREET AROUND 1904. Looking north, the lamp post is at the bottom of Sen. Edward E. Goslin's lawn and the building with the covered porch across the street was Orlando Patton's General Store on the corner of Main and Bridge Streets. This was one of four large general merchandise stores in Federalsburg at the turn of the century, which carried an extensive and well-selected line of dry goods, notions, shoes, hats, gents' furnishings, carpets, crockery ware, groceries, and more. Federal Independent Order of Odd Fellows (IOOF) No. 35 was organized in Federalsburg on October 20, 1899 and met every Tuesday evening in the Odd Fellows Hall over this store. (From the Laurence G. Claggett collection.)

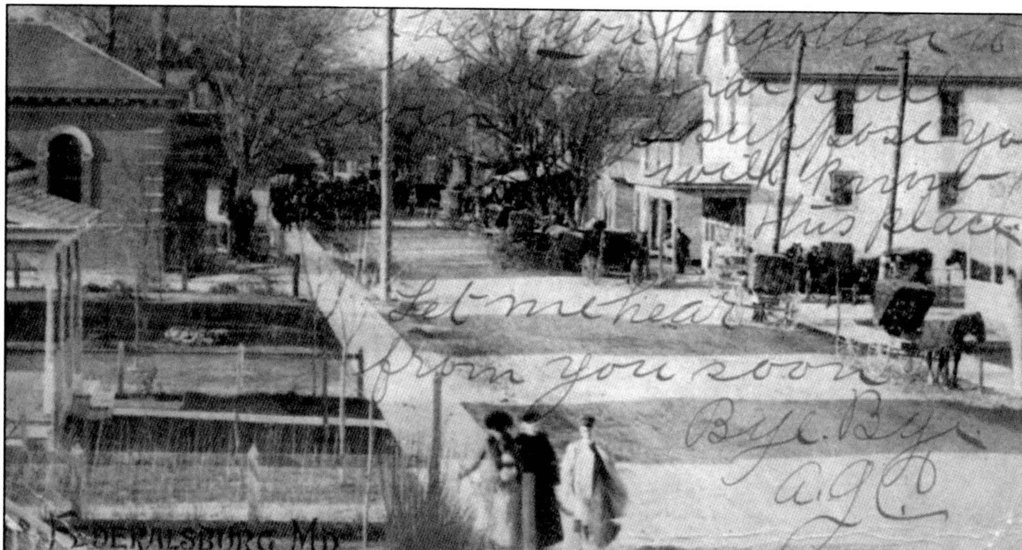

NORTH MAIN STREET. Looking north from Bridge Street, the brick building on the left was the Federalsburg Bank of the Eastern Shore Trust Company. Today, the building has been remodeled and Bank of America is the current owner. The building on the right is Orlando Patton's General Store. (From the Laurence G. Claggett collection.)

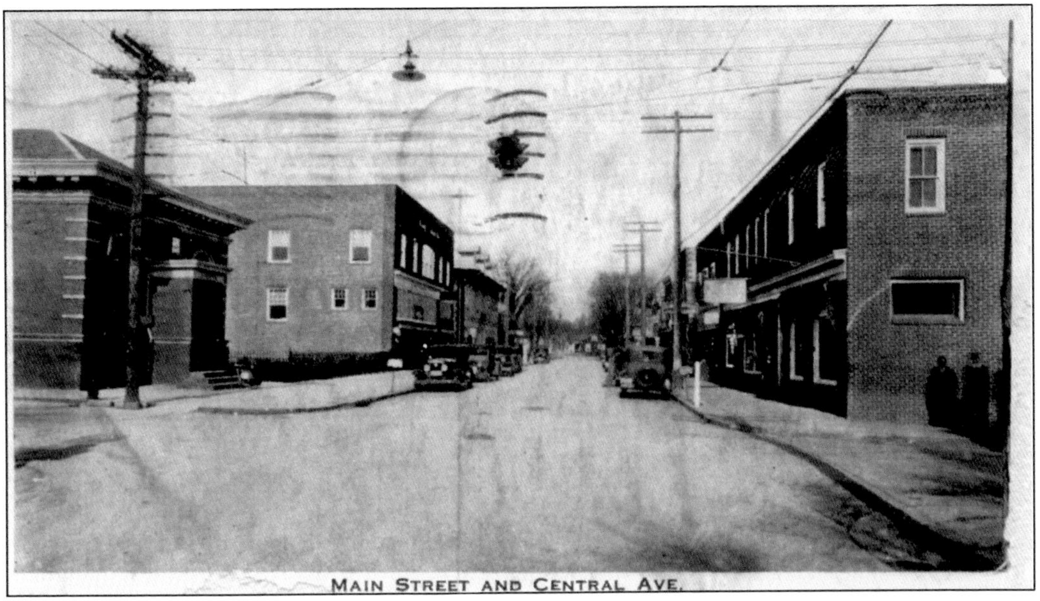

NORTH MAIN STREET LOOKING NORTH IN 1932. The buildings on the right, from left to right, housed the Post Office, Cantner's Drug Store, and Poole's Men's Store. On the left were the Federalsburg Bank, Long and Short, Inc., and the Masonic temple. The street light over the center of the intersection was the only one in town until the second one was installed at the by-pass in the late 1960s. (From the Jeff Porter collection.)

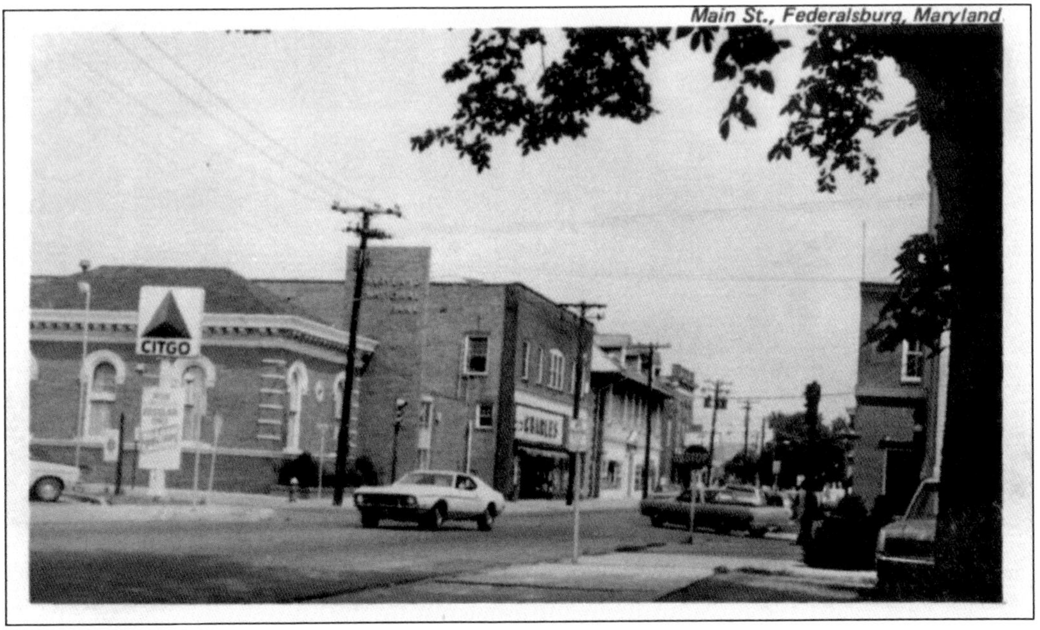

NORTH MAIN STREET. This is the same view as above only years later. The bank has been remodeled, Long and Short, Inc. has become a clothing store, and a service station has replaced the residence on the southwest corner of Main Street. (From the Danny Phillips collection.)

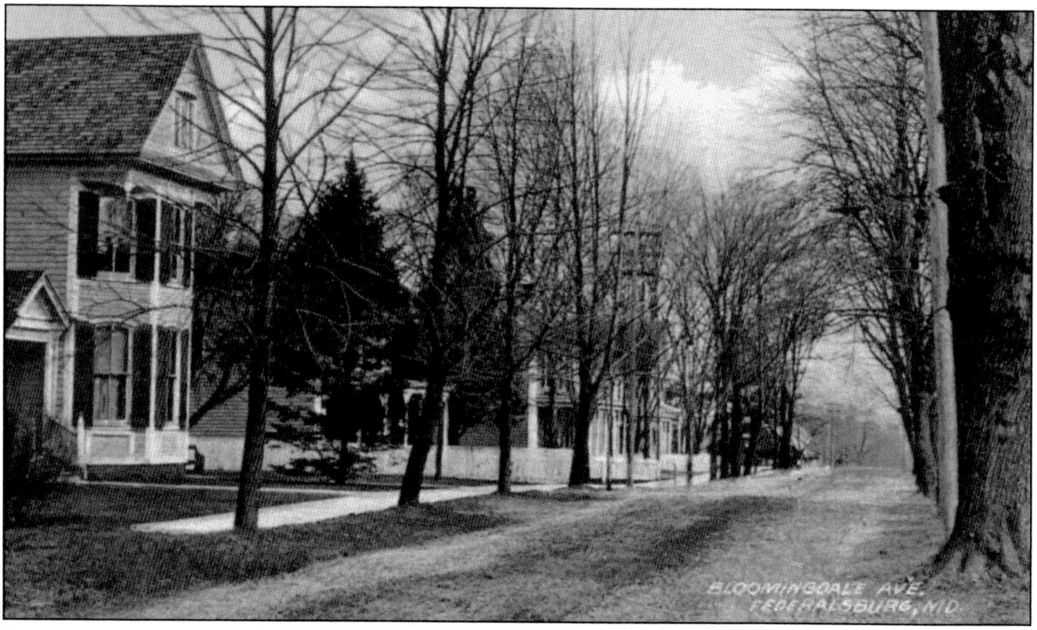

Bloomingdale Avenue Looking South. Bloomingdale Avenue was called Bloomingdale Hill at one time. The house on the left and the one across the street were the last houses on the street when the photo was taken, and one can see where the sidewalk ends. (From the Danny Phillips collection.)

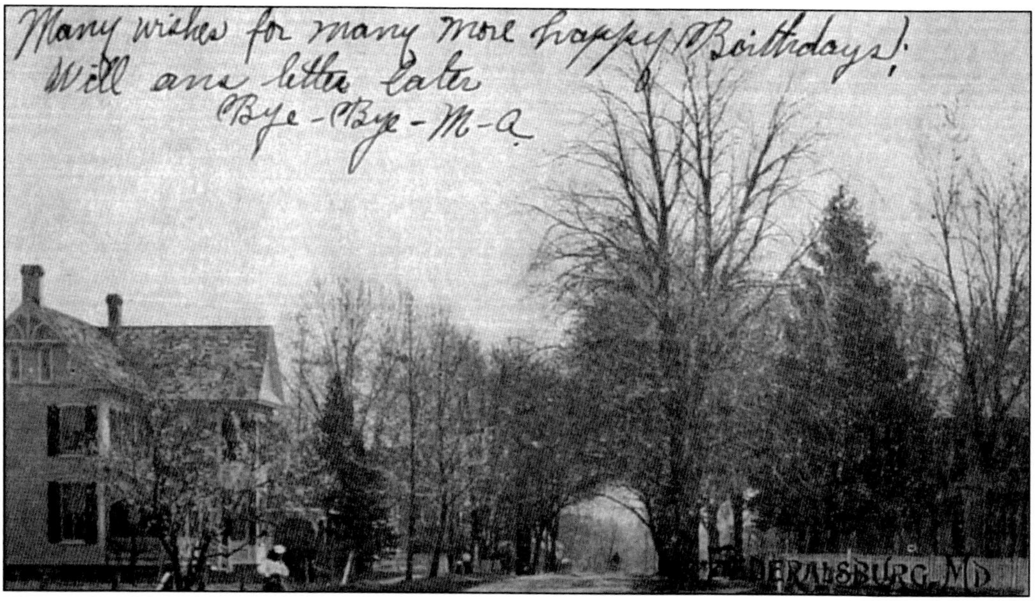

Bloomingdale Avenue Looking South. The house on the left, at 127 Bloomingdale Avenue, is the former home of Miss Mary Davis. Recently, it had been the location for Prints Charming Photography. (From the Laurence G. Claggett collection.)

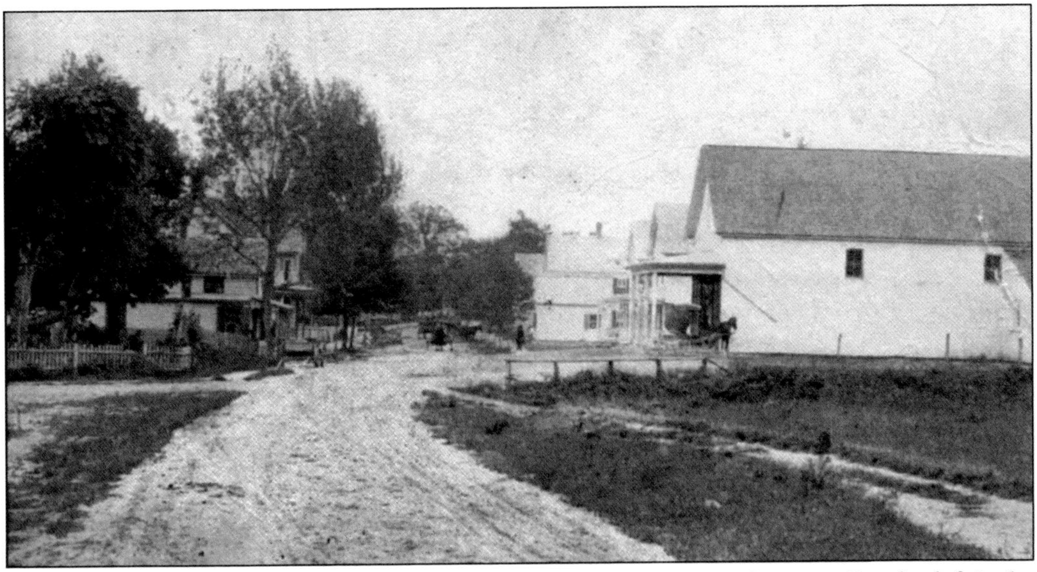

WHERE BLOOMINGDALE HILL (AVENUE) BECOMES NORTH MAIN STREET. On the left is the road going to Idlewild and Denton. The long building on the right was E.E. Nuttle's general store. This location was early on called the "Point." The photo was taken around 1904. (From the Danny Phillips collection.)

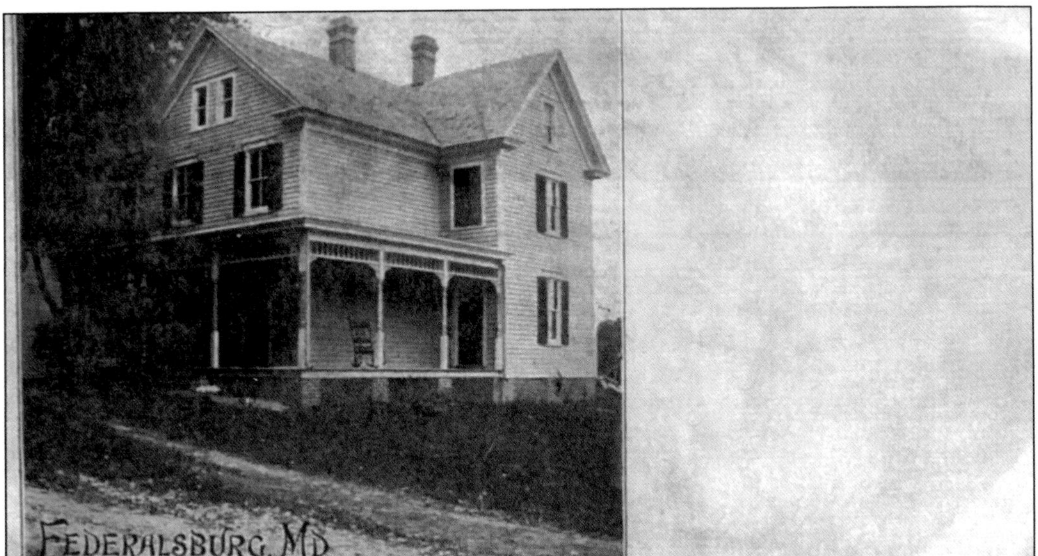

121 BLOOMINGDALE AVENUE. In 1904 this was the home of Charles W. Jefferson, son of Dr. Charles W. Jefferson, who practiced medicine in Federalsburg in the mid-to-late-1800s. The younger Jefferson was a member of the House of Delegates and in 1918 was appointed postmaster of Federalsburg after his brother, Thomas O. Jefferson, relinquished the position. The house was at one time owned by William H. Alburger, who served in the Civil War, Company G of the First Eastern Shore Regiment of Infantry, Maryland Volunteers. In 1877, he operated a plow works/blacksmith shop to the right of the house. The house was passed down to his eldest daughter, Hattie, who married Charles W. Jefferson in 1893. (From the Laurence G. Claggett collection.)

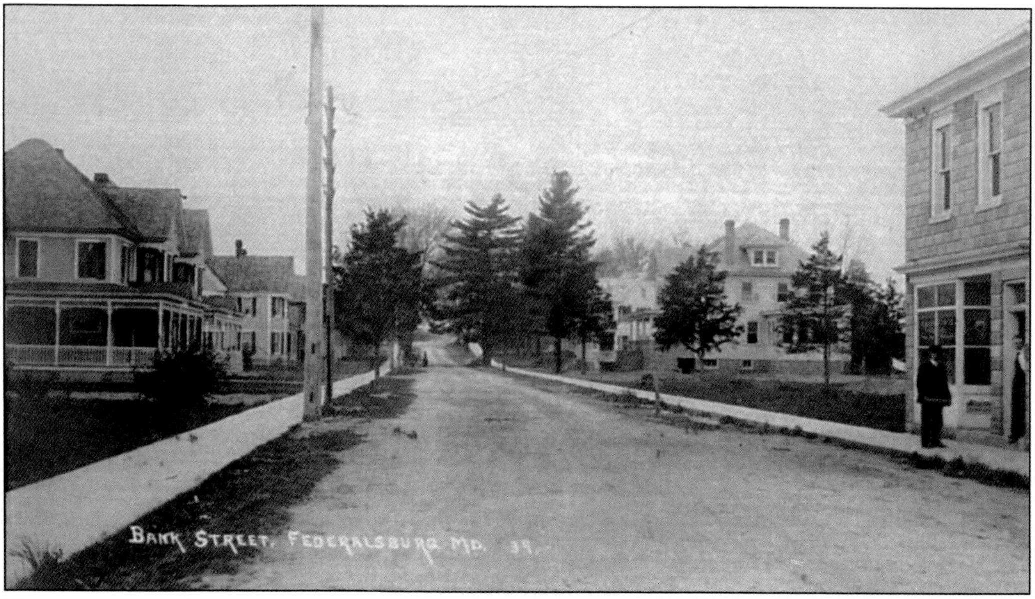

West Central Avenue Around 1932. Still known as Bank Street, the house on the left was the home of O.G. Martino, who worked as a bookkeeper at the Idlewild Mills for a number of years in the early 1900s. On the right the cinder-block building was once occupied by J. Raymond Charles, an insurance agent, and on the second floor is the dental office of Dr. William S. Nabb. Most streets were still not paved in 1932, although many had sidewalks. (From the Laurence G. Claggett collection.)

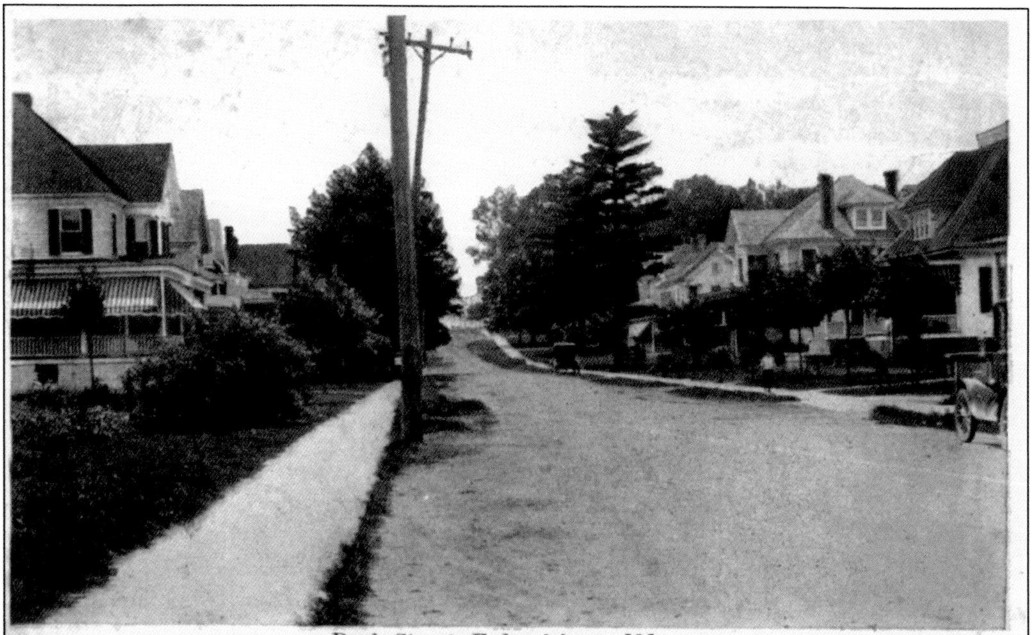

West Central Avenue. The home of Sen. E.E. Goslin sat at the top of the hill many years before these homes were constructed. Notice the addition of the house on the far right, not shown in the above photo. (From the Danny Phillips collection.)

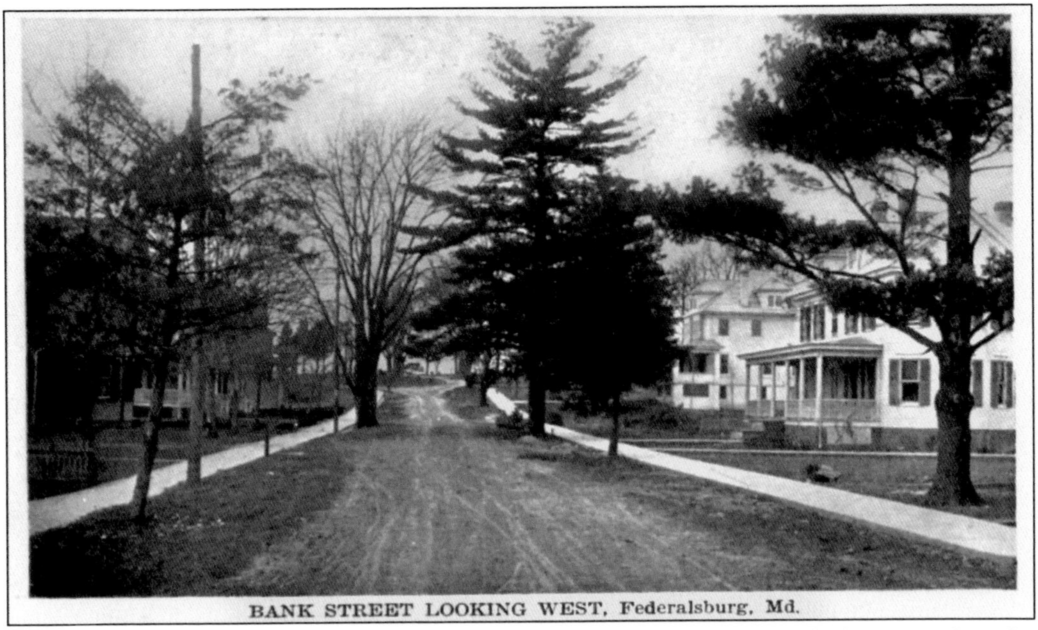

West Central Avenue Looking West. This is a shot taken a little farther west than the previous shots. (From the Danny Phillips collection.)

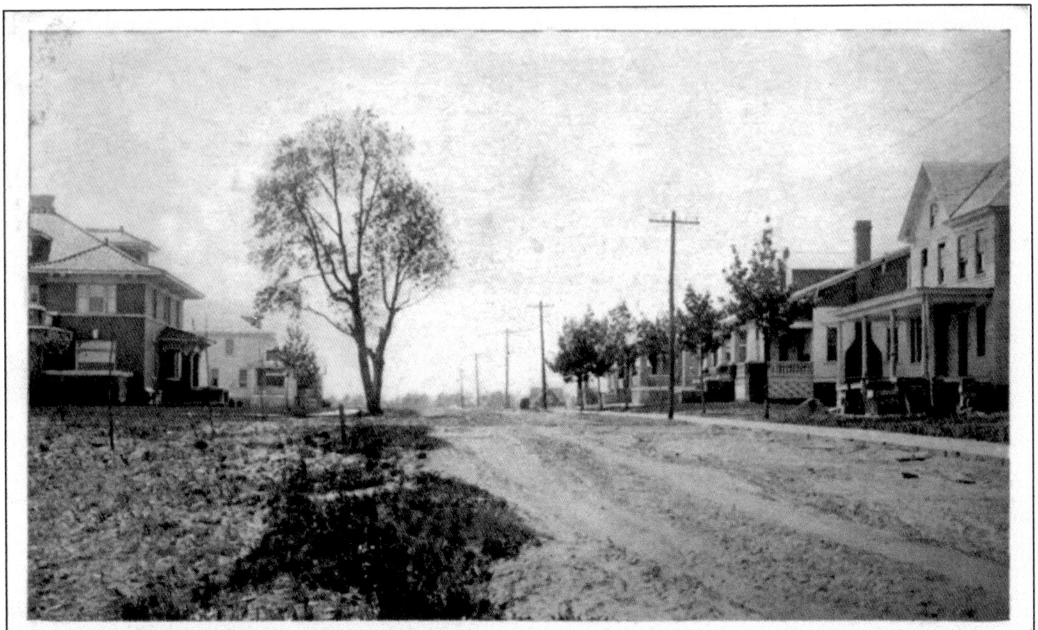

West Central Avenue Looking West. Still called Bank Street, this shows the top of the hill. The home on the left was the residence of Robert W. Messenger and later the home of John E. Elrick, "agent for Vigoro used on lawns, flowers, fruits and vegetables." (From the Danny Phillips collection.)

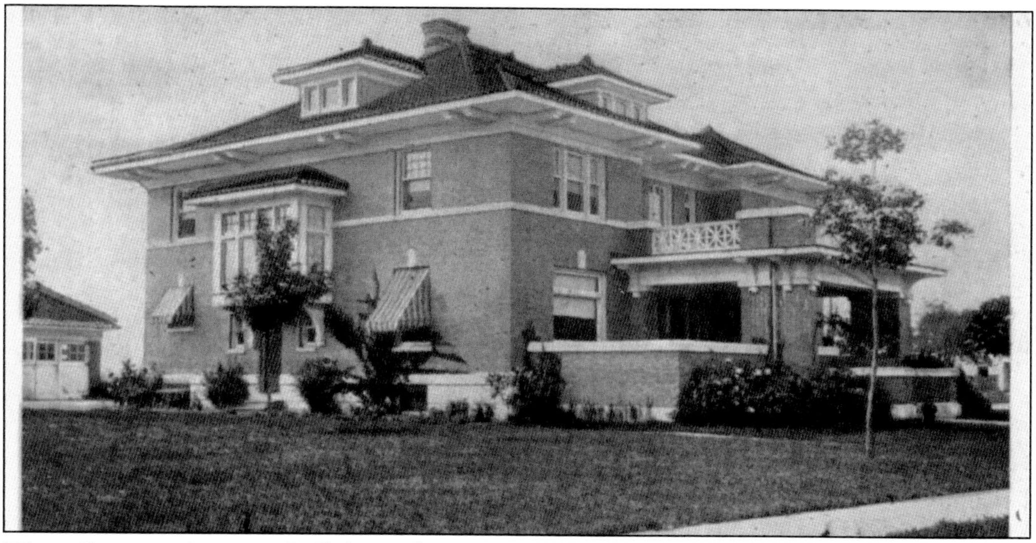

West Central Avenue. Built by Robert W. "Bob" Messenger around 1915, this five-bedroom mansion was constructed of a distinctive yellow brick with a terra cotta roof. Sometime after World War II, Messenger told Judge Marvin H. Smith that he built the house for $15,000. He was born in 1870 and moved with his family to Federalsburg at the age of 10. He served in the Spanish American War. In business, he partnered in many ventures with his brother, H.B. or "Burdette," as he was known. Perhaps their most notable venture was the Eagle Mills built in 1900. Steam-operated and running along the railroad tracks and Marshy Hope Creek, it was one of the best-equipped mills on Delmarva. Large quantities of grain were imported, and the mill's products were distributed by Messenger boats and by rail. Across the tracks from Eagle Mill stood the Federal Can Company, which manufactured cans for the local canneries. The post–World War I collapse and the Depression caused the financial decline and eventual loss of his home and business and Messenger died in 1948. Although he lived in Pocomoke City during his last years, he is buried in Hillcrest Cemetery. (From the Danny Phillips collection.)

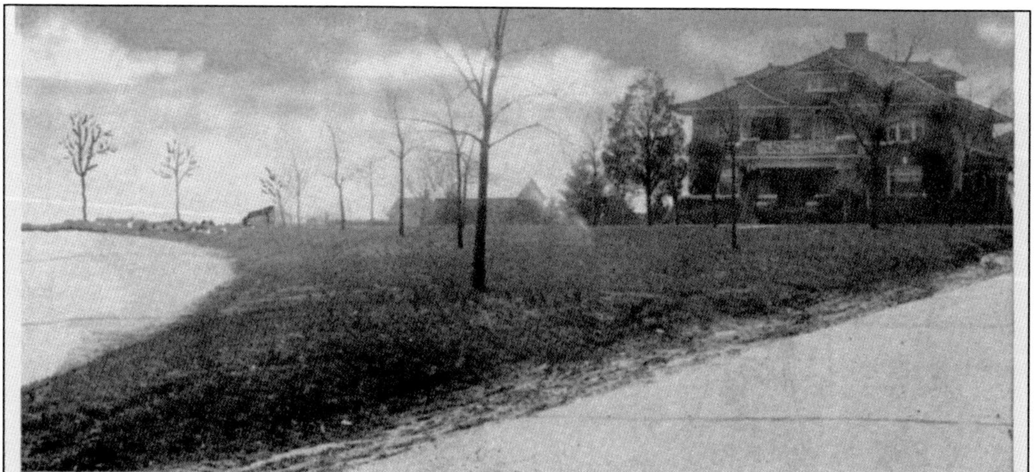

The Triangle. By the time this postcard was made, the name Bridge Street had been changed to West Central Avenue. The "Park" referred to in this photo is now known as "The Triangle." The house on the right was the Messenger/Elrick house. (From the Danny Phillips collection.)

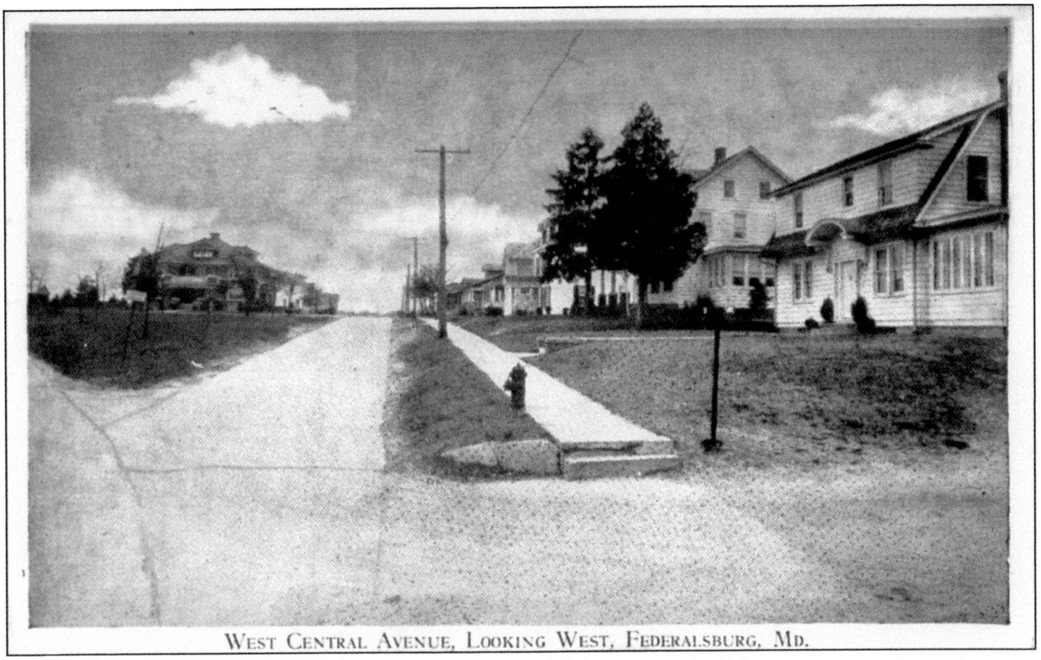

WEST CENTRAL AVENUE. This is another view of "The Triangle." The house on the right now has a porch on the front and a low brick wall around the yard. (From the Francis A. "Sonny" Callahan collection.)

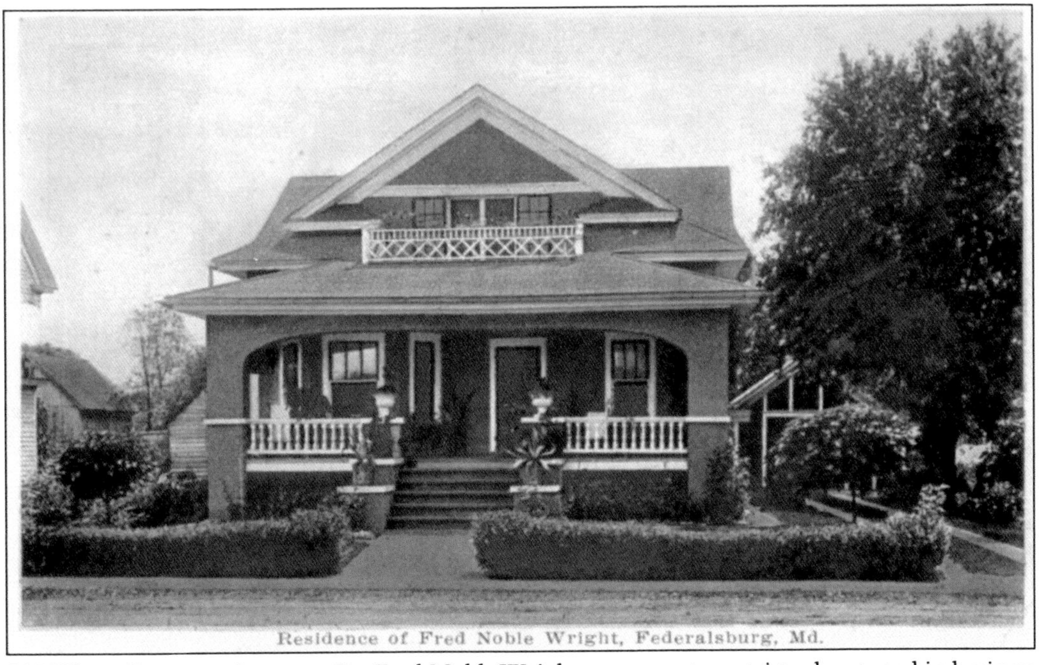

107 WEST CENTRAL AVENUE. Dr. Fred Noble Wright was an optometrist who started in business in 1912. His office was located in his residence. (From the Danny Phillips collection.)

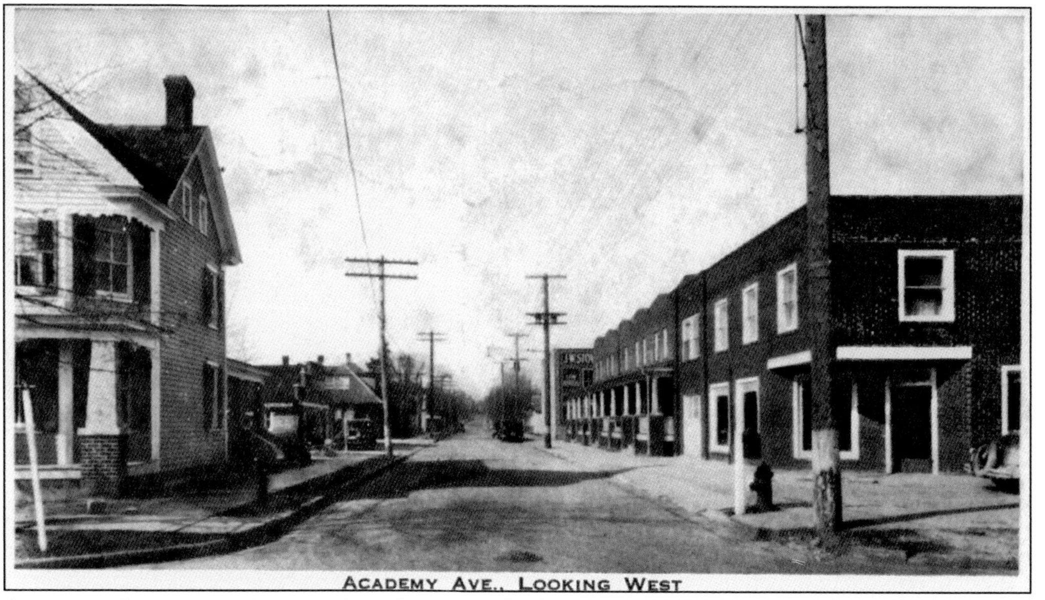

ACADEMY AVENUE AT SOUTH MAIN STREET. The building on the right has been used for various businesses such as the Milk Bar, Hulliger's Barber Shop, and a laundromat. The next set of buildings was known as "The Brick Row" apartments. These were once choice apartments where many residents set up housekeeping. Behind the apartments was J.W. Stowell Printing Company. The house on the left was the home of Stewart E. Hallowell, who ran an automobile shop on Academy Avenue beside his house. (From the Jeff Porter collection.)

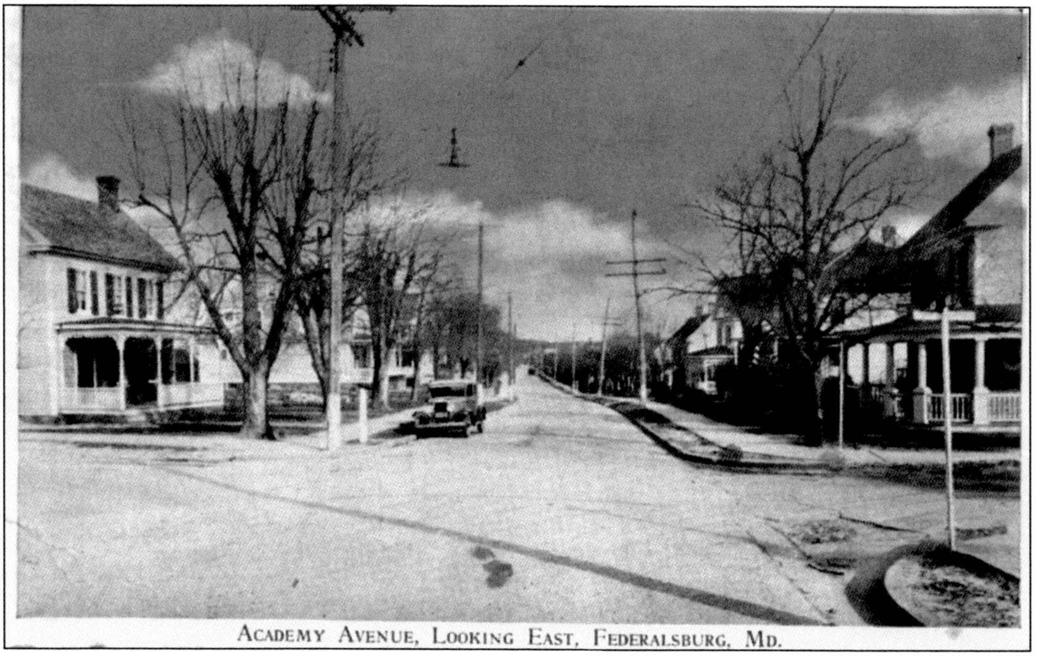

ACADEMY AVENUE AT BUENA VISTA AVENUE. The house on the right corner was the home of Thomas J. Williams, manufacturer and dealer in charcoal in 1904. (From the Danny Phillips collection.)

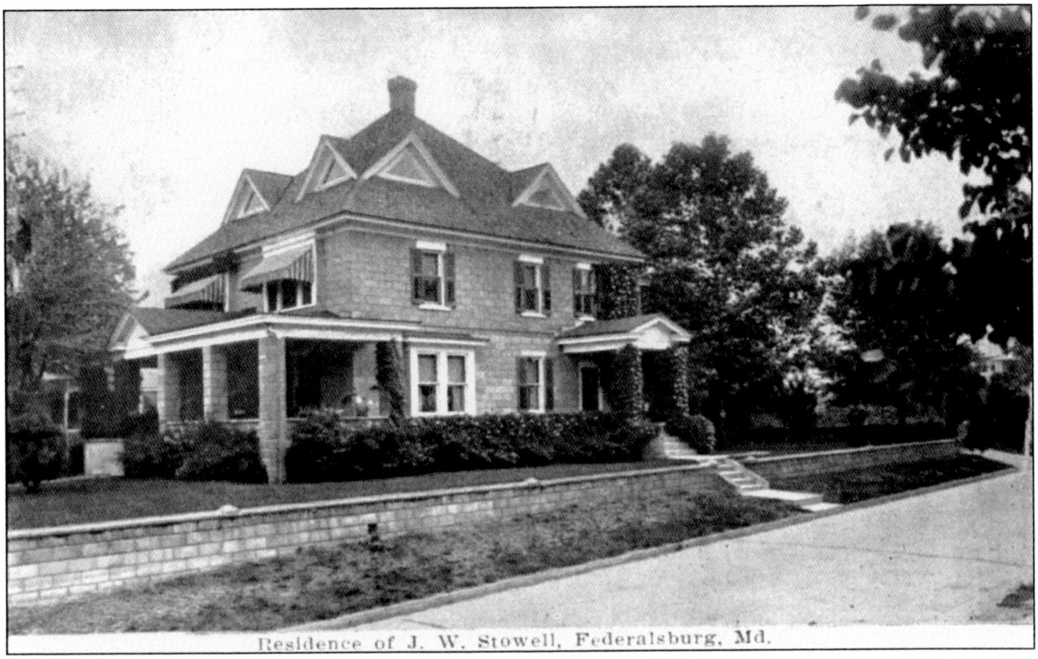

ON THE CORNER OF BUENA VISTA AND ACADEMY AVENUES. This was the residence of John W. Stowell. He owned of J.W. Stowell Printing Co., Inc., which he started in 1889. This company printed numerous materials on Federalsburg, including the *1804–1904 Souvenir Book*, the *1914 Federalsburg Year Book*, the *1932 Historical Souvenir Book*, and many school yearbooks. (From the Danny Phillips collection.)

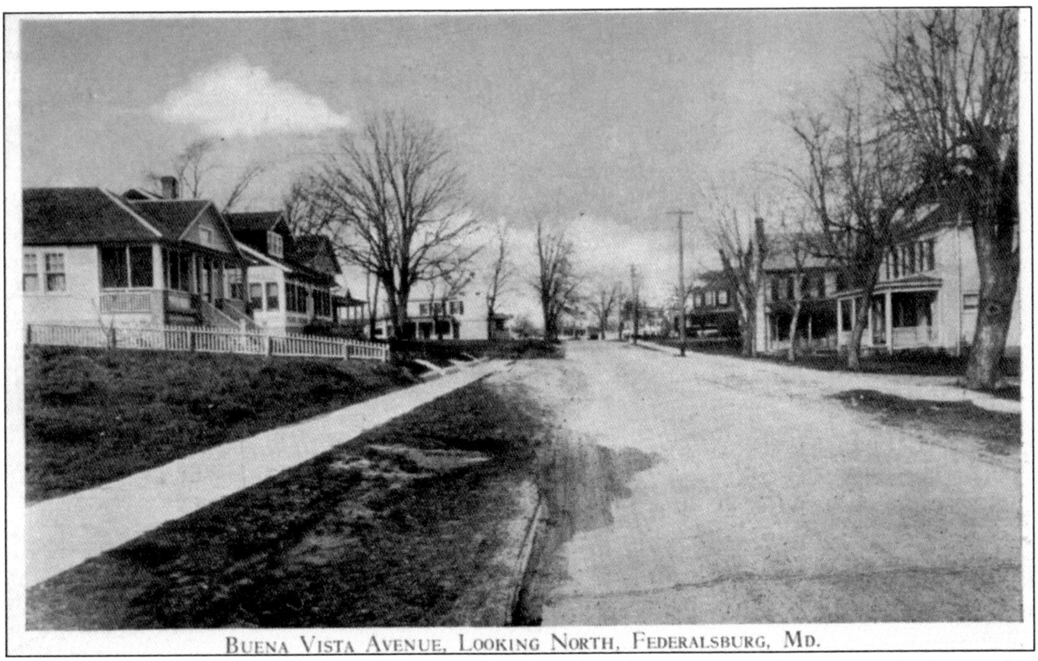

ANOTHER VIEW OF BUENA VISTA AVENUE. This postcard is looking north towards the "Triangle." (From the Charles S. Long collection.)

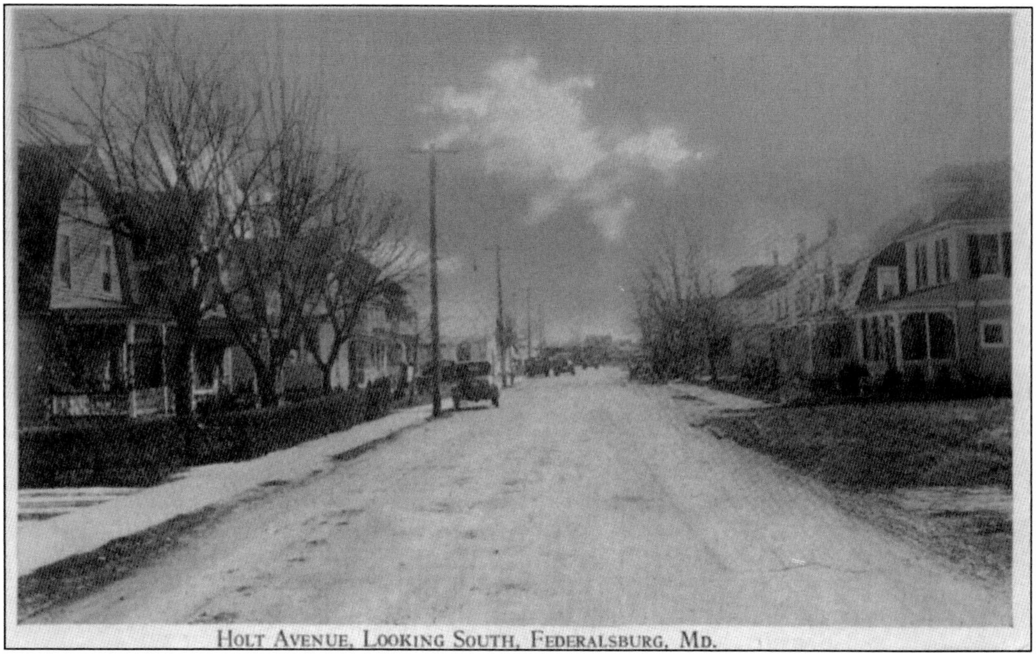

HOLT STREET. Now known as Holt Street, this *c.* 1932 view faces south toward the railroad track. Holt Street was the busy industrial section of the town at one time and included an ice plant and an ice-cream factory. (From the Francis A. "Sonny" Callahan collection.)

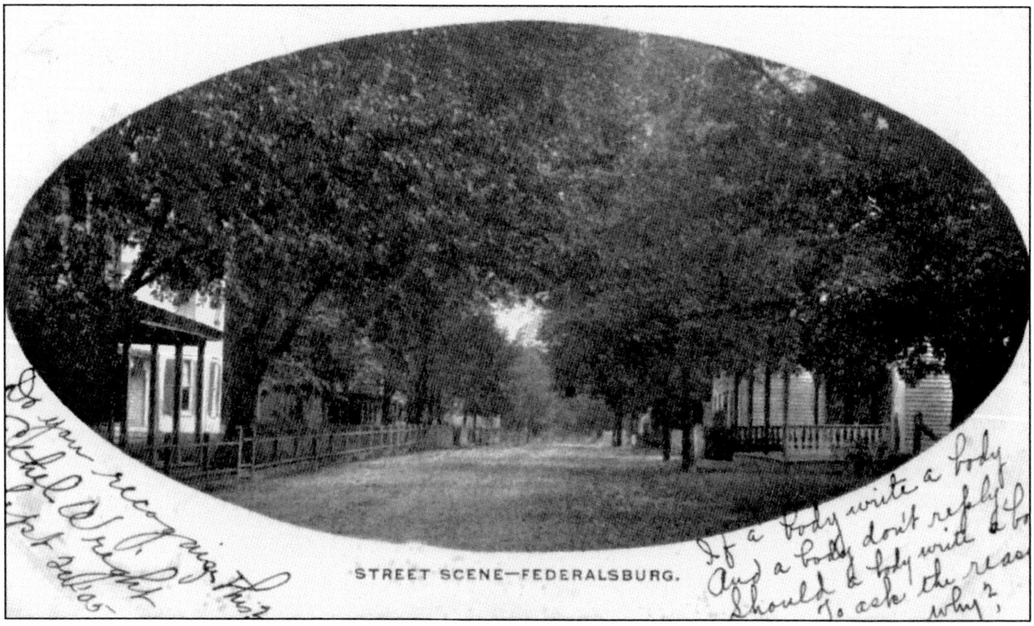

EAST CENTRAL AVENUE AROUND 1904. This is a street scene of Federal Hill, now known as East Central Avenue. Notice the personal verse written on the front: "If a body write a body, And a body don't reply, Should a body with a body, To ask the reason why?" (From the Charles S. Long collection.)

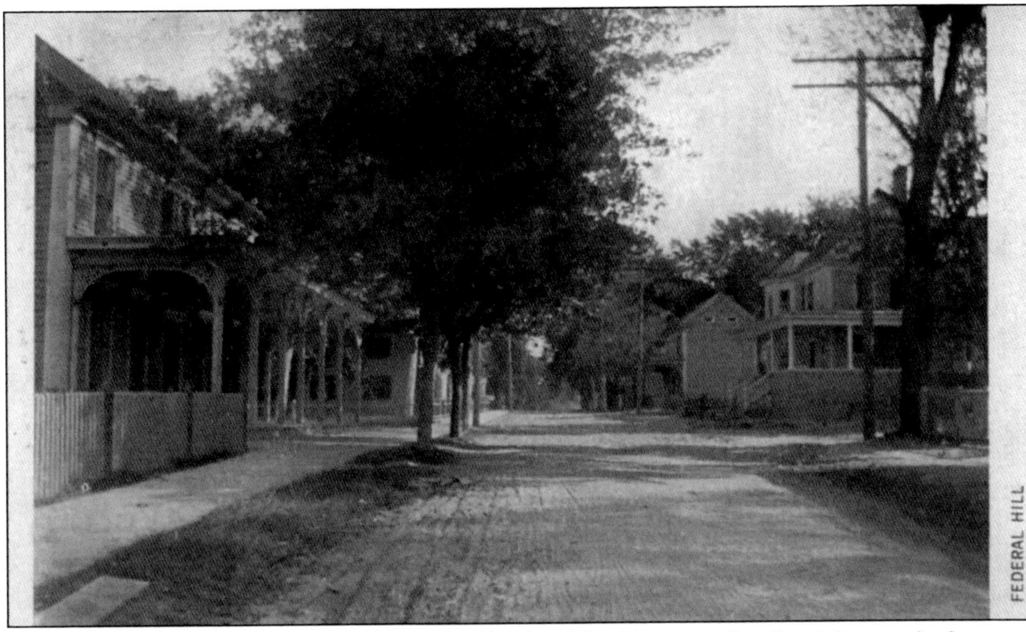

EAST CENTRAL AVENUE. This is a view of Federal Hill looking east. On the right was the home of Dr. Robert Kemp Jefferson, which sits on the corner of East Central and Reliance Avenues. (From the Francis A. "Sonny" Callahan collection.)

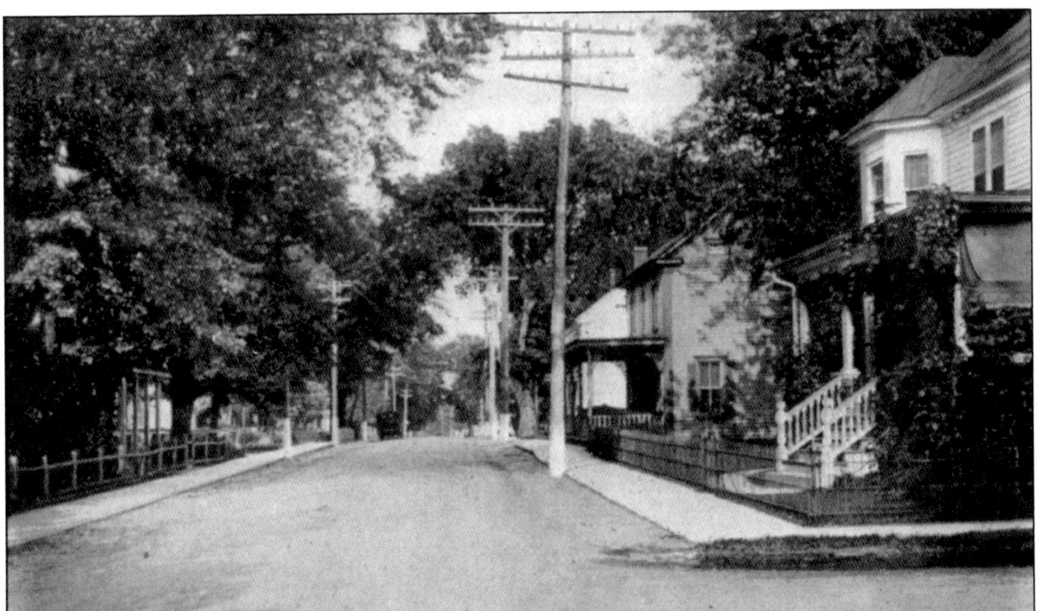

201 EAST CENTRAL AVENUE. This is a closer view of Dr. Robert Kemp Jefferson's home. He practiced with his father at 209 East Central Avenue until Dr. Charles W. Jefferson died in 1893. He built this residence in 1906 and his office was located in the basement. Ellenor Merriken wrote that "Dr. R.K. Jefferson lingers in the memory of many an old-timer as the perfect family doctor of all times." Later the house was residence of John R. Hargreaves, a member of the Maryland House of Delegates. (From the Danny Phillips collection.)

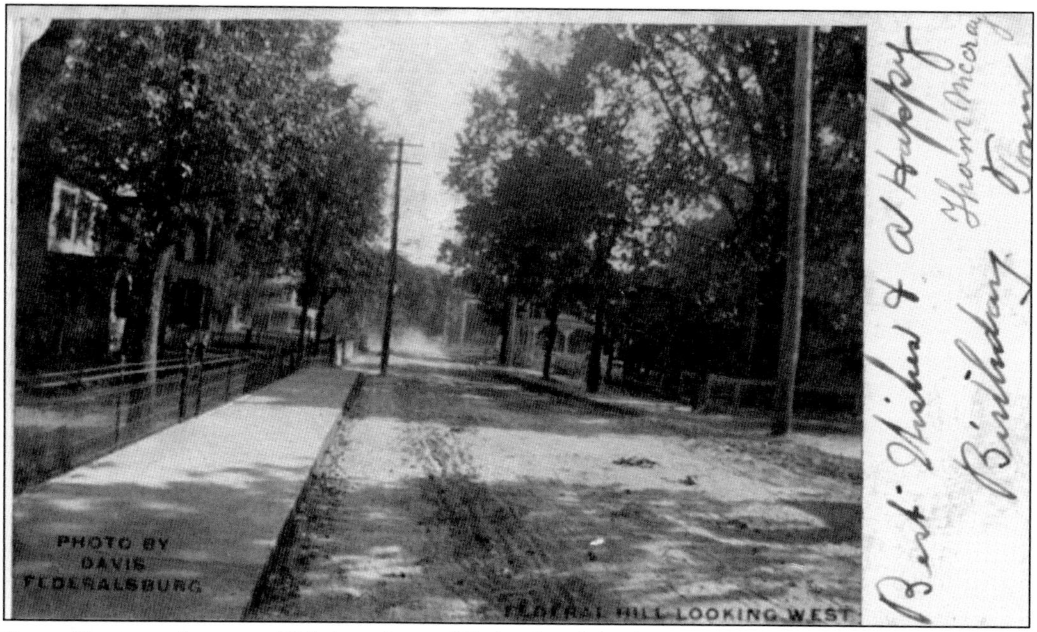

East Central Avenue. This is a view of Federal Hill looking west towards the bridge. Notice the address on the front of the postcard, which was addressed only as Thom McCray Town. If you were addressing the postcard to a local resident the only address needed was "Town." (From the Danny Phillips collection.)

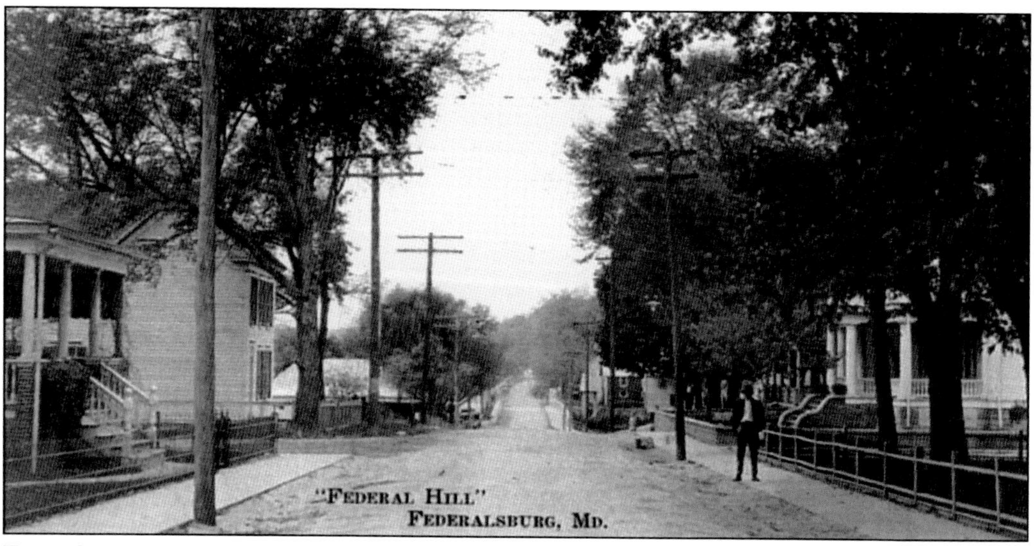

East Central Avenue. This is another view of Federal Hill looking west. The house on the near left, which was the home of Dr. R.K. Jefferson, is now the home of Mr. and Mrs. Howard Bradley. The next house on the left is no longer there. On the right was the home of Maryland state senator Wilmer Fell Davis, a prominent citizen and leader in both local church activities and politics who served Caroline County for several terms. He also owned a local feed, poultry, and egg-distributing plant and was an agent for Mutual Life Insurance Co. of New York. The home is now residence for his son and daughter-in-law, Mr. and Mrs. Wilmer Fell Davis Jr. (From the Laurence G. Claggett collection.)

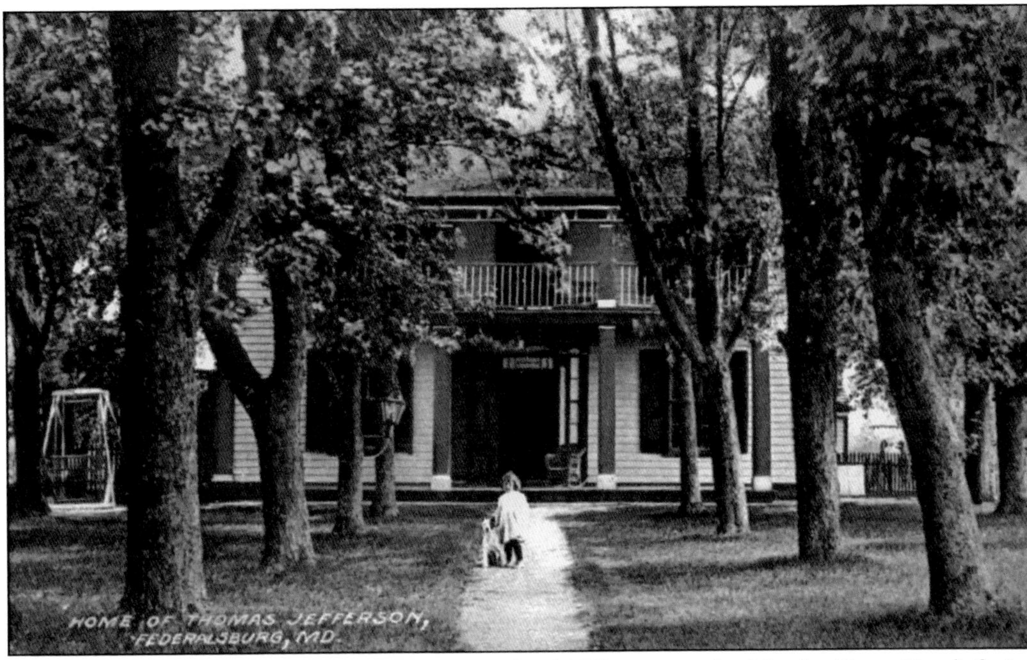

East Central Avenue. This home sat on Federal Hill next to the Marshy Hope Creek facing north. In 1904 it was the residence of Mrs. Rhoda Elliott. The house later belonged to Thomas O. Jefferson. Mr. Jefferson was a druggist and owned Jefferson Drug Store. He was also the town postmaster. He started a bakery down the hill beside the Marshy Hope Creek for two of his sons. The little girl with the dog in the photo is a daughter, Ruth Jefferson, who was born in 1903. Notice her message on the postcard sent on April 1, 1911. Later the Zaffere family bought the business and also the house. The house has since been torn down and a modern brick residence stands in its place. (Both from the Danny Phillips collection.)

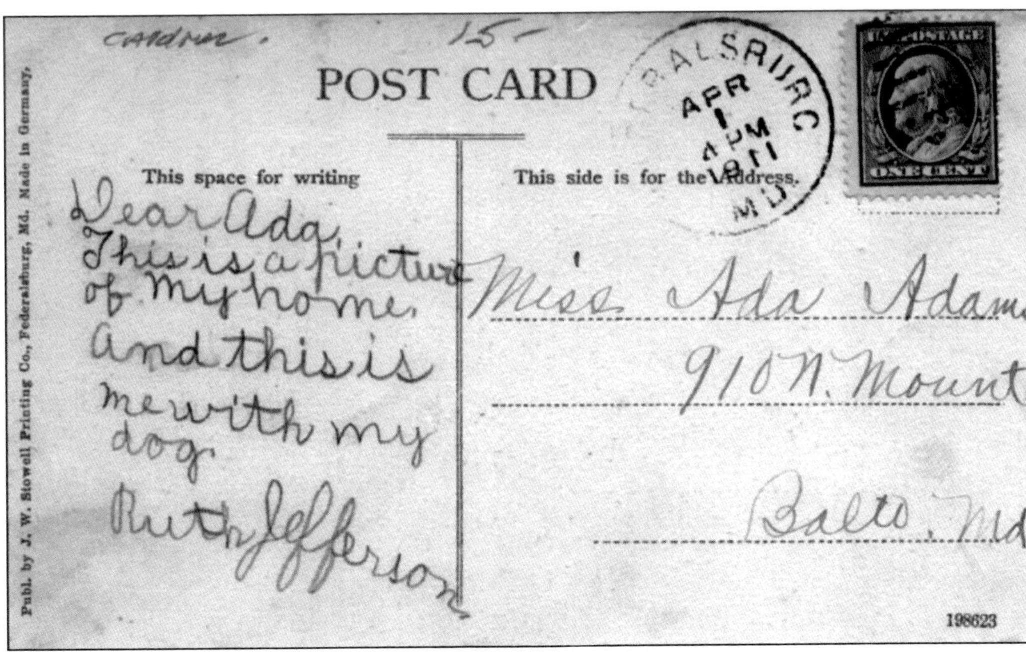

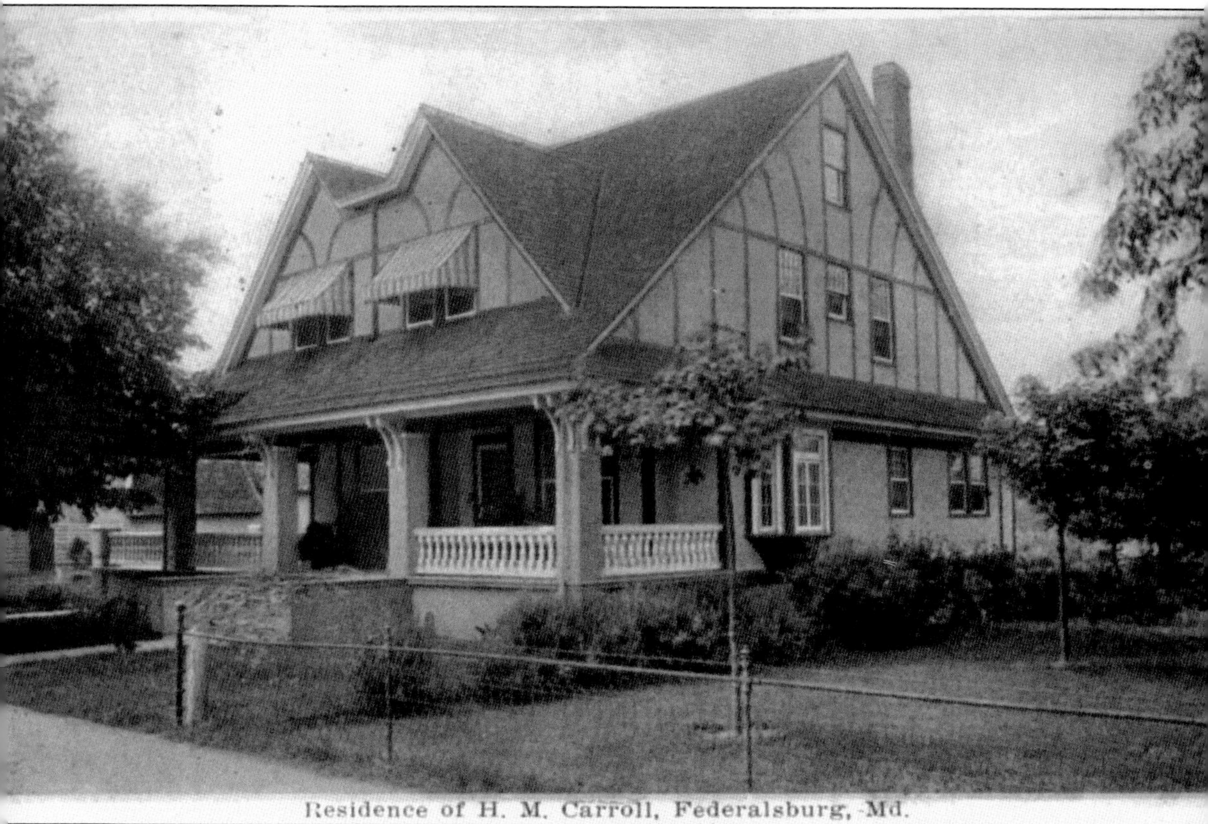

EAST CENTRAL AVENUE. This was the residence of Harry M. Carroll, and later his son J. Russell Carroll, who was a postmaster for Federalsburg. The house looks the same today as it did in 1932 when the photo was taken. (From the Danny Phillips collection.)

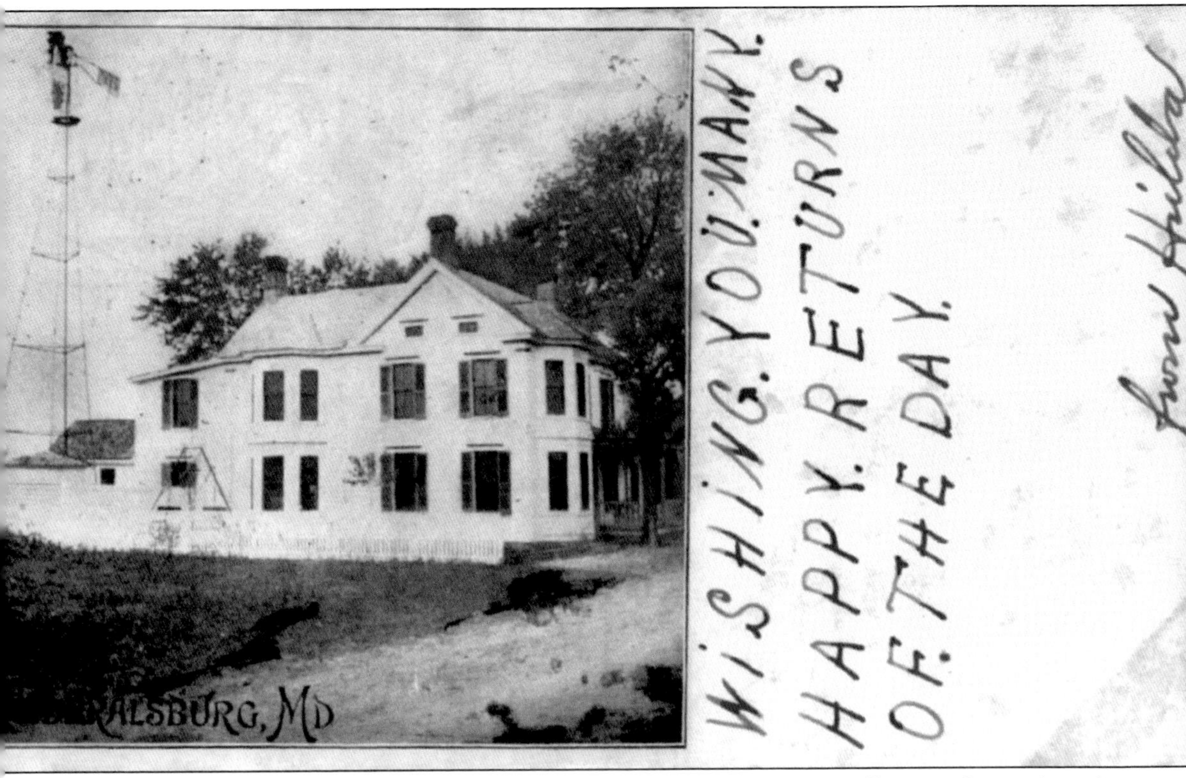

East Central Avenue. This was once the residence of Dr. Charles W. Jefferson, who graduated from the University of Maryland School of Medicine in 1852 and practiced medicine at his residence until his death in 1893. According to Ellenor Merriken, "he became one of the most-noted physicians of the Peninsula, and was sent for far and near, both in consultation and regular practice. He was known to be one of the kindest, most liberal, and upright of men, and while his friends were legion, he had no enemies." (From the Danny Phillips collection.)

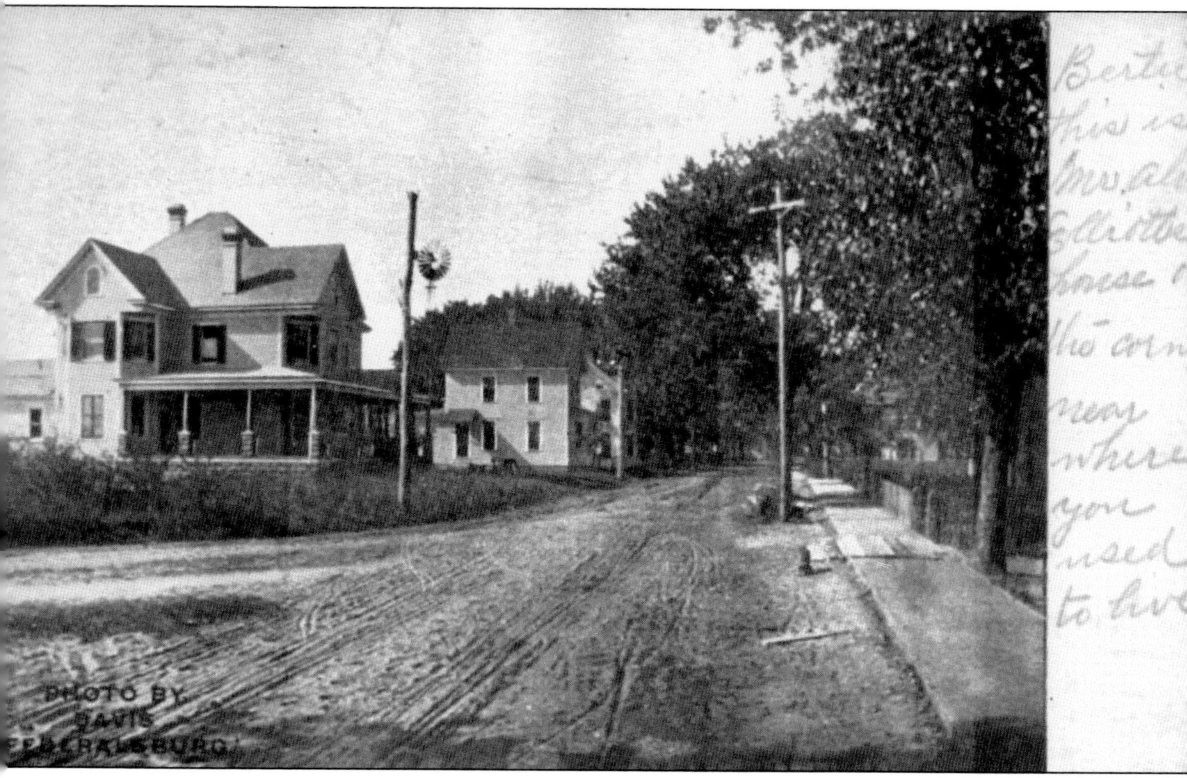

EAST CENTRAL AVENUE LOOKING WEST. On the left, you can see Liberty Road forking left. The house on the left was the residence of Rufus F. Noble and later his son, T. Sewell Noble. They operated a general merchandise store on the corner of South Main Street and Academy Avenue under the name R.F. Noble & Son, which sold furniture, dress goods, shoes, and groceries. (From the Francis A. "Sonny" Callahan collection.)

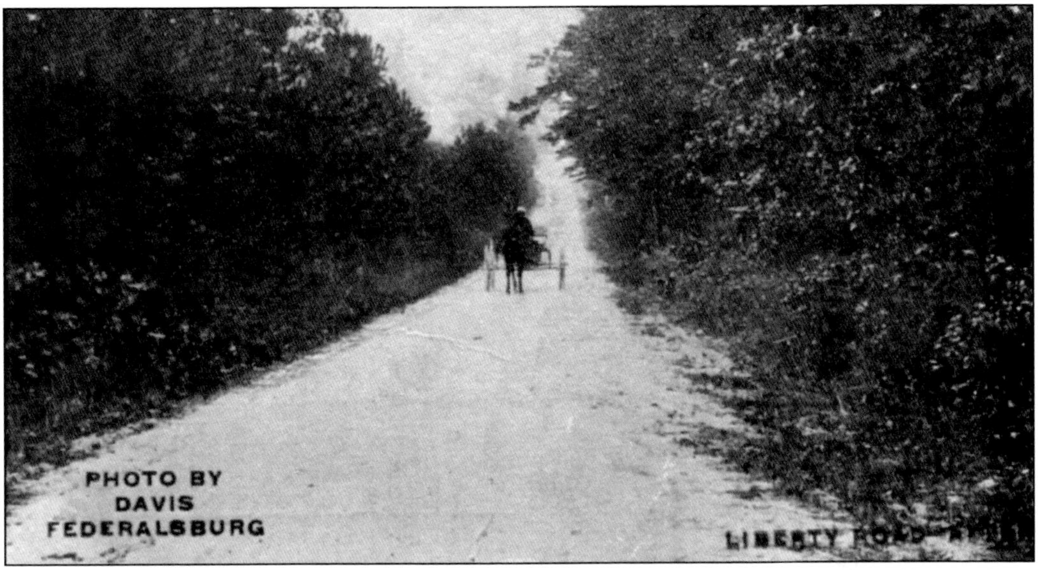

LIBERTY ROAD IN 1904. The Liberty Road was the first road improved around Federalsburg. About two miles long, it was one of the finest examples of shell-road building to be found anywhere, having been kept carefully repaired with the center well rounded up. Though put through a bed of pure yellow sand, the lime dust has combined with the sand along the sides of the road and gradually formed a soil that has grassed in and has added materially to the general appearance. The early 20th-century progress in shell road construction helped label Federalsburg as being "in the very front rank of Peninsula towns." (From the Charles S. Long collection.)

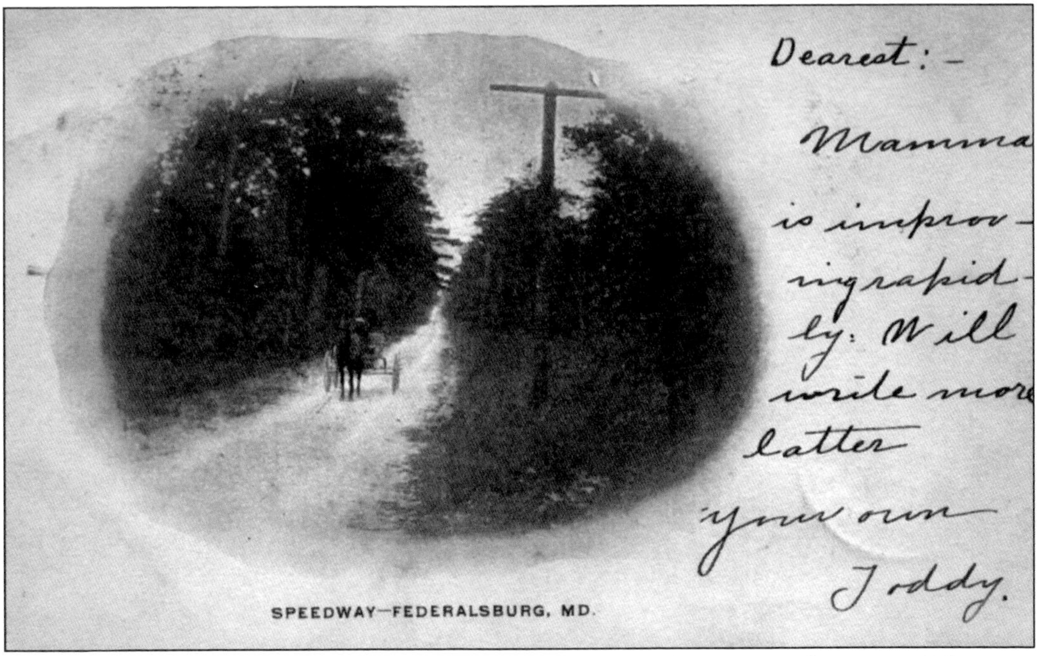

RELIANCE ROAD. Formerly known as Miles Branch Road, this served as a road between Federalsburg and Seaford, Delaware. It was known as the "Speedway." The 1904 photo shows a horse-drawn wagon on the road. (From the Francis A. "Sonny" Callahan collection.)

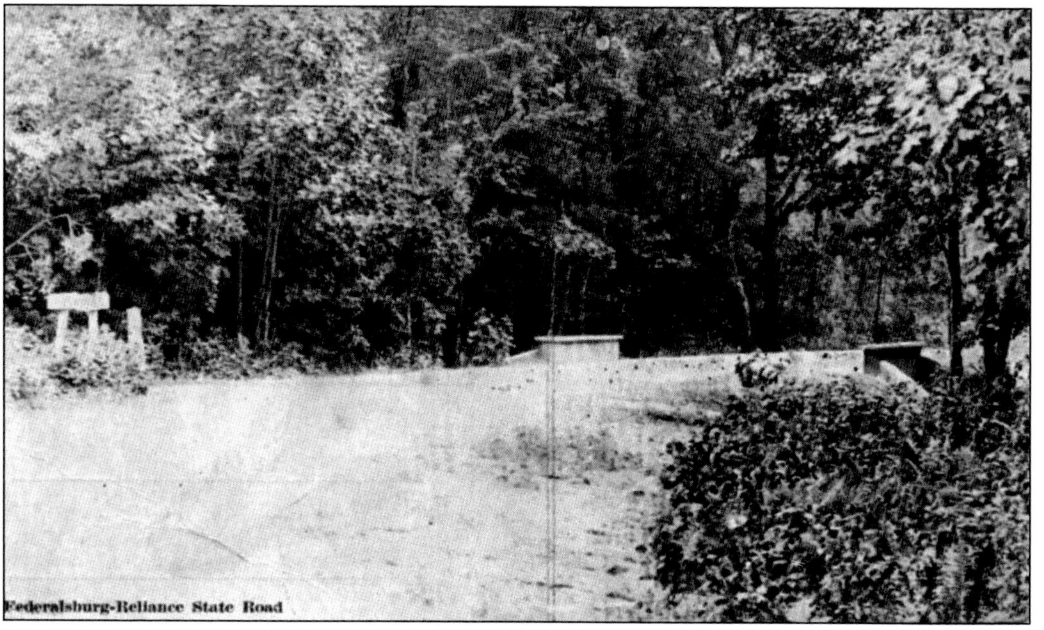

FEDERALSBURG-RELIANCE STATE ROAD. This is another view of the Reliance Road between Federalsburg and Seaford, Delaware. (From the Danny Phillips collection.)

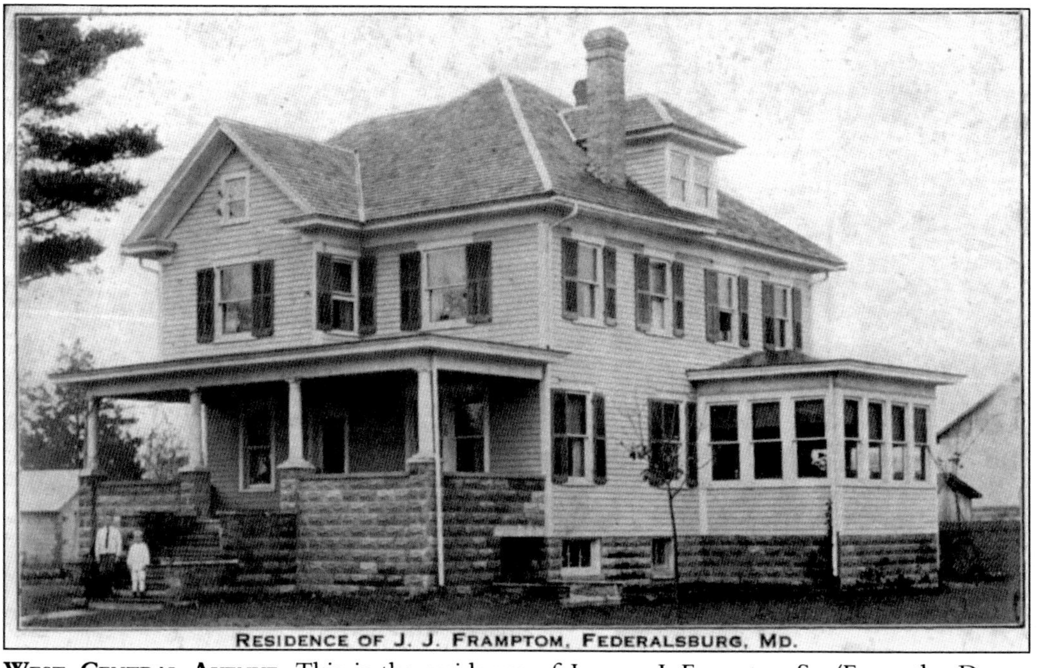

WEST CENTRAL AVENUE. This is the residence of Jerome J. Frampton Sr. (From the Danny Phillips collection.)

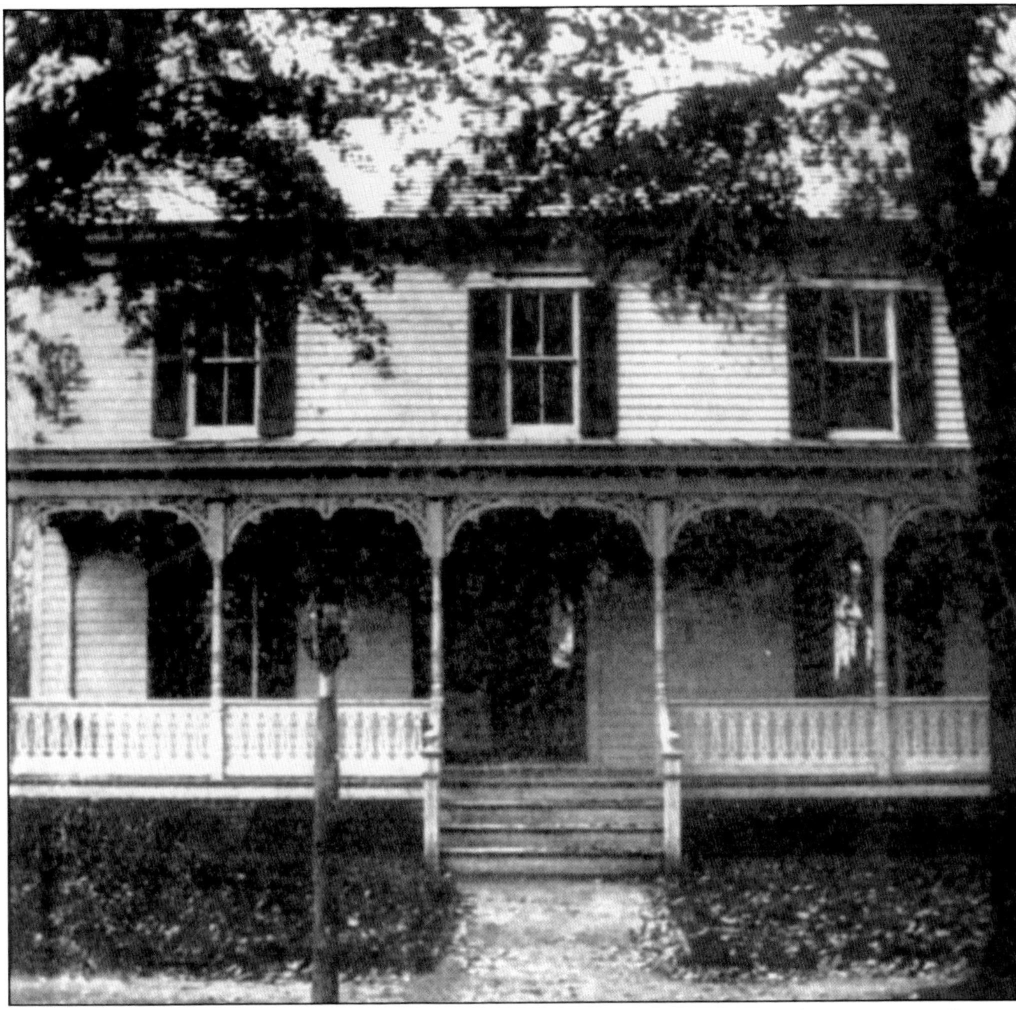

J.T. Frampton Residence. This was the residence of Joseph T. Framptom, who was a manufacturer and dealer in all grades of carriages, surreys, buggies, and wagons. He started this business in 1864. When his son Jerome J. Framptom Sr. graduated from college, he joined the firm as an undertaker and in 1893 their main business became undertaking. (From the Danny Phillips collection.)

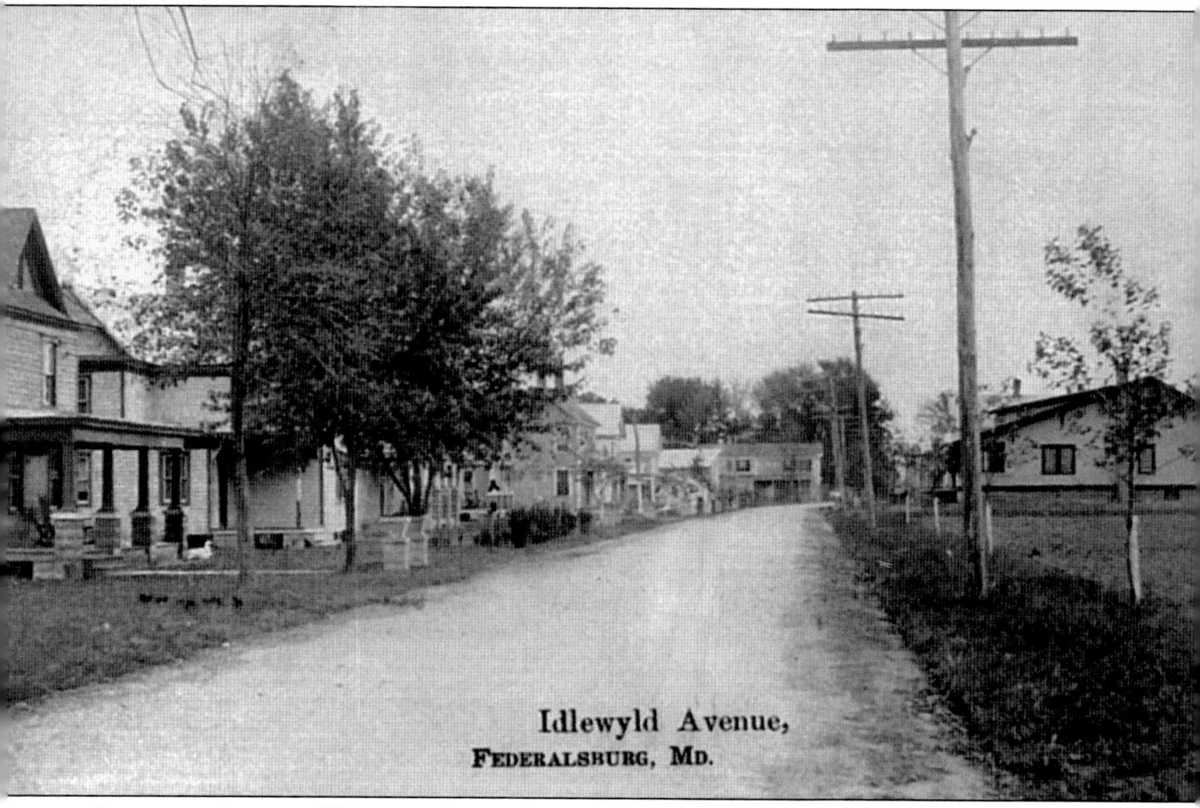

IDLEWYLD AVENUE. This street is now known as Old Denton Road (or Denton Road). The community is still known as Idlewild (or Idylwild, Idlewyld, or Idlewilde.) This area has also been called Walkertown. (From the Laurence G. Claggett collection.)

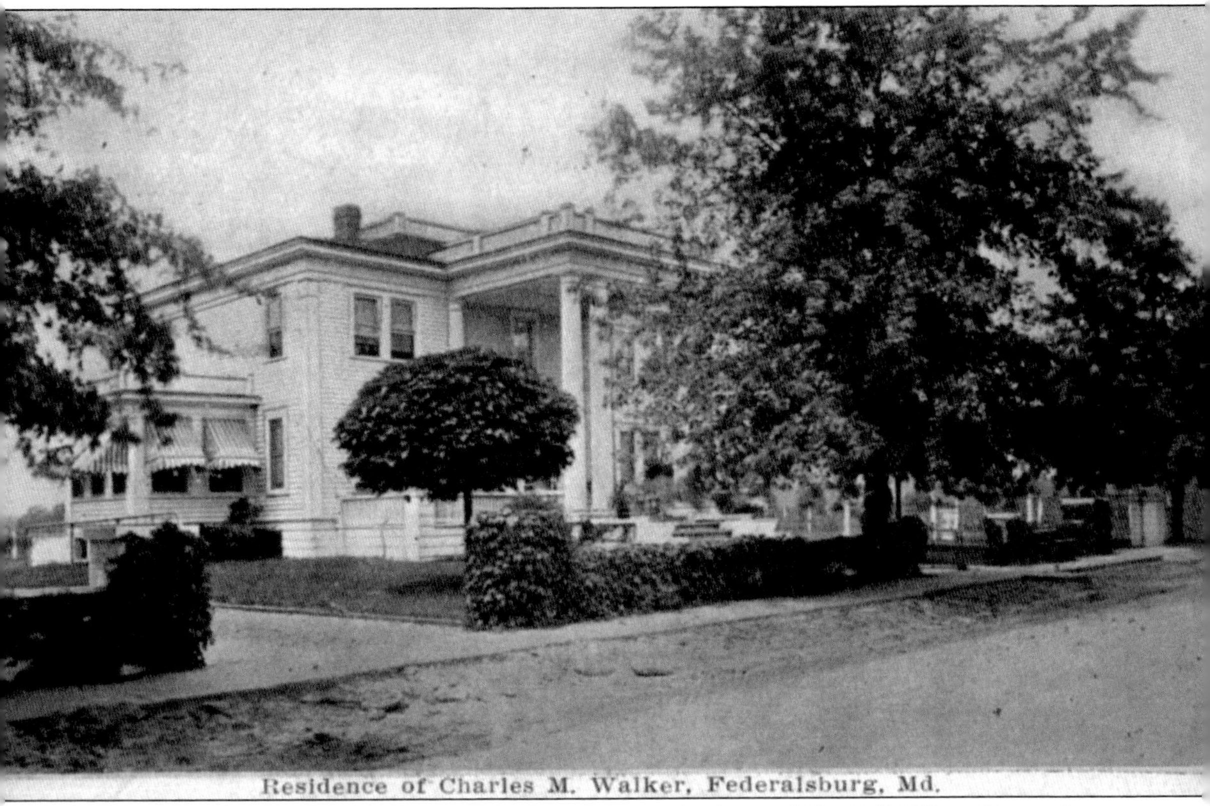

516 Old Denton Road. This was the residence of Charles M. "Charlie" Walker. He was born in Reading, Pennsylvania on January 25, 1876. It is not known when or how he arrived in Federalsburg, but, according to Jean Andrew, "he gained a reputation as a contractor, building many houses in the area to the extent that he renamed what was called Idlewild for many years to Walkertown." He named this house "Lillyshall." The house next door was built for his sister and named "Idlewild." Although he had many real estate interests, painting was his primary interest. He did hundreds of paintings, including landscapes, fantasies, portraits of his neighbor ladies, water scenes, and florals. His large paintings of Biblical scenes hung in some of the local churches. Walker died in March of 1952. (From the Danny Phillips collection.)

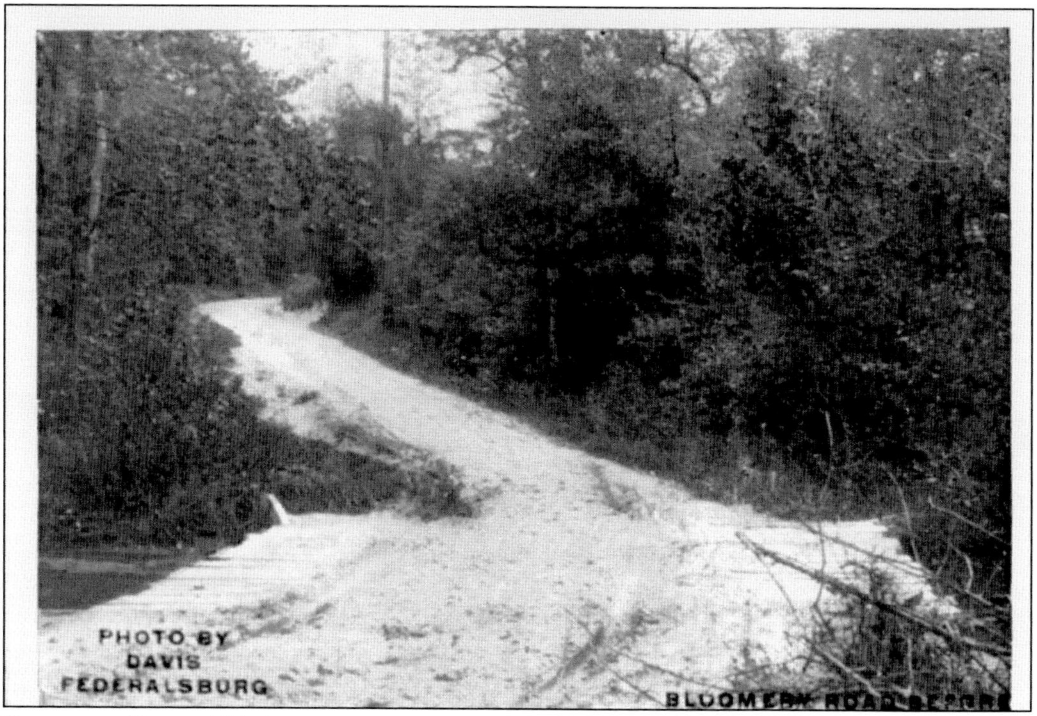

Bloomery Road. This is a country road about five miles to the northeast of Federalsburg. The old dirt road is narrow and wooden boards are laid over the stream to provide a crossing. (From the Danny Phillips collection.)

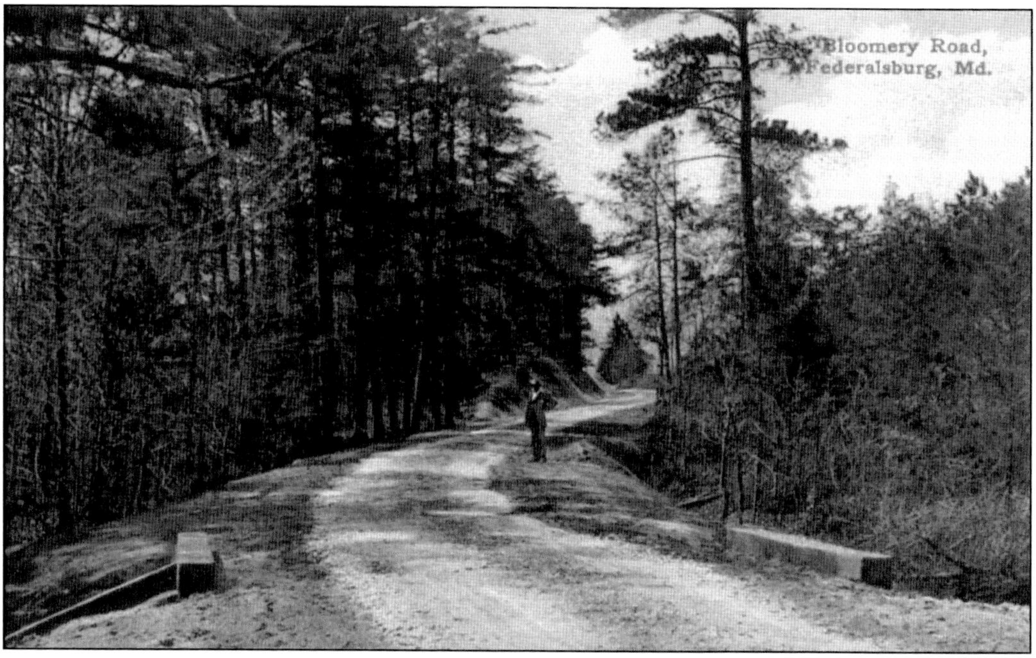

Bloomery Road. This scene shows the dirt road has been widened and additional work has better secured the bridge crossing. (From the Danny Phillips collection.)

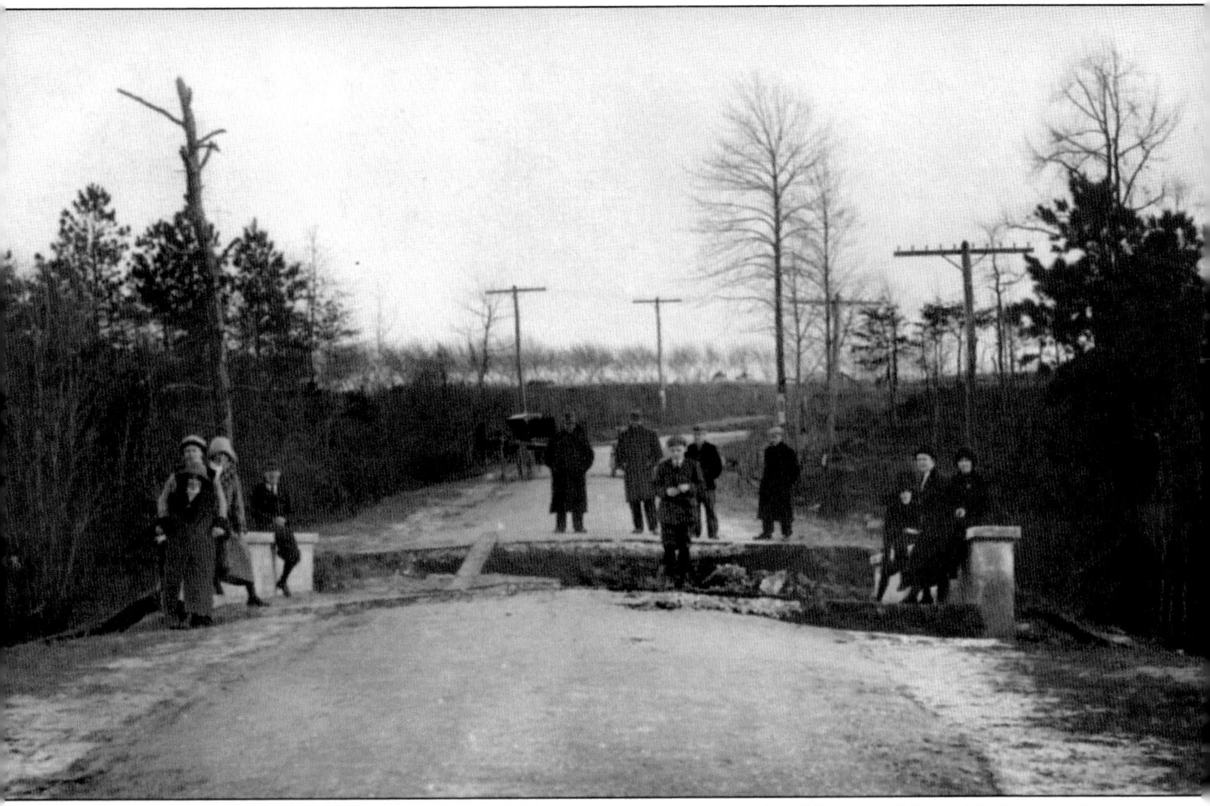

Bridge Out. This is possibly the Faulkner Bridge near Federalsburg with a 30-foot gulley caused during the flood of August 15, 1919. Or, perhaps it was the Bloomery Bridge, which was completely wrecked during this flood. Floods have been a recurring problem to roads, bridges, homes, and businesses around the town. (From the Francis A. "Sonny" Callahan collection.)

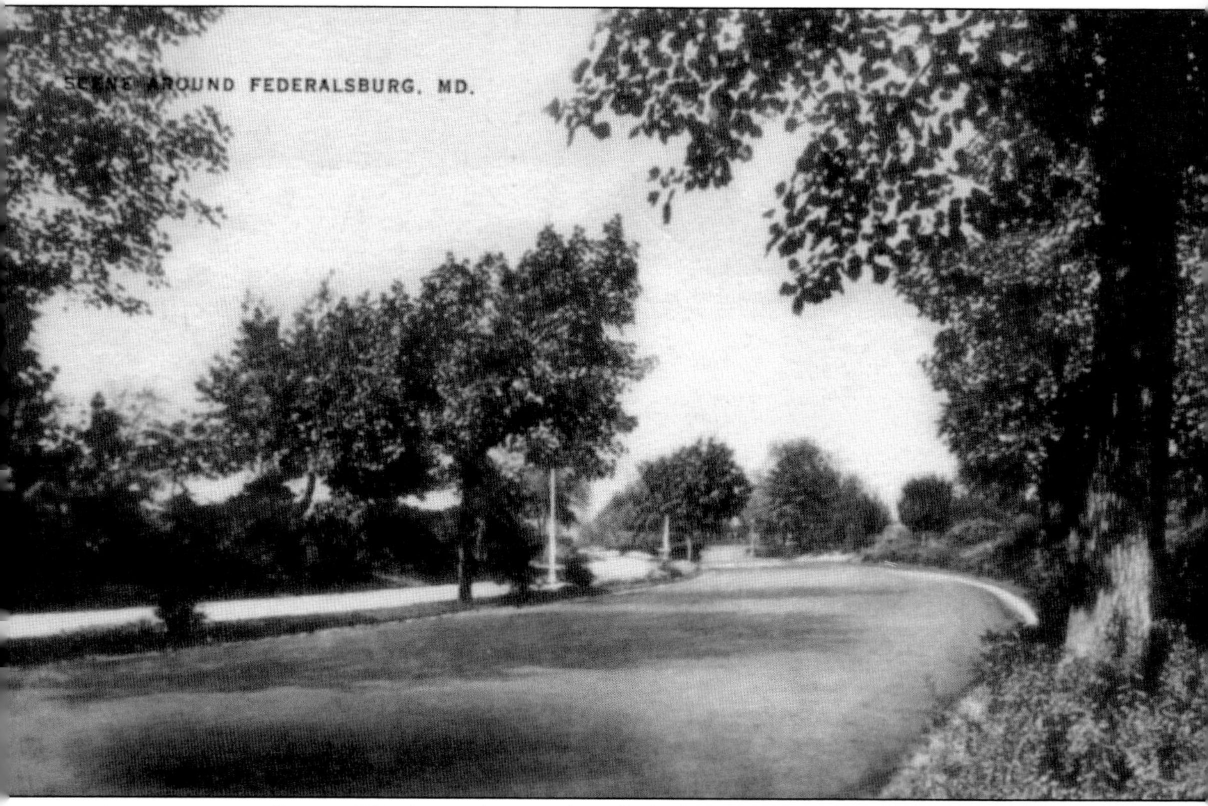

FEDERALSBURG SCENE. This is another unidentified photo portraying a beautifully scenic road possibly from around Federalsburg. (From the Danny Phillips collection.)

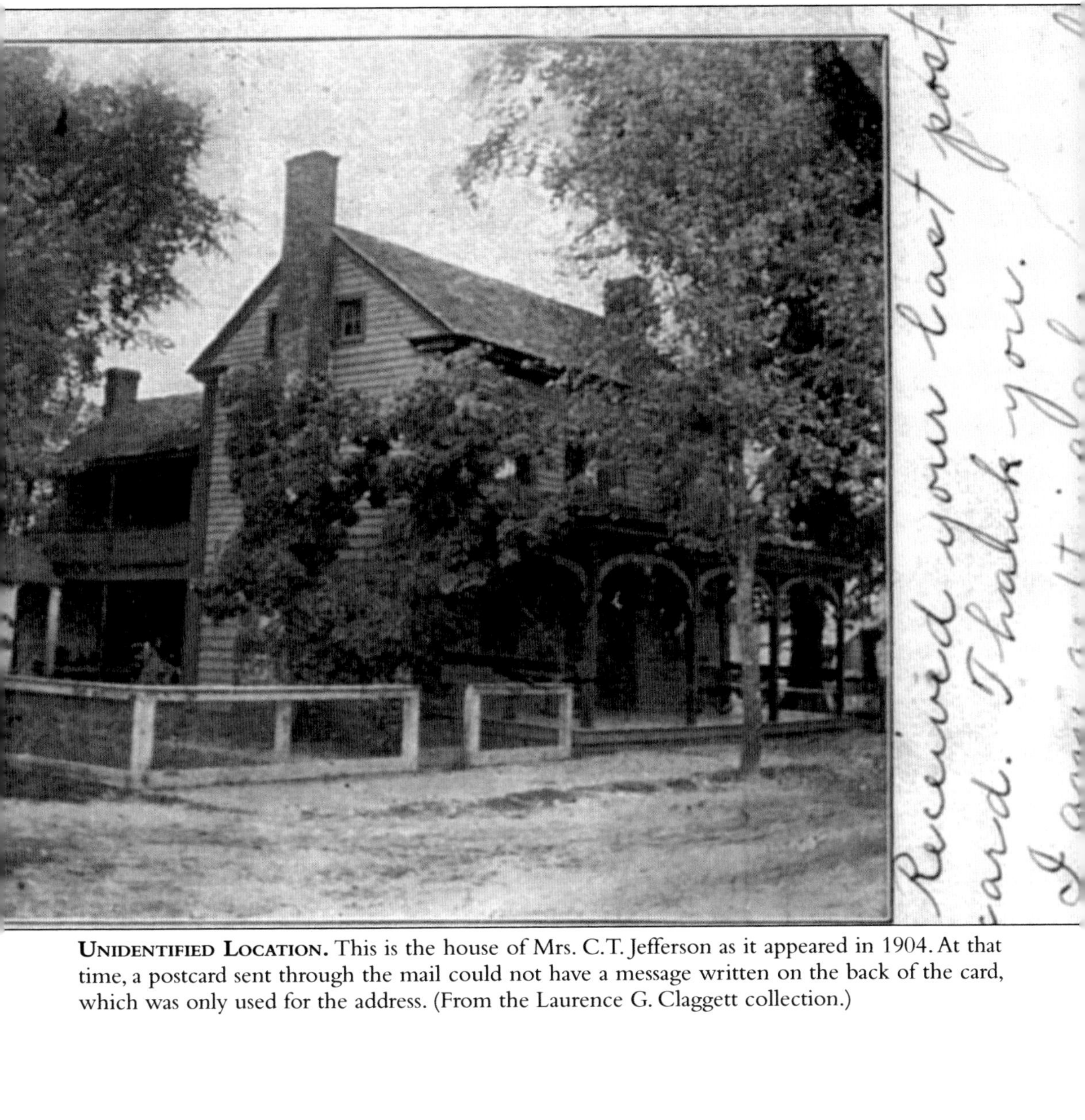

UNIDENTIFIED LOCATION. This is the house of Mrs. C.T. Jefferson as it appeared in 1904. At that time, a postcard sent through the mail could not have a message written on the back of the card, which was only used for the address. (From the Laurence G. Claggett collection.)

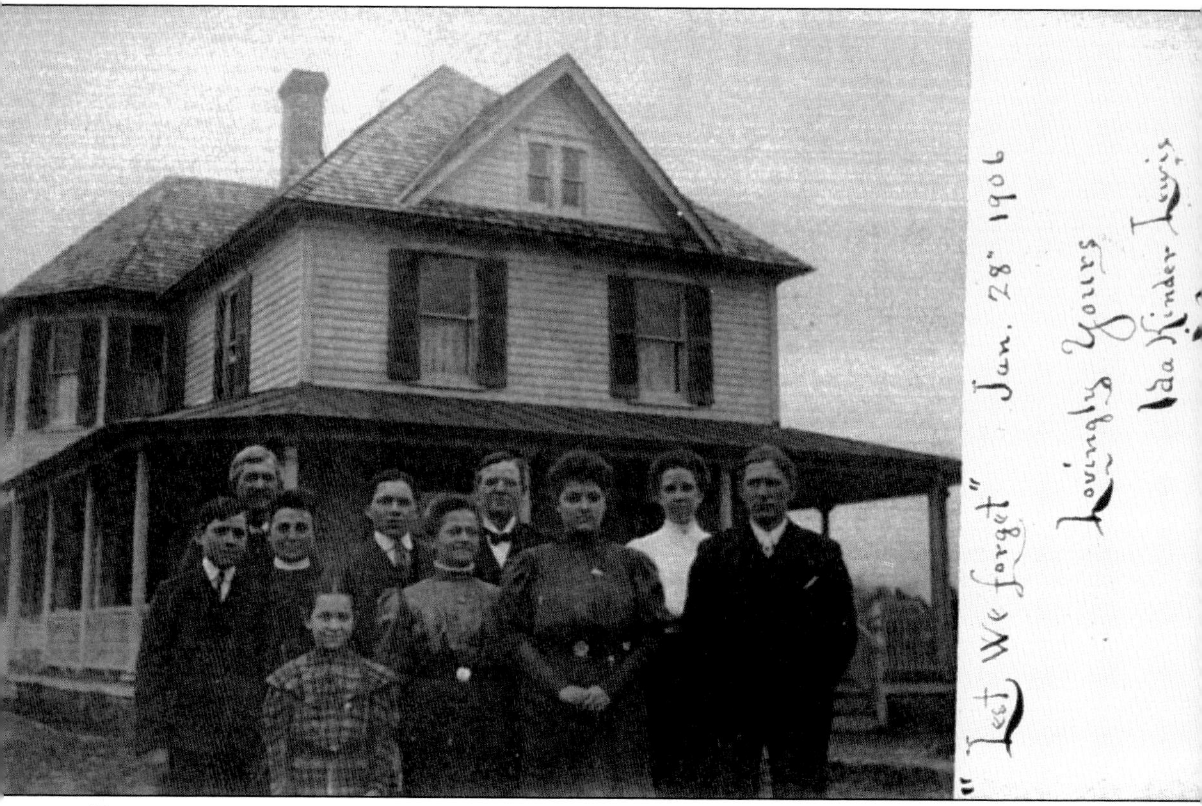

POSTCARD FROM FEDERALSBURG. This postcard was sent from Federalsburg to Oak Grove, a Delaware settlement a few miles off the Federalsburg Reliance Road. The house is unidentified. The sender, Mrs. Ida F. Kinder Lewis, was born July 28, 1864 and died June 3, 1913. She was married to Charles S. Lewis. While they lived a number of years in California, they were very active in the planning of the renowned Davis, Noble, and Kinder family reunions. Their only child, a daughter, lived only 15 months. The only person identified in the photo is the man standing on the right. He was J. Raymond Charles, the first Federalsburg Volunteer Fire Company president. He was an insurance agent (except for life) and was in business with H.E. Kinder. He was also the promoter for the 1932 Historical Souvenir Book which originally sold for 75¢. (From the Laurence G. Claggett collection.)

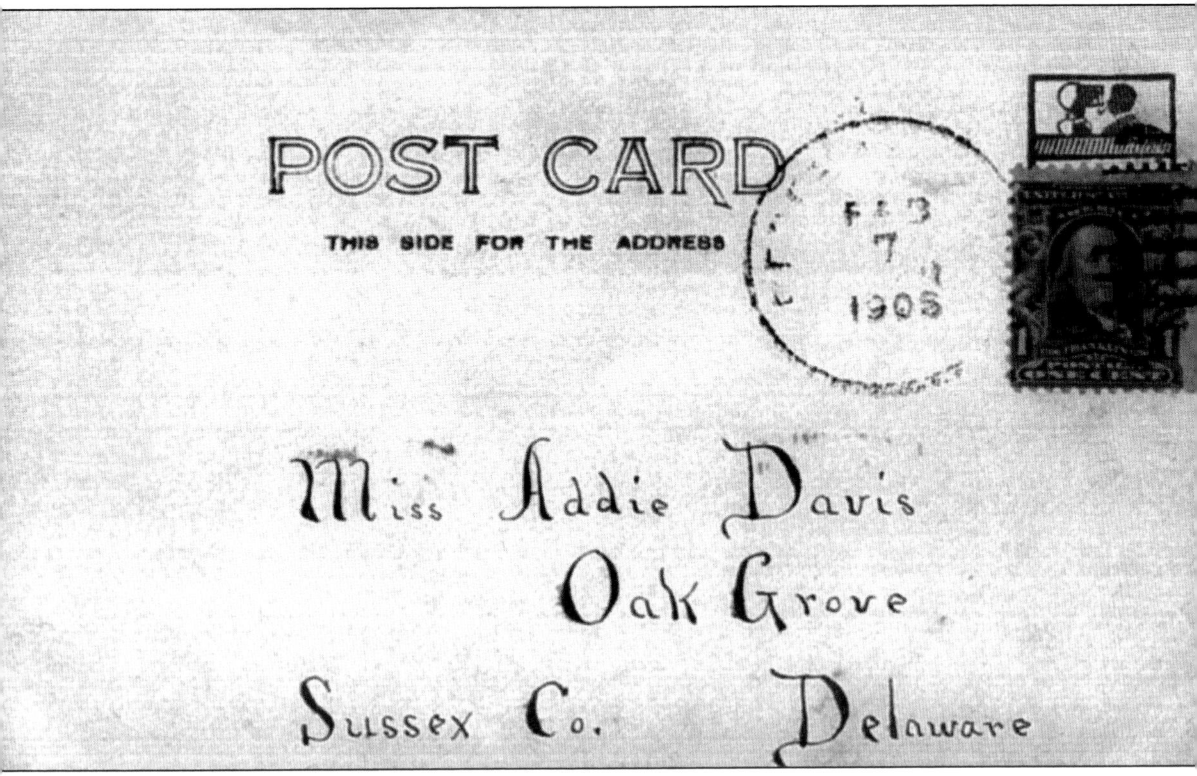

Postcard from Federalsburg. This is the address side of the postcard featured on page 44.

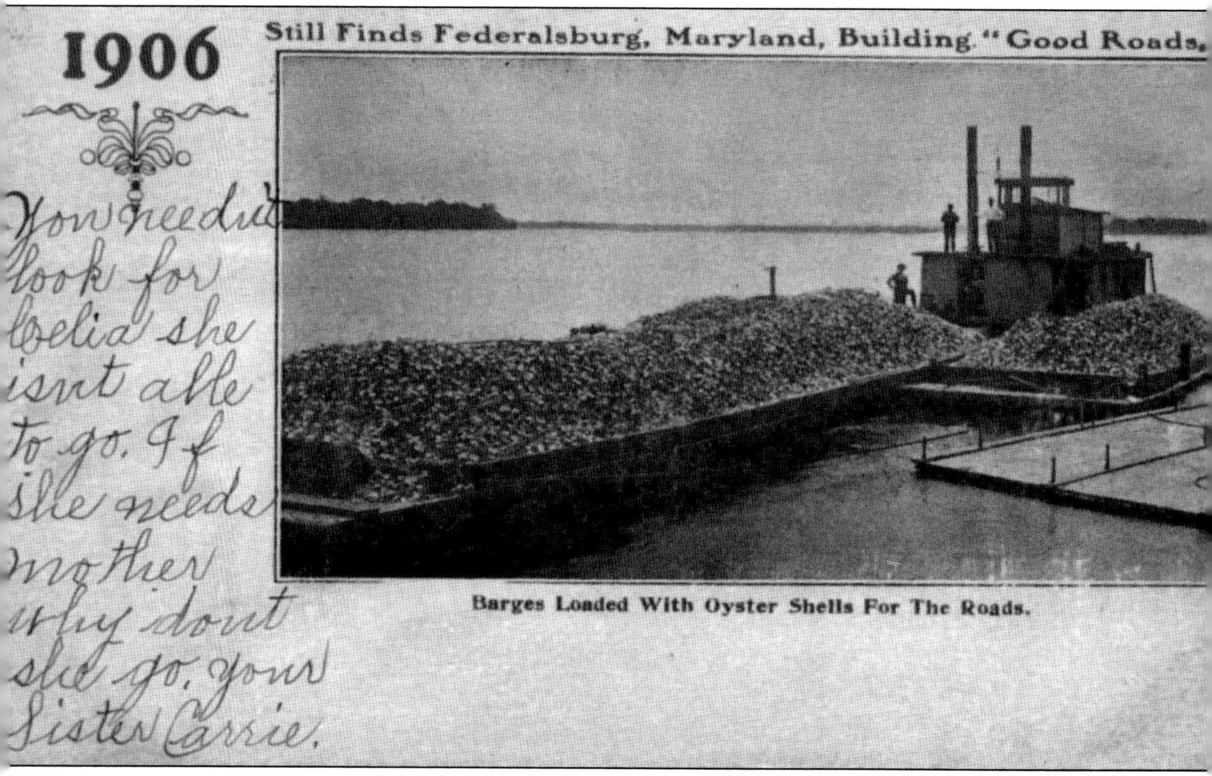

OYSTER SHELL ROADS. Prior to the turn of the century, wagon loads were limited to what a team of horses could pull over the sandy road with the driver walking. A drive over this type of road was described as enervating and depressing in the extreme. Then someone got the idea of covering roads with oyster shells, as was being done in other parts of the county. At that time oyster shells were in abundance and were a disposal problem as are our automobile tires today. Shells could be purchased for 2 1/4¢ per bushel. Of the roads surrounding Federalsburg, two miles of Liberty Road was the first one improved around 1900. Mr. H.B. Messenger of Federalsburg arranged the rail shipment of shells and he persuaded local residents who had an interest in improving Liberty Road to haul the shells to the road by horse-drawn wagons. A farmer could now haul two and three times as much as they formerly did on the same roads. The drive was then described as "a relaxation and a positive enjoyment and leaves one feeling as if he had just listened to a beautiful piece of music or witnessed a fine sunset." Other roads soon were shelled, including Faulkner's Hill Road, shelled 7/8 of a mile and then the Miles' Branch Road (Reliance Road), shelled 1 5/8 miles and completed in the spring of 1903. In the winter of 1903 the Easton Road was shelled as far as Friends' Corner, 5/8 of a mile. (From the Archie Palamaras collection.)

Two

Business and Industry

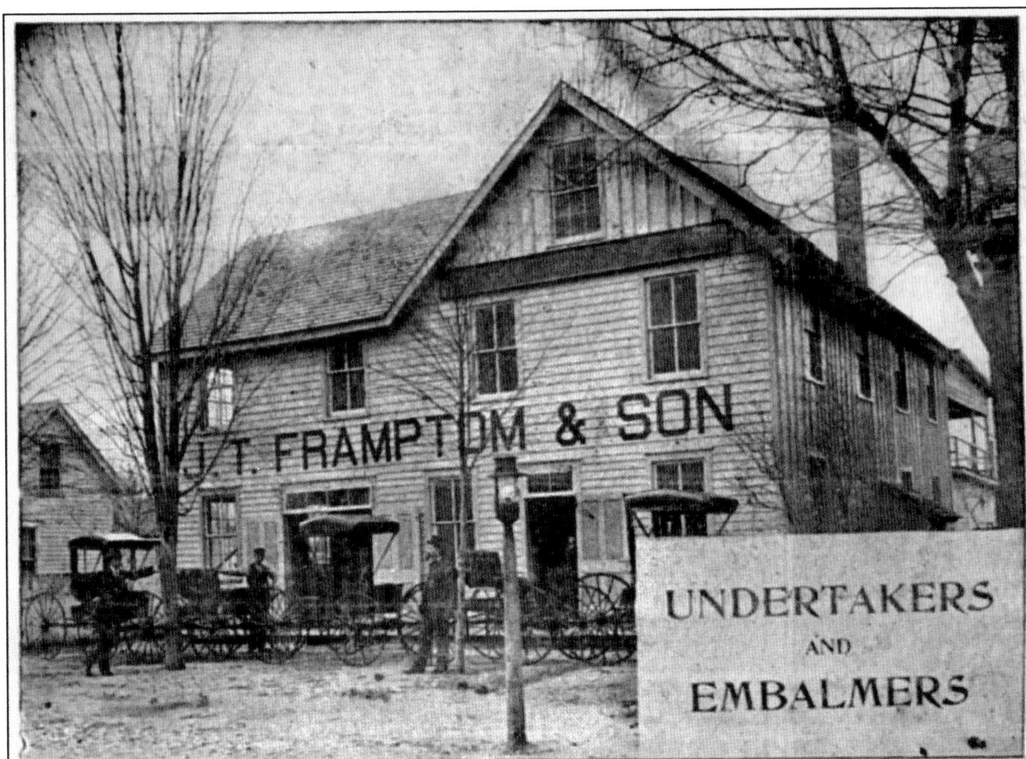

Oldest Business. The oldest business establishment in Federalsburg began in 1864 when Joseph T. Framptom started a livery and undertaking business. They became one of the best and most up-to-date establishments on the Peninsula. In 1893, J.J. Framptom graduated from college in embalming and became an expert in this line. (From the Federalsburg Historical Society, Inc. Collection.)

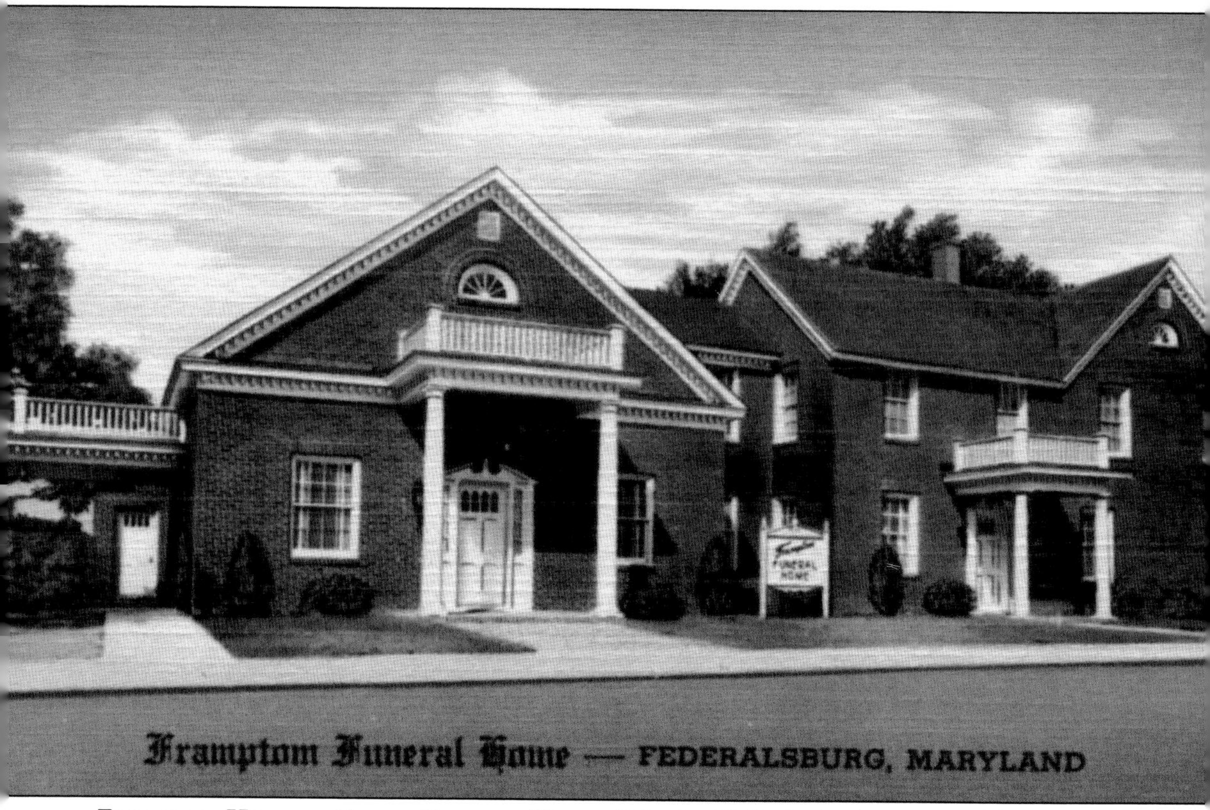

FRAMPTOM-HAWKINS-ESKOW FUNERAL HOME, P.A. In 1972, the business was sold to Donald and Margaret Hawkins. Mr. and Mrs. Hawkins ran the business until 1988 when they sold it to their daughter and son-in-law, Margaret "Janie" and Michael Eskow. They, along with their daughter and son-in-law Christy and Roman Coale, ran the business, which still ranks as a leading establishment within the town under the name Framptom-Hawkins-Eskow Funeral Home, P.A. (From the Danny Phillips collection.)

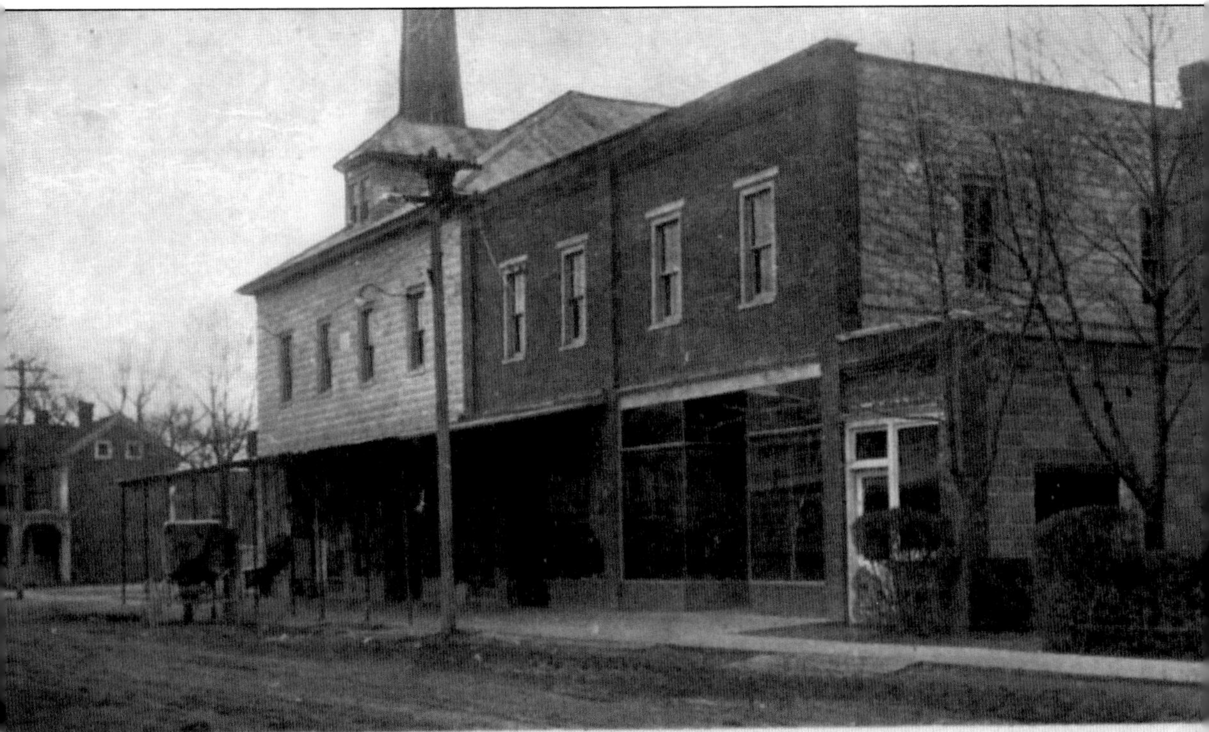

FIRST NATIONAL BANK, Federalsburg, Md.

West Side of South Main Street around the Turn of the 20th Century. These buildings have housed many businesses, including Fox's $.05 to $1 store, Western Auto, Eastern Shore Public Service Co., H.M. Black Style Shoppe, J.F. Patchett & Son Plumbing and Heating, and Guy S. White grocery. The little office on the right served as an office at one time for John N. Wright of the canning industry. The second floor at one time housed a movie theater known as the "Peanut Gallery" and at other times served as living quarters for several families. The current businesses include Great Wall Chinese Restaurant, Mother's Southern Kitchen, J.W.'s Fresh Cutz & Curlz, and What's Your Destination Transportation. The First National Bank opened in this building before they constructed a building across the street at the corner of South Main Street and East Central Avenue. In 1914, the annual meeting of the stockholders elected the following board of directors (prominent men of their time): E.E. Goslin as president, Bayard Nichols as first vice-president, Thomas S. Holt as second vice-president, W.R. Breeding, O. Hignutt, C.R. Neal, E.L. Morris, H.A. Joyce Jr., Charles M. Walker, Thomas J. Todd, and Charles Kinder. E.J. Hammond served as cashier and Philetus Jefferson as assistant cashier. (From the Danny Phillips collection.)

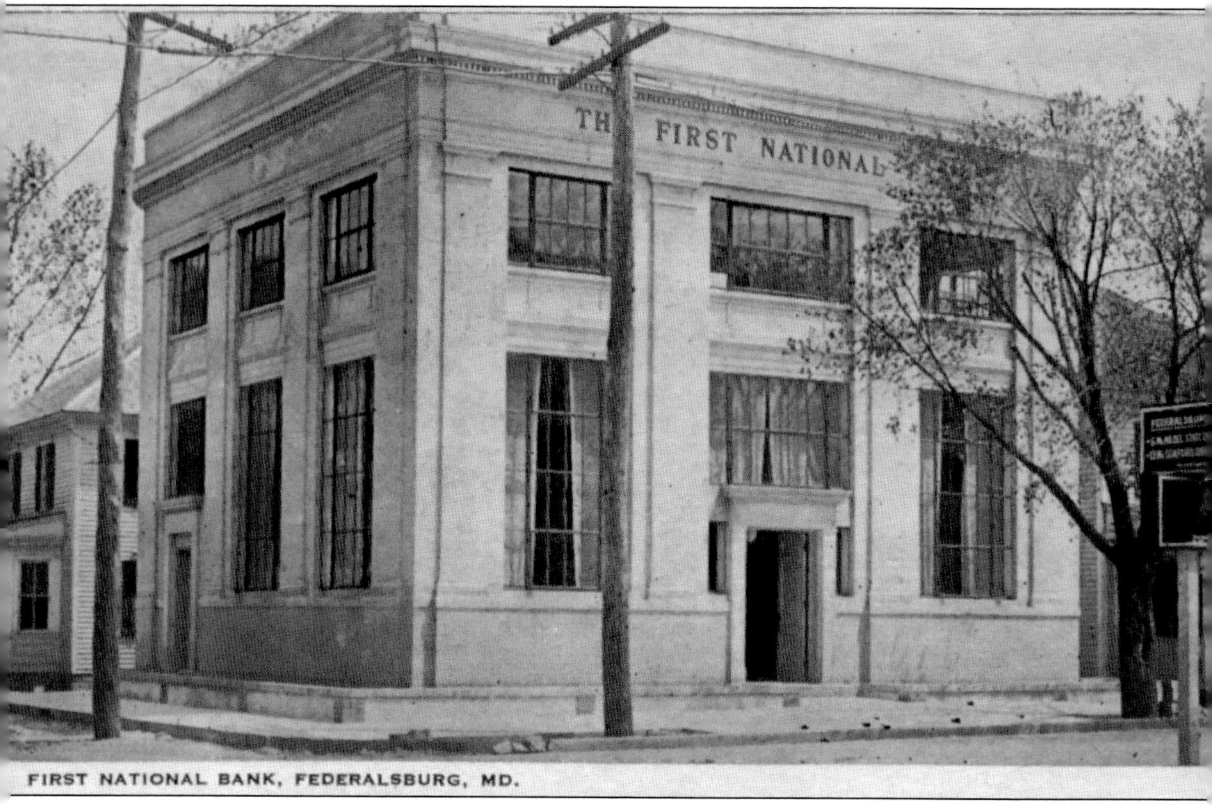

FIRST NATIONAL BANK. According to Ellenor Merriken, Federalsburg had a disastrous fire in 1903 that destroyed several buildings in the heart of town before it was brought under control. Mark Wright's Hardware Store, which stood on this corner, was destroyed. Dr. George Galloway then had a home and office built on the southeast corner of Main Street and somewhere during the late 1910s and early 1920s the house was moved further east on East Central Avenue to make way for the new bank building (see house on the left side of postcard). According to Gloria Durham, who managed the Denton National Bank in Federalsburg, the First National Bank paid off all customers during the bank panic and it is believed the bank closed around 1931. The building then housed the Hotel Russell, where you could dance every evening and buy sandwiches, a soda, or ice cream. Later the building became the home office of Holt Oil Company. During the 1960s, the Denton National Bank purchased the building and opened a branch. While the name has changed names several times, it has remained a bank since this time and is currently home of BB&T Bank. (From the Jeff Porter collection.)

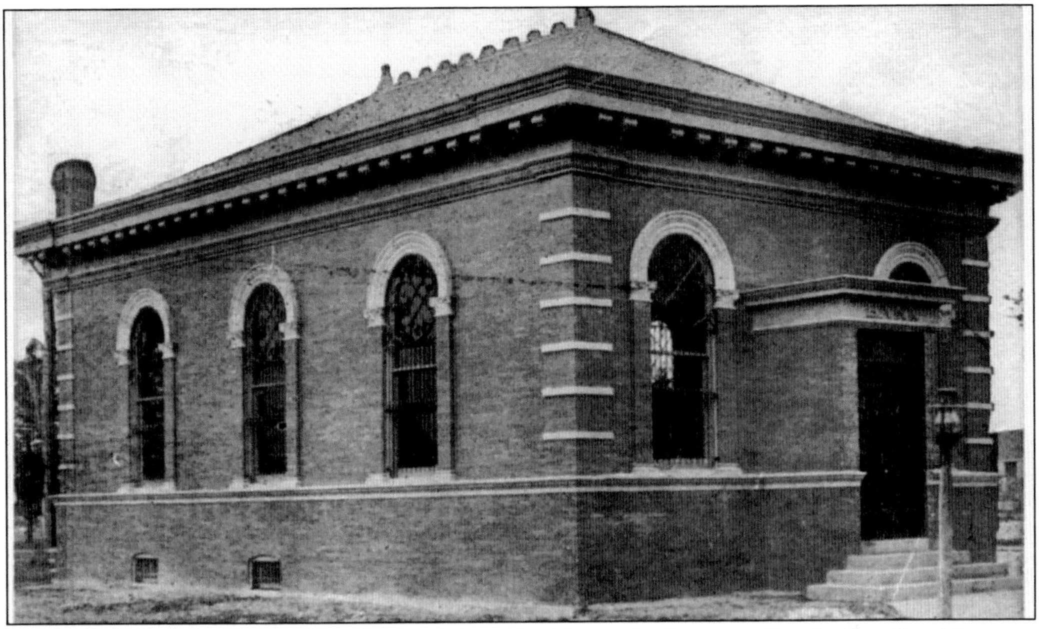

FEDERALSBURG BANK. These images of the Federalsburg Bank were taken before the side street was built, first known as Bank Street and now as West Central Avenue. Main Street was still a dirt road. Notice in the lower postcard the appearance of light poles. Federalsburg was still being lighted by oil lamps at the turn of the century and in 1904 the lighting bill was about $150. John F. Disharoon, owner of the Idlewild Mills, found a way to harness available water power for electricity and formed the Idlewild Electric Light, Heat, and Power Company to provide electricity to the town. In December 1906, the town of Federalsburg was lighted by electricity for the first time. (From the Danny Phillips collection.)

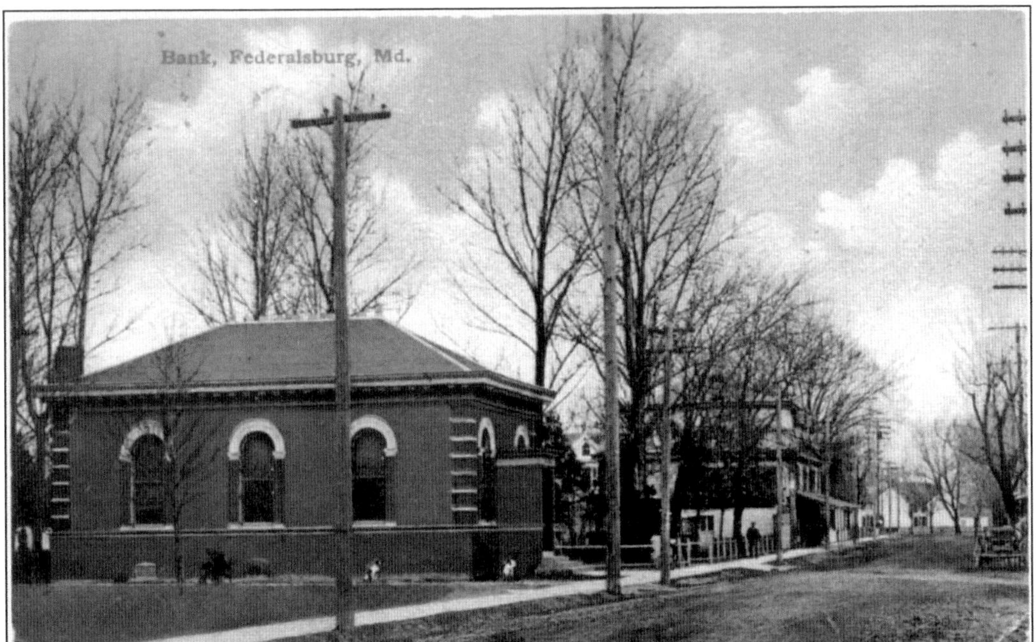

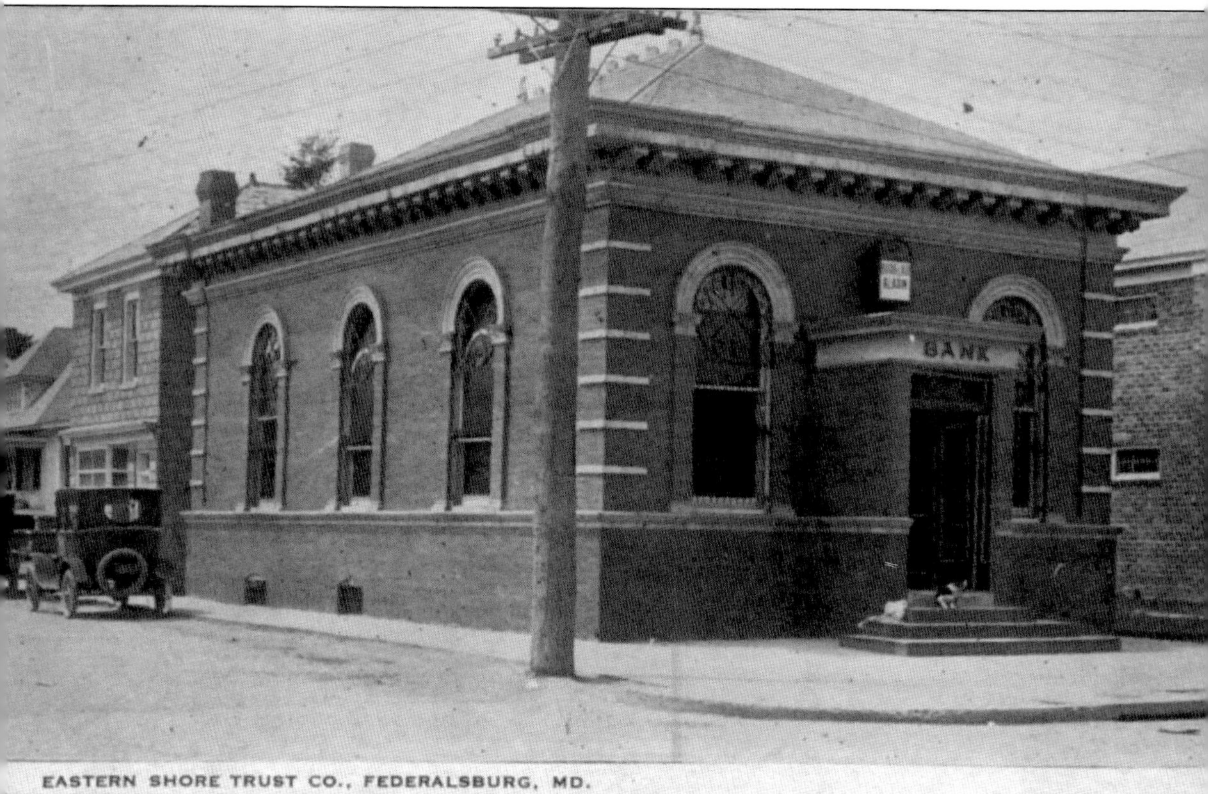

FEDERALSBURG BANK. Messrs. Thomas H. Chambers, Harry W. Davis, John M. Wright, and Fernandes Davis first approached the citizens of Federalsburg to establish a local bank. While they met with some opposition and much indifference, they persisted in their purpose and finally succeeded in securing sufficient capital. A suitable building, for temporary quarters, was erected by Mr. Chambers, and the bank opened for business on the 21st day of September, 1901 and proved a success from the beginning. Business steadily increased in volume under the following board of directors: Thomas H. Chambers, president; Fernandes Davis; J. Marcus Wright; Rufus F. Noble; Edward E. Nuttle; Alex. Noble; Francis P. Corkran; and George E. Noble. Mr. Harry W. Davis served as cashier and Mr. Harvey D. Williams as the teller (assistant cashier). The directors of the Federalsburg Bank of the Eastern Shore Trust Company purchased a lot on the corner of North Main Street and the new street that opened on the south side of Sen. Edward E. Goslin's lawn upon which would be built "a handsome banking house which will be an ornament to the town and reflect credit upon the management of the institution." (From the Danny Phillips collection.)

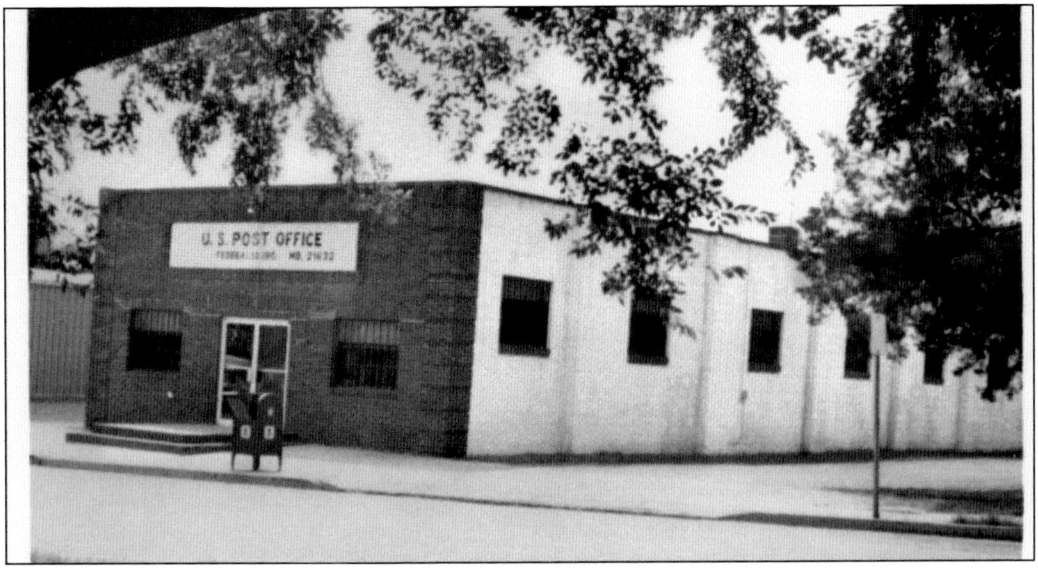

Post Office. The U.S. Post Office operated in several locations on North Main Street until this building opened October 1, 1952. While some improvements have been made, this building still serves the citizens of Federalsburg today. Postal employees at the 1952 dedication included Bruce Hartzell, Ridgely Brown, Gordon Butler, Virgil Turner, Clark Andrews, Arthur Johnson, Bobby Westfall, Russell Carroll, Francis Turpin, William "Pete" Galloway, Edgar "Husky" Fisher, Byron Griffith, Ed Williams, Frank Bradley (postmaster), and Raymond Bennett Jr. (Top postcard from the Danny Phillips collection; bottom postcard from the Federalsburg Historical Society Collection.)

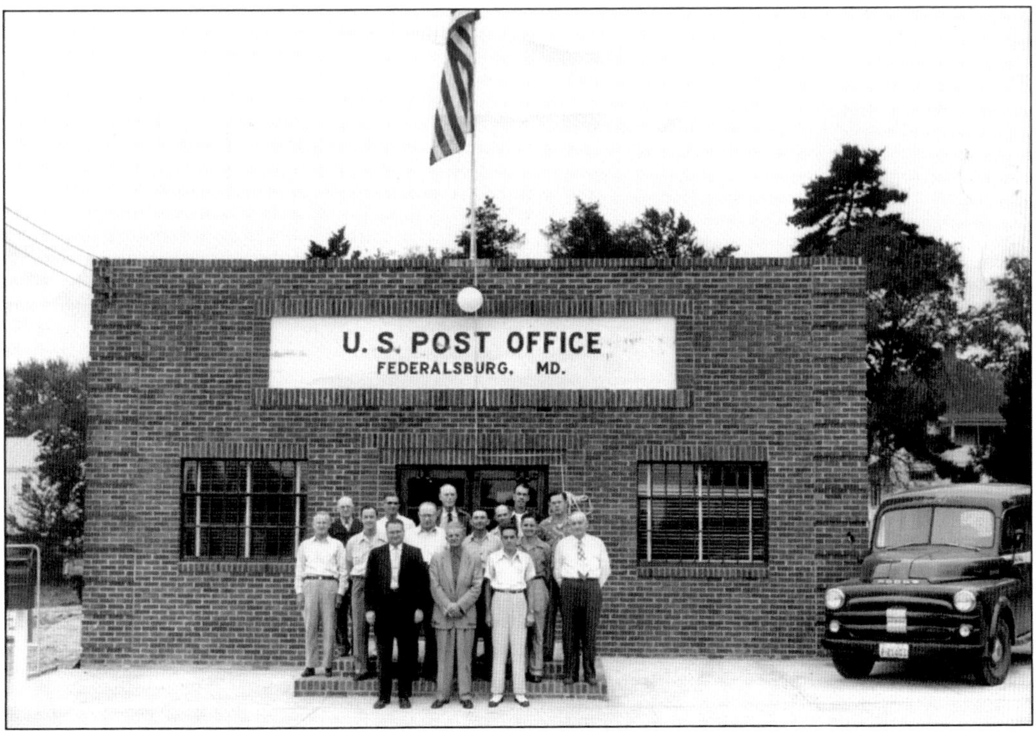

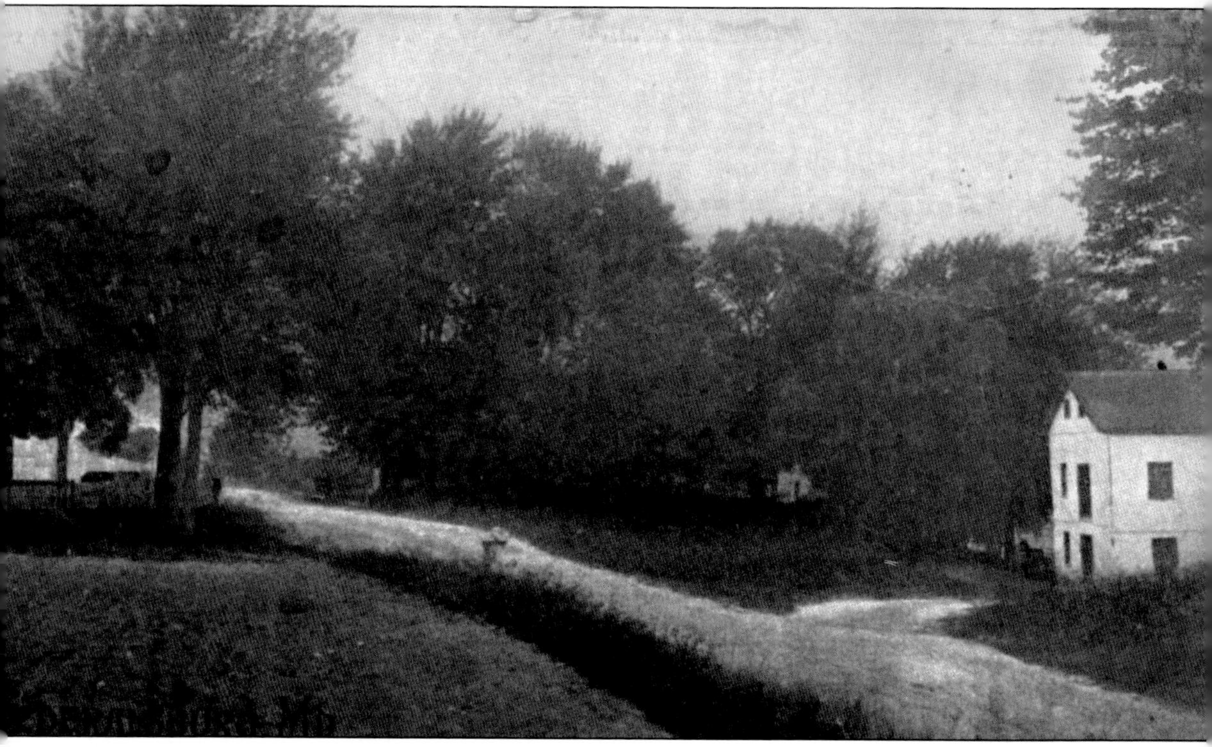

IDLEWILD MILL. The old Idlewild Dam on the Marshyhope Creek just above Federalsburg was constructed around 1704. With its tremendous watershed and fast down-grade water-power the grist mill became very active. The deed for this property was originally written on parchment and paid for in tobacco. It has been written that some of the ground corn for George Washington's army came from this mill. The mill changed hands many times as did the name. James Faulkner sold the mill to Solomon Bartlett in 1734 and Thomas Lewis operated the mill from 1791 to 1809. James B. Robbins continued to run the mill until 1825 when he disposed of his entire holdings to Meshack and John Elliott, of Sussex County, Delaware and the mill became known as Elliott's Mill. They made many improvements and added a carding machine (wool fleece was carded and combed and made into rolls for household spinning wheels) and a saw mill (sawed lumber for building homes, boats, and sailing vessels) to the operation. A wooden bridge was constructed over the dam with side railings on both sides and was strong enough to carry most any load. In 1858, John Francis Elliott (the son of the original purchaser) sold the mill properties to John W. Brown, son of Eccleston Brown, who was another big land owner and prominent citizen. The mill then became known as Brown's Mill. Additional improvements were made to the mill to take care of the ever-increasing business. (From the Laurence G. Claggett collection.)

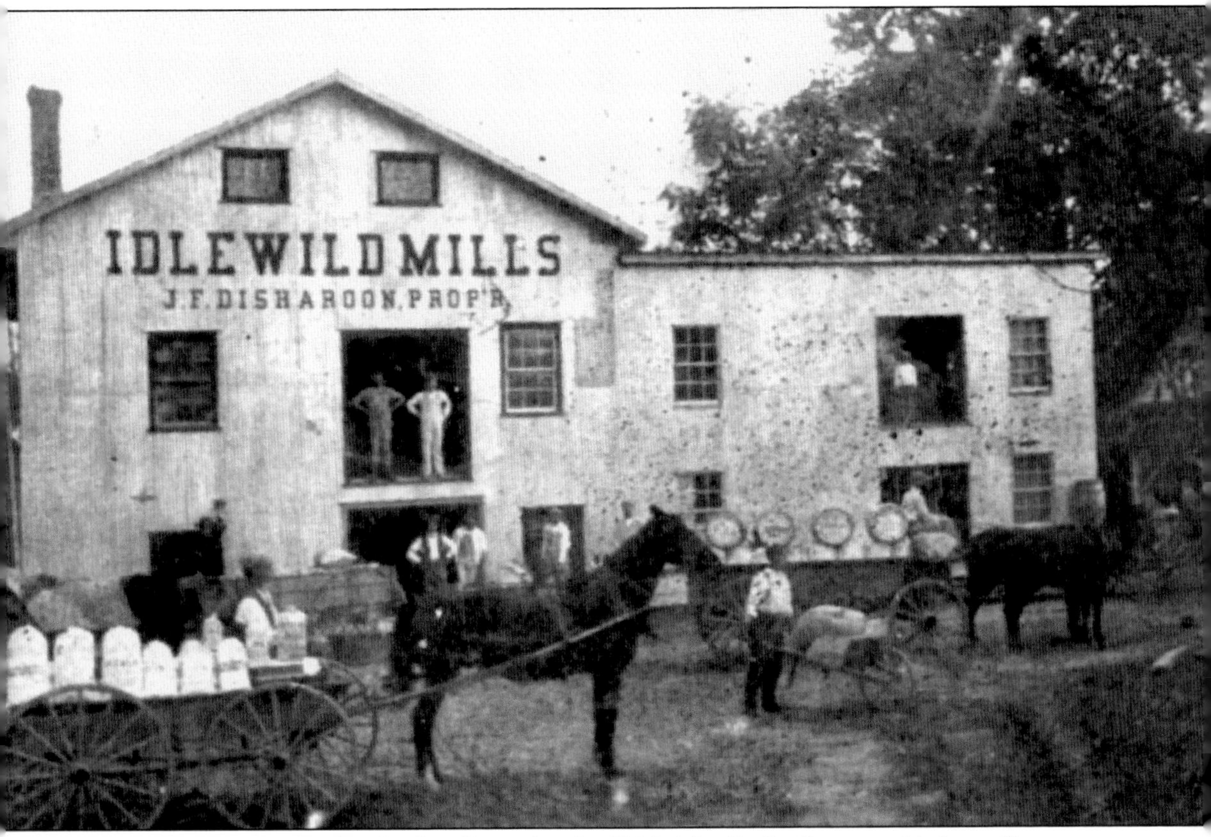

Idlewild Mill. After her husband's passing in 1894, Mrs. Lydia Brown sold the mill property to John F. Disharoon and it became known as the Idlewild Mill. Once again, improvements were made and the old paddle wheels were supplanted with a group of powerful turbines. Steam engines turned the dynamo, which used sawdust as fuel to fire the boiler. With the abundance of water power now available, Mr. Disharoon utilized some to provide electricity to his home and to the mill. Later, he organized the Idlewild Electric Light, Heat and Power Co., which was capable of furnishing electricity to Federalsburg. In 1908, he formed a stock company with the prominent businessmen of Federalsburg. The company provided power to Hurlock and East New Market and later to Preston and Secretary. In 1912, the mill property was sold once again. In 1915, the Idlewild Mill burned and was never rebuilt. However, one of the original walls is still standing along one of the banks "as a reminder of what was once the finest water-powered grist mill on the shore." (From the Mary Holt collection.)

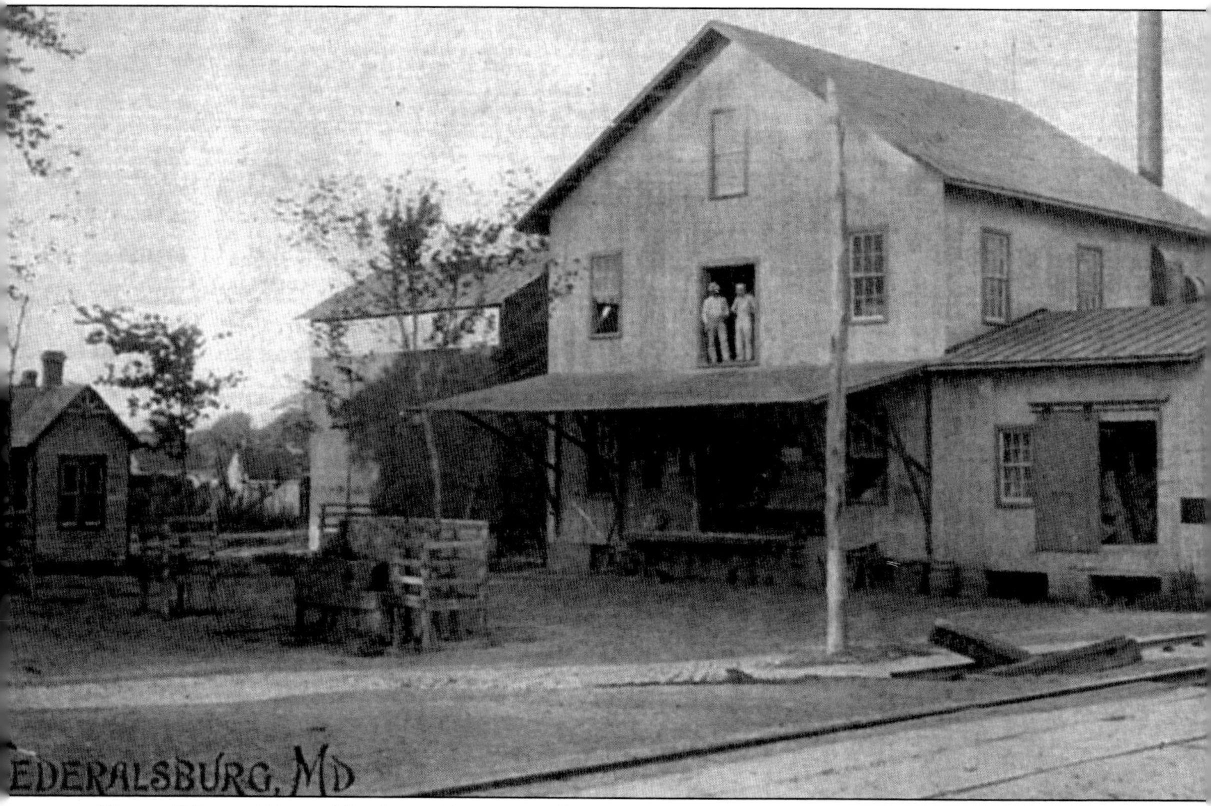

EAGLE MILLS. Henry Burdette Messenger, known as H.B. or Burdette, was named after one of two brothers, Andrew and Henry, who emigrated from Yorkshire, England in the late 1630s. The name was passed from generation to generation until H.B.'s father, Henry A., passed the name to him. Henry A. moved the family to Federalsburg around 1880 seeking a warmer climate than Massachusetts. H.B. also had a brother, Robert William, known as R.W. or Bob. The family started in the cannery business around 1887 and owned or partly owned at least 10 canneries on the Delmarva peninsula. In 1900, H.B. built the powerful and well-equipped Eagle Mills. Due to some dry seasons, water power would fail to do all the work called for at the other mills and caused much inconvenience to the people of the town and surrounding country. It was situated at the lower end of town, along the water and the railroad. It gathered grain and distributed its products by its own boats and by rail, with ample capacity and power, and fitted with the most improved machinery. In 1904, it was heralded as the best-equipped mill on Delmarva. For a period of two years, the Idlewild Mill was idle until a disastrous fire, starting from the boiler, destroyed the Eagle Mill in 1911. While this mill was rebuilt, Idlewild Mill went back into operation until the Eagle Mill reopened. Later this operated as Federalsburg Flour Mills under G.T. Bell & Son. (From the Laurence G. Claggett collection.)

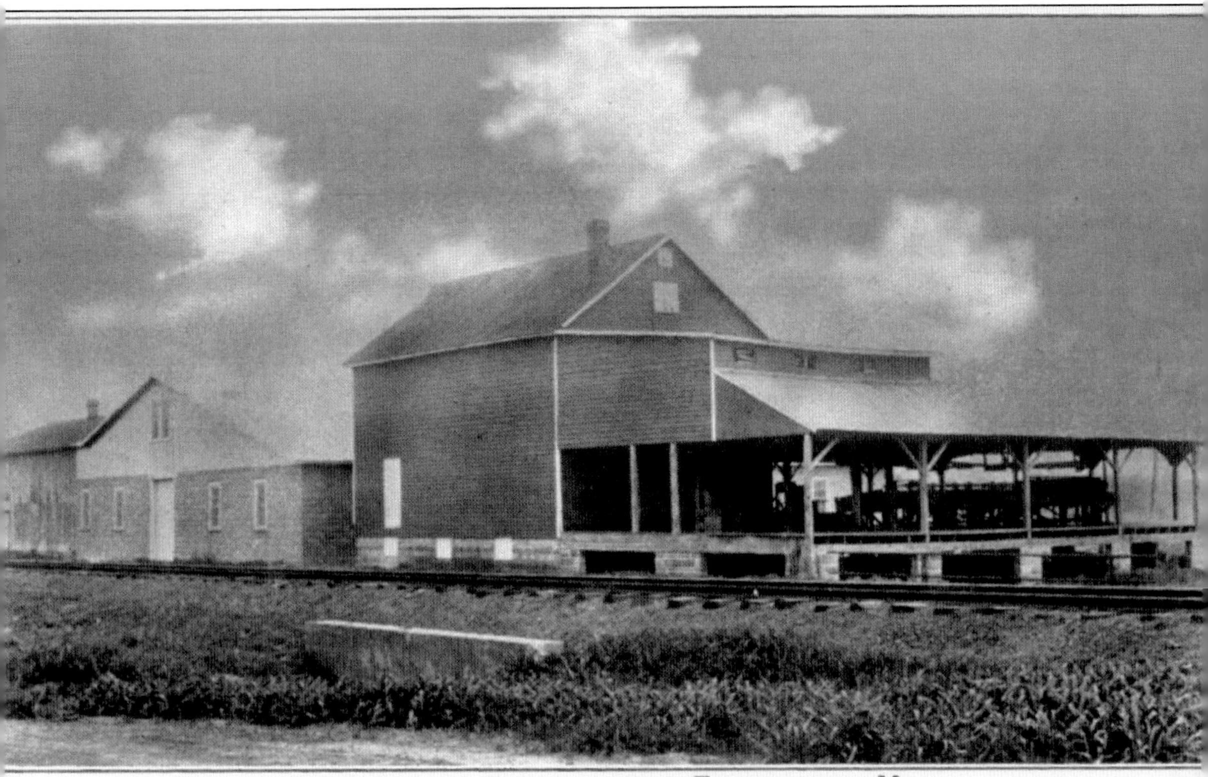

FRUIT PACKING ESTABLISHMENT, FEDERALSBURG, MD.

JOHN N. WRIGHT JR. This postcard shows the John N. Wright Jr. pickle factory, potato house, and packing shed. The establishment was located on the southwest side of Railroad Avenue. Mr. Wright was a buyer and seller of fruits, produce, and evergreens with pickles as a specialty. The company offered high-quality canned goods and guaranteed "absolute protection, prompt service, and reasonable rates." He owned and operated several canning factories and created hundreds of jobs for working people, many of whom depended on the canning season in former years to make enough money to tide them over winter when jobs were scarce. Mr. Wright also sold insurance and coal, was an agent for Western Union Telegraph, and served as a notary public. They were the last canneries in operation in Caroline County, but ceased that part of the business in 1997. Today, the family still operates a farming operation at this location. (From the William F. Gray Jr. collection.)

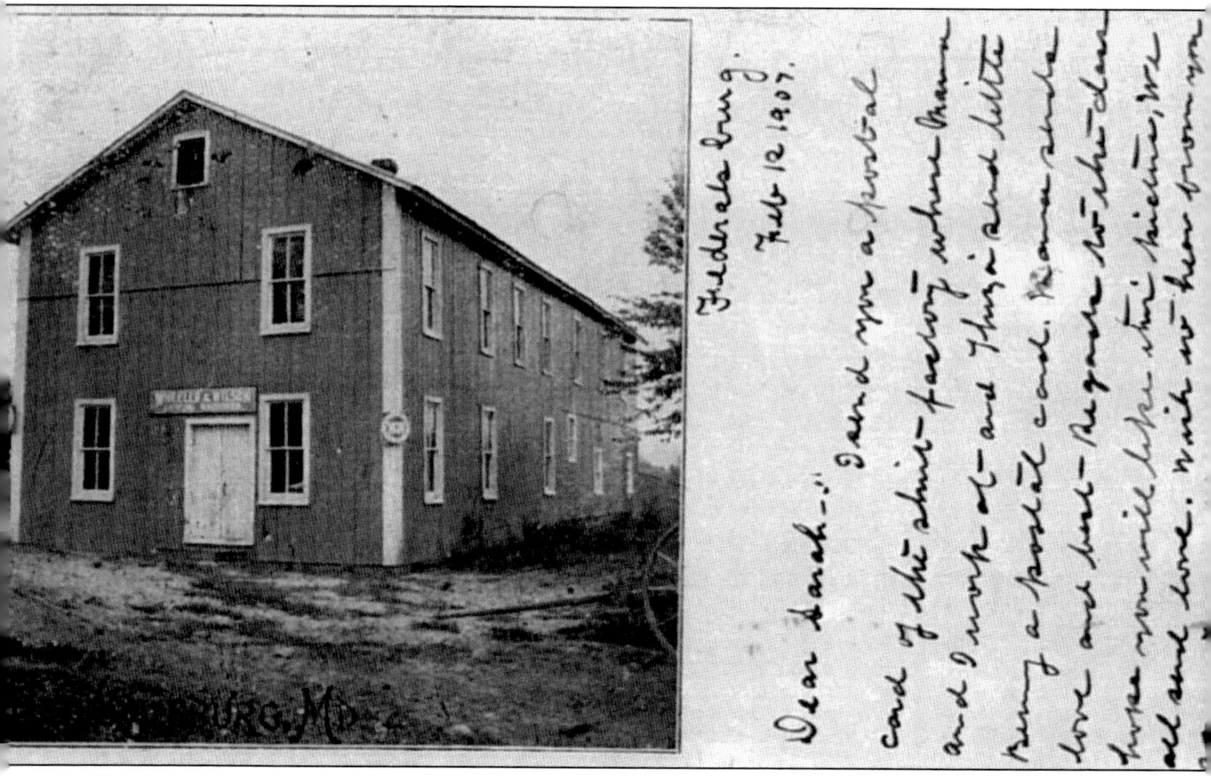

FEDERALSBURG SHIRT FACTORY. One industry in the early 1900s employed mostly female help, about 50 hands, in Federalsburg. The Federalsburg Shirt Factory was a large two-story building fitted with about 40 machines that were driven by a gasoline engine. The business was also an agent for Wheeler and Wilson and Singer Sewing Machines. The output of the factory was about 400 dozen shirts per week. Mr. A.R. Messick was the manager in 1904. Prior to the time of the shirt factory operation, which was located on Bloomingdale Avenue, the location was the establishment of W.H. Alburger, a wheelwright (blacksmith). (From the Laurence G. Claggett collection.)

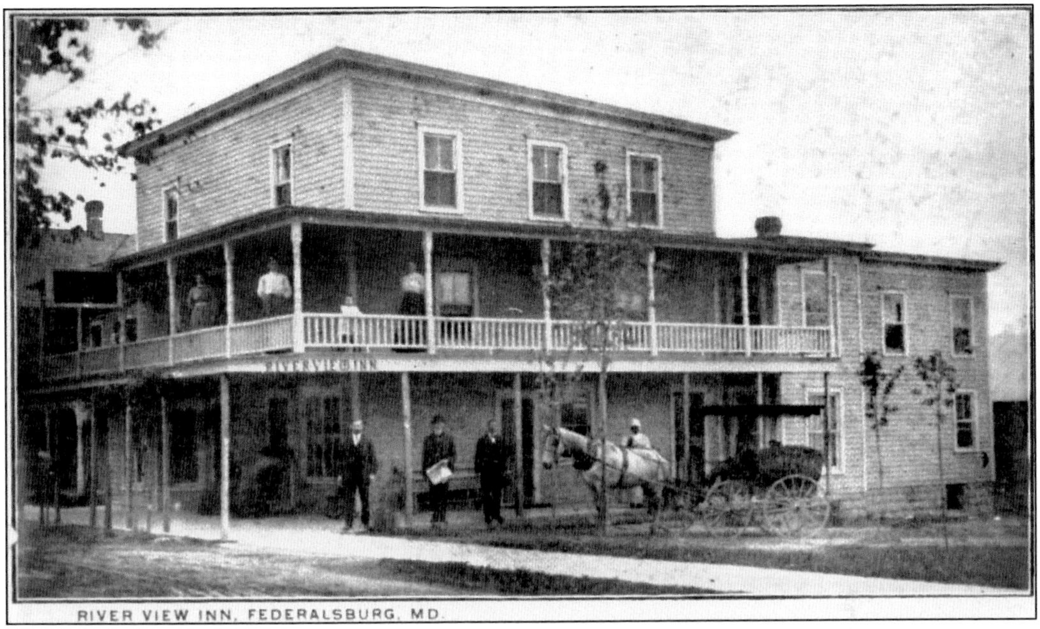

RIVERVIEW INN & BAKERY. In 1902, William T. and Ida Adams returned to Federalsburg and opened the Riverview Bakery on South Main Street (photo below taken around 1904.) Believed to be the first bakery on the Eastern Shore, it was first prophesied to fail because "no one would eat bakers' bread when they could make their own." But once the public learned they could have fresh bread every day without the tedious work, the business flourished. After the original bakery burned, Ida Adams went to work established a hotel business while rebuilding the bakery. The inn was expanded to three stories and 22 beds. The dining room served meals, desserts, and ice cream to many a customer. In 1927, Mr. Adams passed away; Ida Adams served meals in the dining room until 1944 when she was 78 years old. She still continued to run the inn, supervised several apartment rentals and garages, and was agent for the Red Star Bus Lines. (From the Danny Phillips collection.)

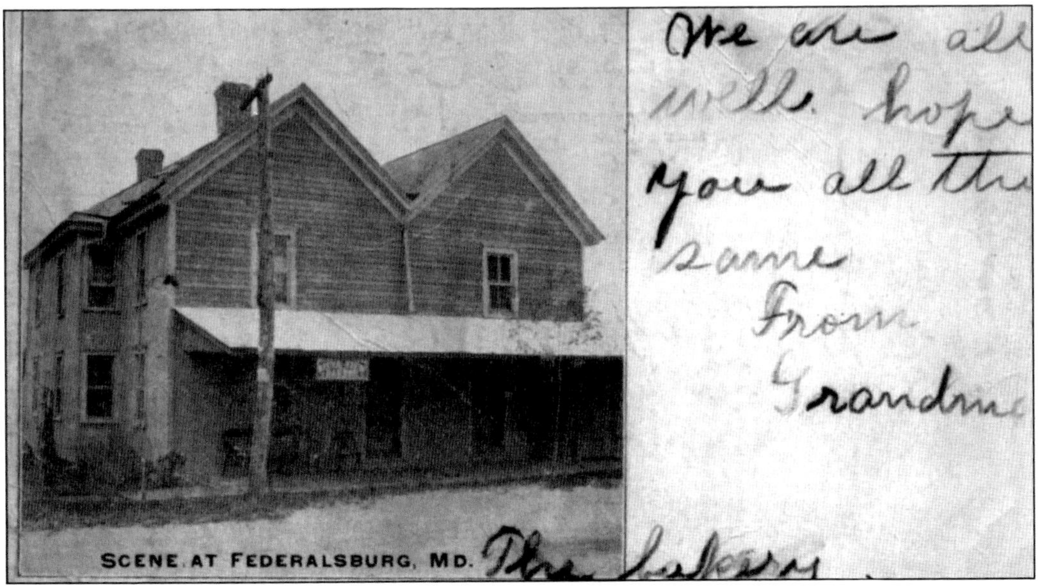

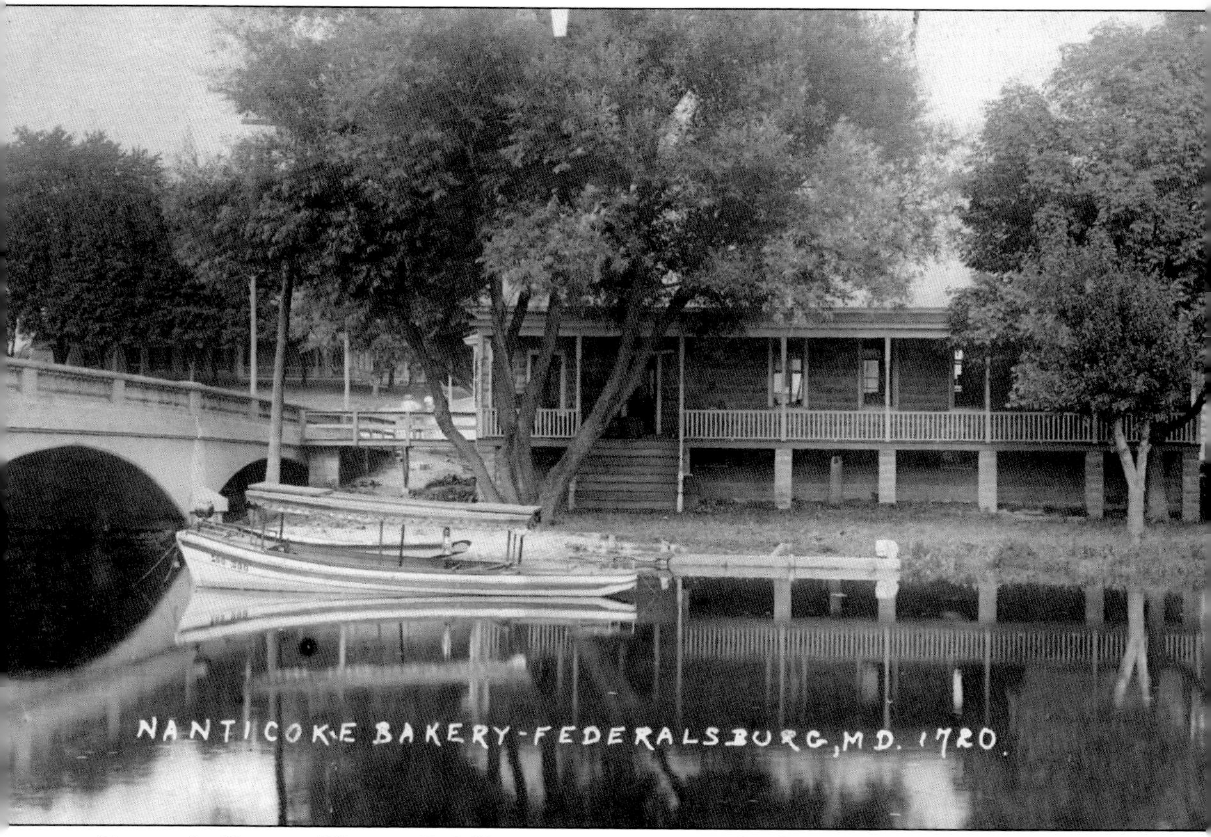

ZAFFERE'S BAKERY. Thomas O. Jefferson was proprietor of Jefferson Drug Store in town and was appointed postmaster of Federalsburg in 1897. In 1918, he built a bakery for his two sons, Philetus A. and Jerome D. The bakery was purchased from the heirs of the late Thomas Jefferson around 1923 by Emil Nicolai, who greatly improved the bakery and made it one of the finest-equipped baking plants on the Delmarva peninsula. In October 1926, Mr. Nicolai was fatally injured when he was cleaning a dough mixer and his hand caught in some of the machinery, drawing his arm in up to the elbow. He suffered greatly from shock and loss of blood and died at Easton Hospital the next day. Mr. Frank Zaffere had a retail bakery in Middletown, Delaware but saw the available Federalsburg bakery as an opportunity to grow. Frank and Anna Mabel Zaffere improved the business and grew the wholesale bakery business to include multiple routes. Sons Frank Jr. and Philip and daughters Mary and Agnes also worked in the business. Some of the local residents who were route salesmen and employees were Dawson Anthony, Barnie Beauchamp, Gilbert Breeding, Bill Cluley, Byard Davis, Ralph Davis, Lily Mae English, Ben Happersett, Lee James, Paul Jester, Larry Meredith, Henry Porter, Alfred Sherman, Roger Short, Ralph Shufelt, Roland Shufelt, Clarence Taylor, Jim Taylor, Philip Towers, Melvin Tull, and Ralph Tull. (From the Danny Phillips collection.)

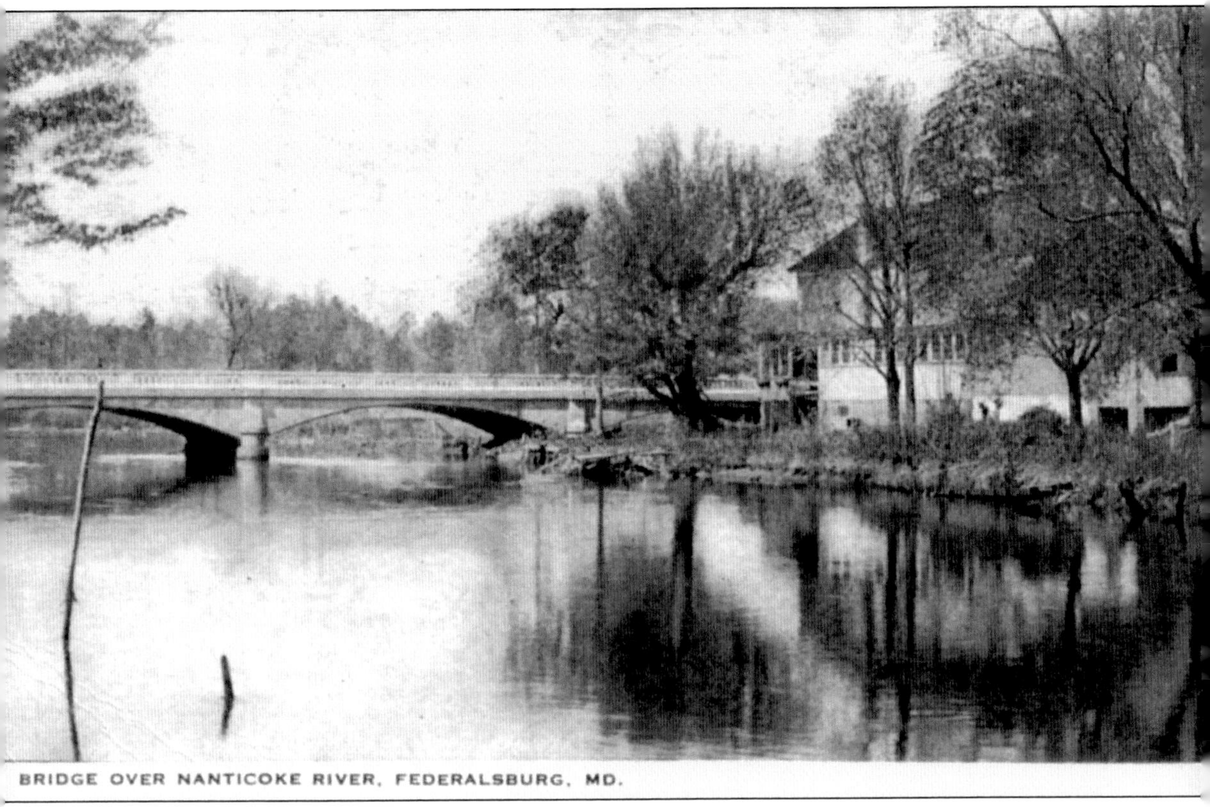

ZAFFERE'S BAKERY. The bakery's location next to the river was quite picturesque; however, there were several floods, especially the great flood of 1935, which caused great damage to the business. According to Ellenor Merriken, "The demand for Zaffere's fine quality baked goods and Sally Ann bread had about outgrown the limit of production at these premises, and after Mr. Zaffere passed away, Mrs. Zaffere, Frank Jr., and Philip moved to a new location and built one of the finest and most modern bakeries on the eastern seaboard." A baking business still operates today at this location under the General Mills label. Fond memories are told by those lucky enough to have visited the small shop located on the East Central Avenue side of this building. Many tales are told about the hobo buns, a large delicious sweet treat, that could be purchased for only a nickel. Other special memories are shared by those who fished beside the bakery on the Marshyhope Creek where the fish gathered en masse to feast on the dough scraps that ended in the waters. (From the Danny Phillips collection.)

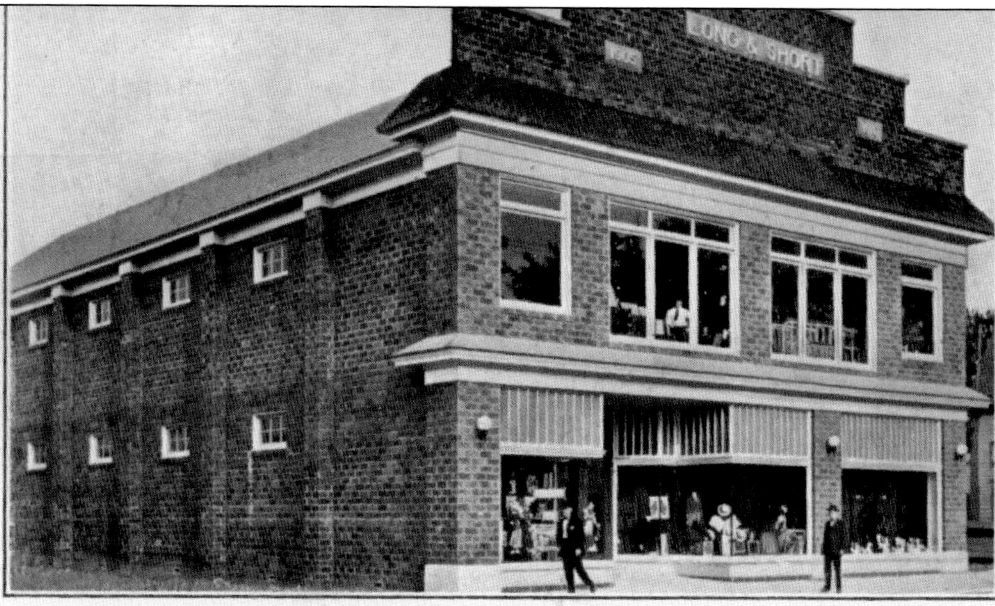

LONG & SHORT'S DEPARTMENT STORE, FEDERALSBURG, MD.

LONG AND SHORT. Long and Short, the downtown department store, opened in 1905, featuring nationally advertised products and claiming to give the public the best dollar-for-dollar value. Some of the merchandise available included dry goods and notions, ready-to-wear clothing, shoes and hats, home furnishings, appliances, and hardware. Prompt delivery was offered for a 50-mile radius around Federalsburg. Employees offered courteous and efficient service. Ellenor Merriken recalled in her book *Herring Hill* several clerks, including Mattie Rosser, May Sparklin, and Bessie and Helen Liden. Jean Andrew, Mrs. Merriken's daughter, recalled the clerks would put your money and sales ticket in a carrier on a line which would go up to the office and return a short while later with your change and receipt. The postcard below shows Long and Short after they incorporated in 1927 and after a third-story addition. (Top postcard from the Charles S. Long collection; bottom postcard from the Danny Phillips collection.)

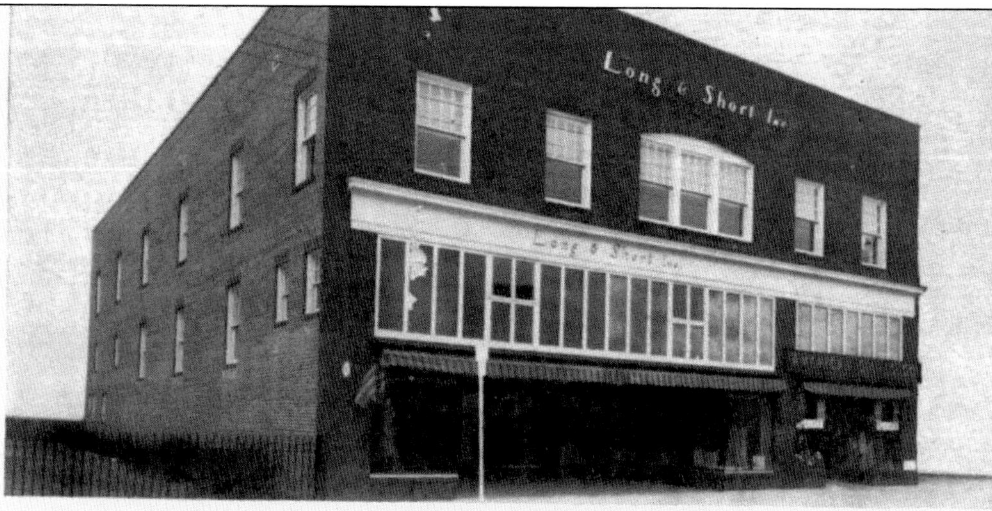

DEPARTMENT STORE. FEDERALSBURG. MD.

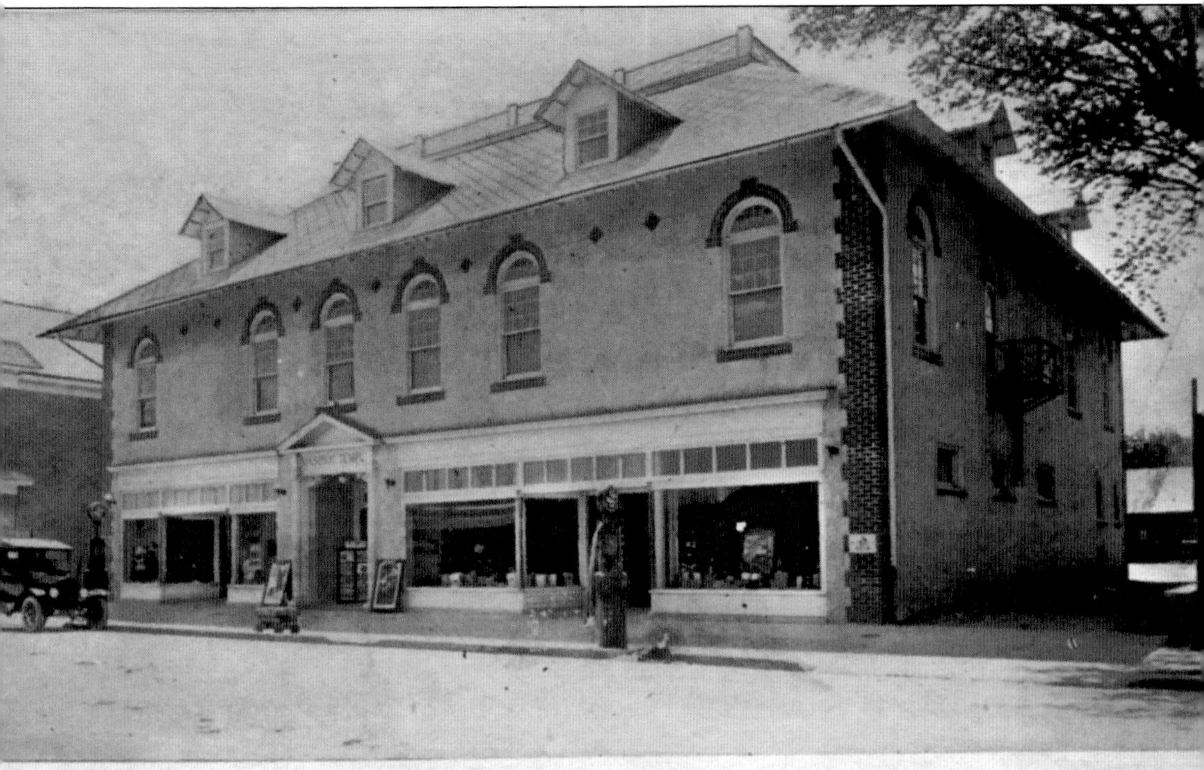

MASONIC TEMPLE, FEDERALSBURG, MD.

NANTICOKE LODGE. Nanticoke Lodge No. 172 A.F. & A.M. was instituted by a charter derived from the Most Worshipful Grand Lodge of Masons in Maryland on November 16, 1875. In 1918, the Temple was completed at a cost of $32,000. Covey and Williams, a Ford agency, occupied the first floor and the second floor housed the lodge and a public hall that held dances, movies, minstrel shows, and other entertainment. In front of the building are theatre billboards and several old-fashioned gas pumps. No longer evident in the photo is the iron rail that ran across the sides of the building; horses were tied to this rail. Businesses have changed throughout the years. Today Meredith's TV & Appliances, Inc. and Tammie's Floral Fantasy occupy the first floor space. (From the Jeff Porter collection.)

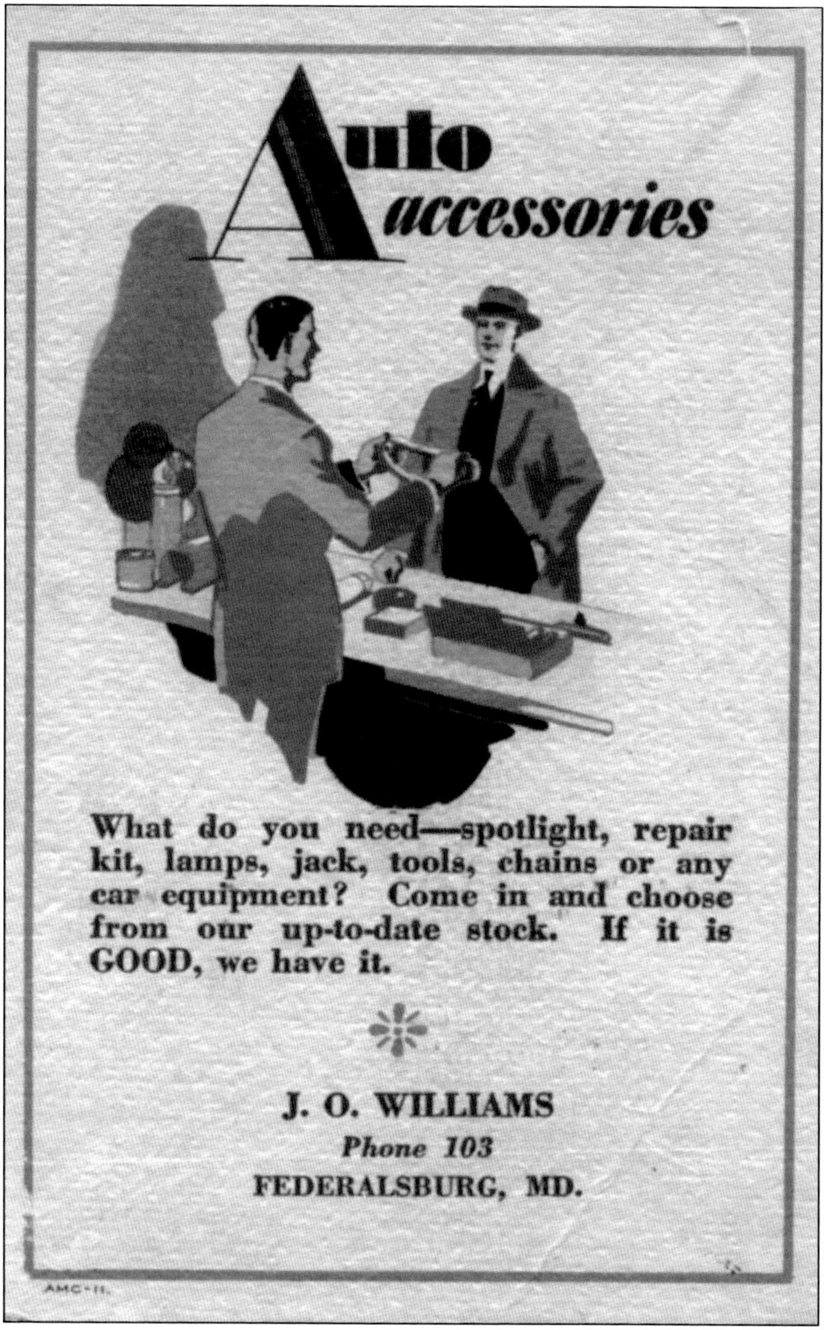

FORD DEALERSHIP. Jacob O. Williams owned the authorized Ford dealership in Federalsburg in the 1920s and later took a partner, Allison "Allie" H. Covey, around 1937. Along with cars, he serviced the vehicles and sold auto accessories. Later, Covey and Williams included a general hardware, a builders supply store, and electrical appliances. Notice the three-digit telephone

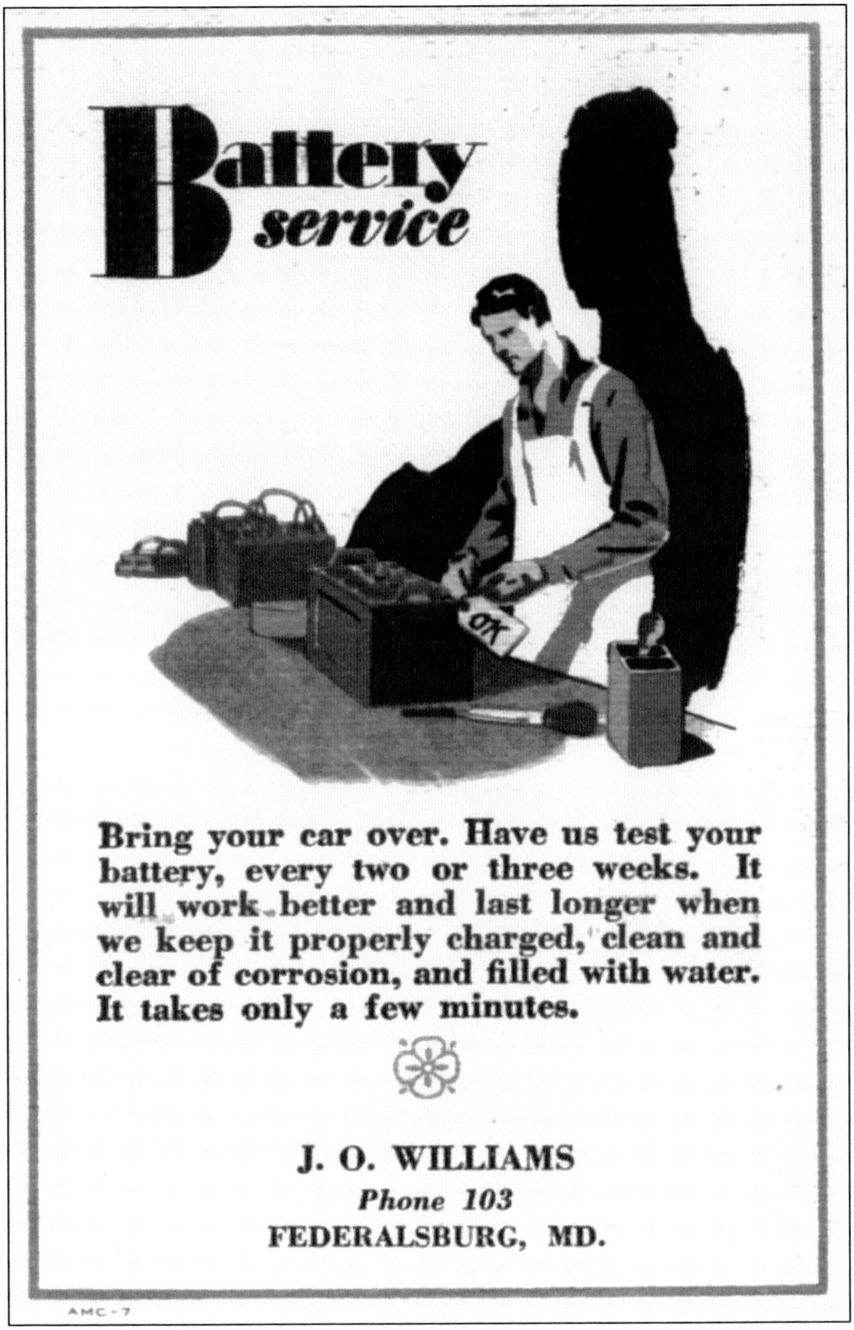

number. They actually had two numbers to call, 33 and 103. Later they went to 3601 and 3611 and eventually to PL4-3601 and PL4-3611 (PL 4 standing for Pleasant 4.) (Both from the Danny Phillips collection.)

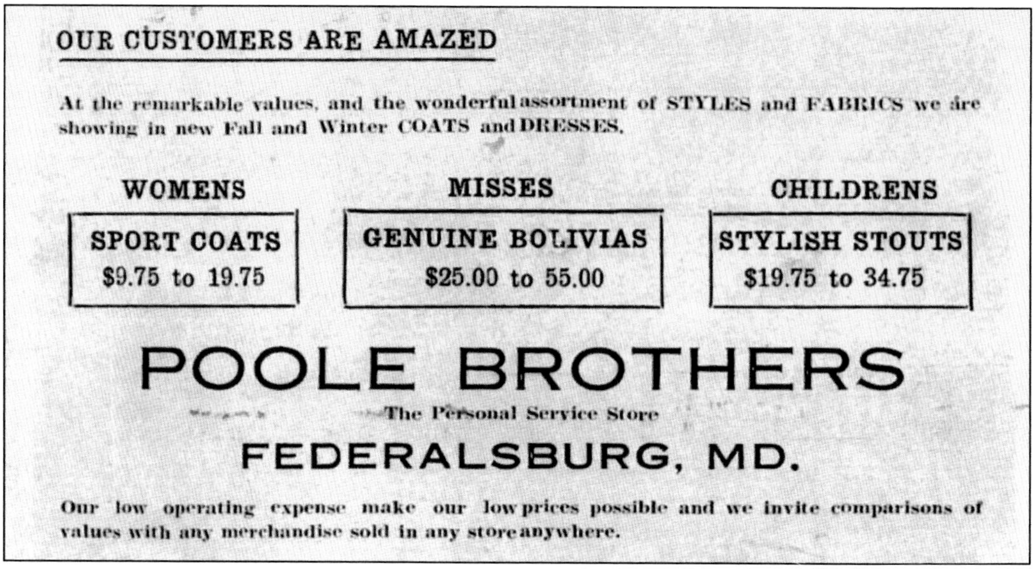

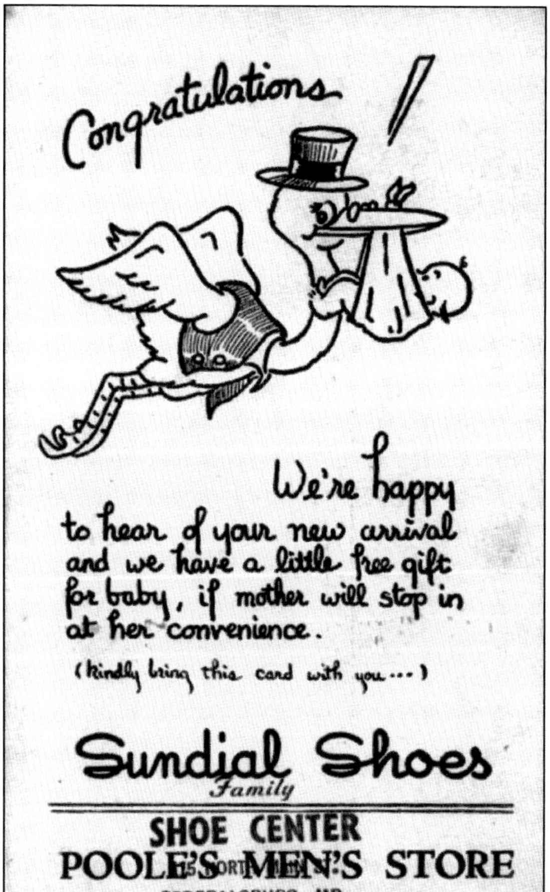

Poole Brothers. Early on, there must have been a family operation in women's and children's clothing. Later on, Poole Brothers was called the Federalsburg Women's Shop or Earle G. Poole Co., Inc. They provided ready-to-wear clothing, furnishings, and footwear. Clinton S. Poole was owner and proprietor of Poole's Men's Store and provided similar items for men and boys. Both of these postcards were mailed out as advertisements for the businesses. (From the Laurence G. Claggett collection.

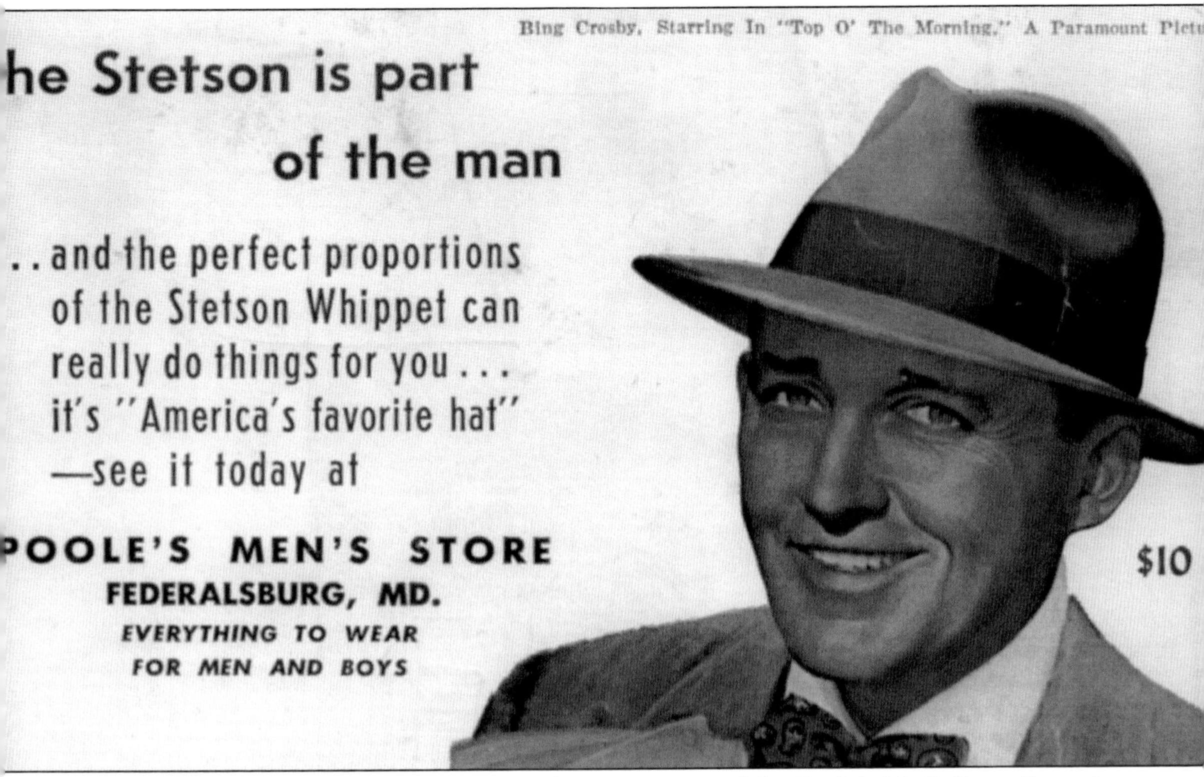

Poole's Men's Store. This is another advertising postcard for Poole's Men's Store. Even the local stores used movie stars to advertise their merchandise. (From the Danny Phillips collection.)

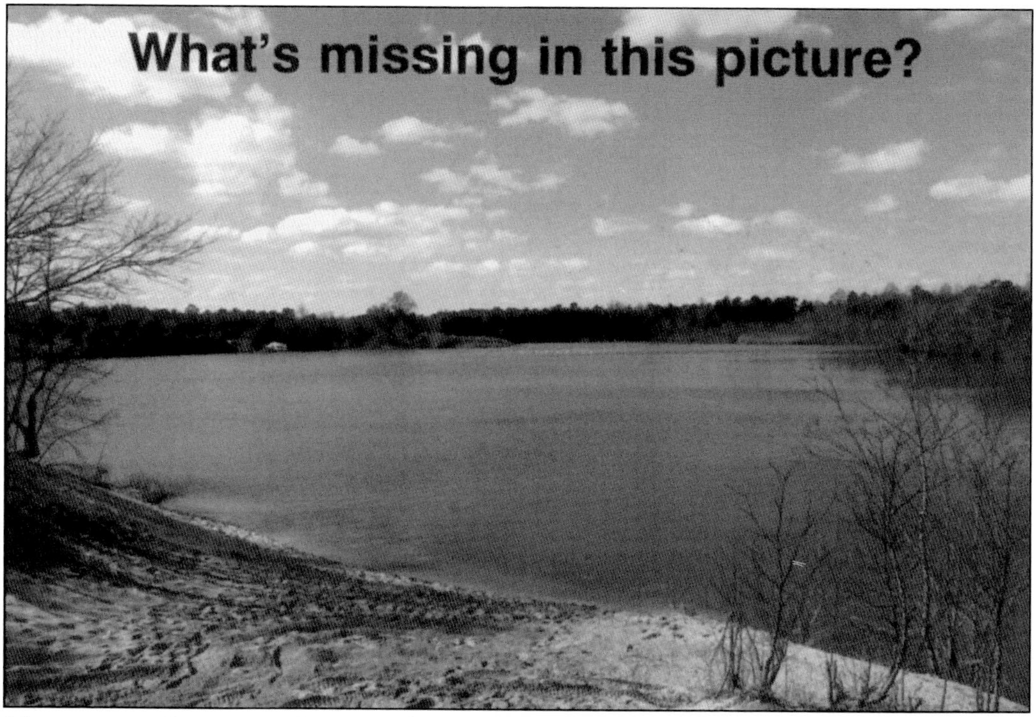

Marshyhope Sand and Gravel. The Marshyhope Sand and Gravel organized locally in the 1970s and distributed several catchy advertising postcards. The message on the back of the top postcard reads, "You—our customer!" The message on the bottom back reads, "You think this is beautiful—wait 'til you see our sand!" (From the Charles S. Long collection.)

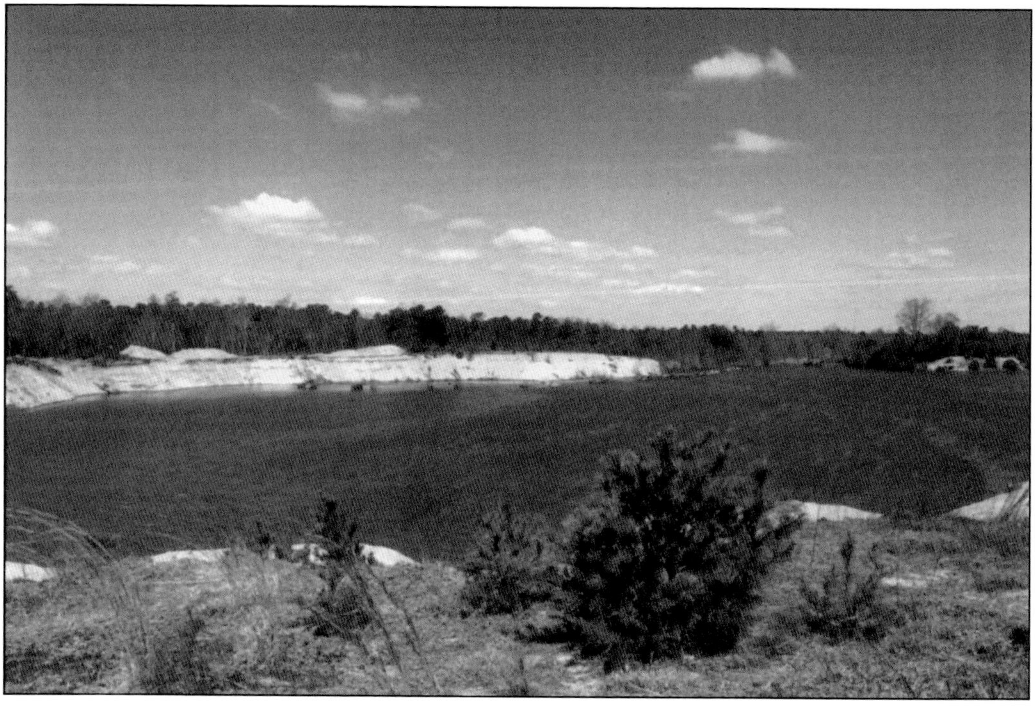

Three

The Railroad and The River

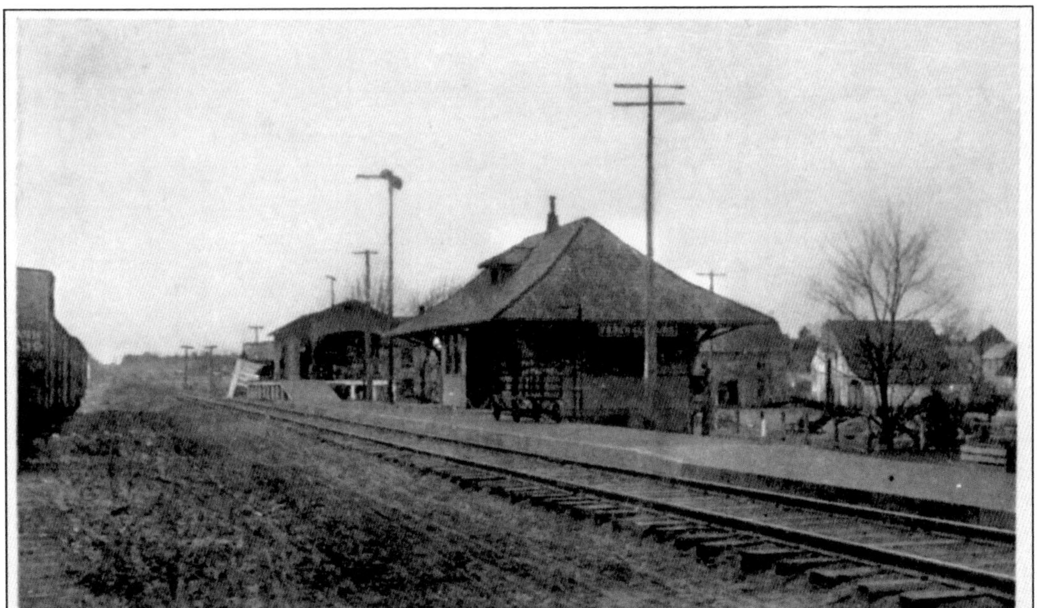

Railroad. The Seaford and Cambridge division of the Pennsylvania Railroad was opened for traffic on October 12, 1868, although at that time it extended only from Seaford to East New Market. This date marked a new era in the history of Federalsburg, for it was that railroad, with its refrigerator-car accommodation, which made New York, Philadelphia, and other Northern cities markets for the perishable products of local gardens and orchards. (From the Danny Phillips collection.)

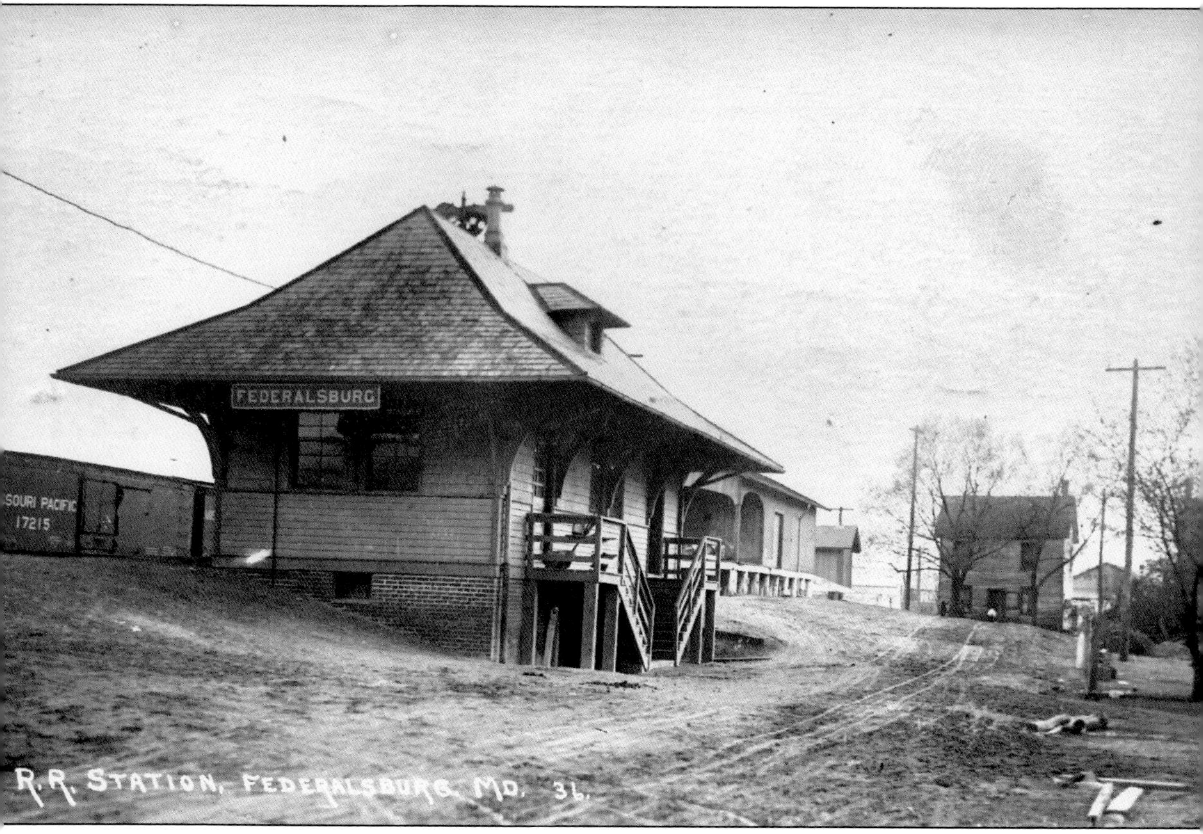

RAILROAD. This is an early photograph of the railroad station. The building serves today as the headquarters for the Maryland and Delaware Railroad Company. This short line railroad currently operates over 120 miles of track on the Delmarva Peninsula. The main commodities handled are corn, grain, and soybeans, but they also haul fertilizer, lumber, paper products, chemicals, and other products.

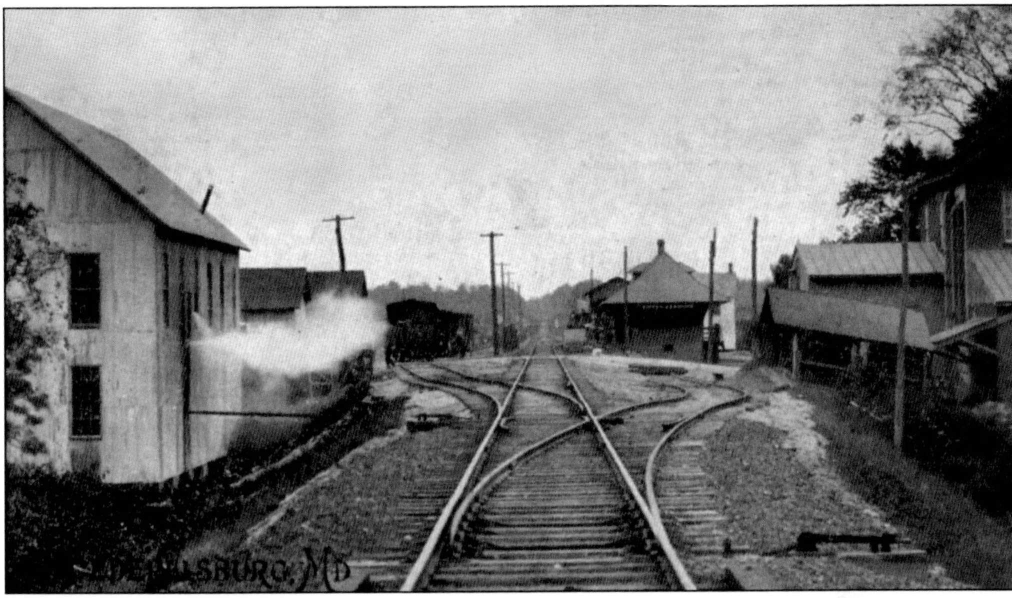

Railroad. The railroad was built through Federalsburg between 1867 and 1868. The first engine came over the rail in the spring of 1868 and blew loud and long blasts as it came around the east curve. Everybody headed for the station to welcome the monster. Prior to the coming of the railroad it was necessary to drive to Bridgeville, Delaware, a distance of 10 miles, to catch a train going north. Stage coaches made daily trips carrying the mail and passengers. As Cambridge and Easton had no rail facilities at that time, coaches left here for those points with mail and passengers upon the arrival of the Bridgeville coach. (Top postcard from the Francis A. "Sonny" Callahan collection; bottom postcard from the William F. Gray Jr. collection.)

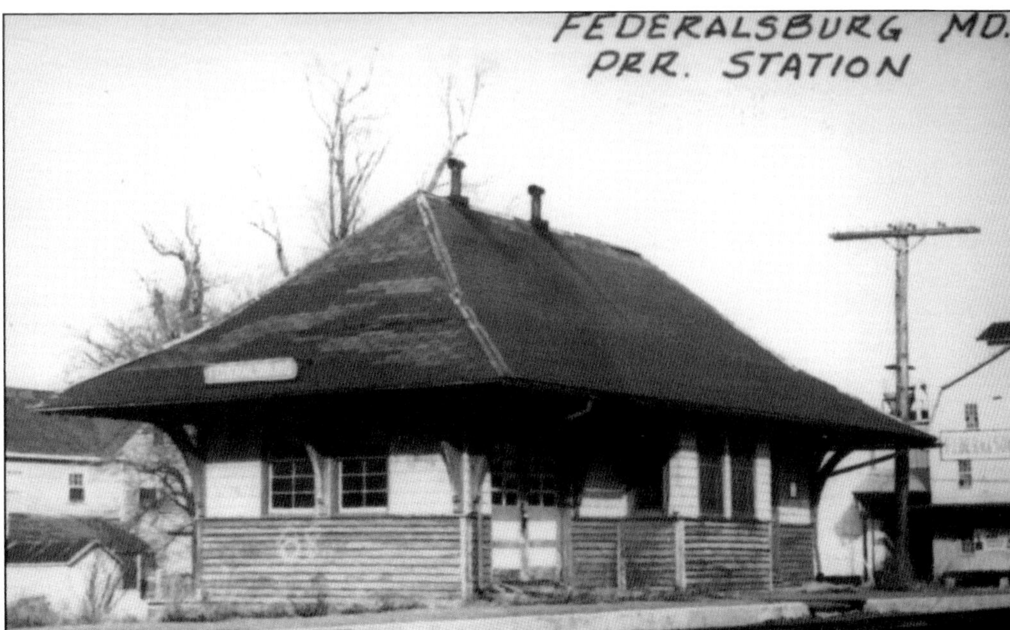

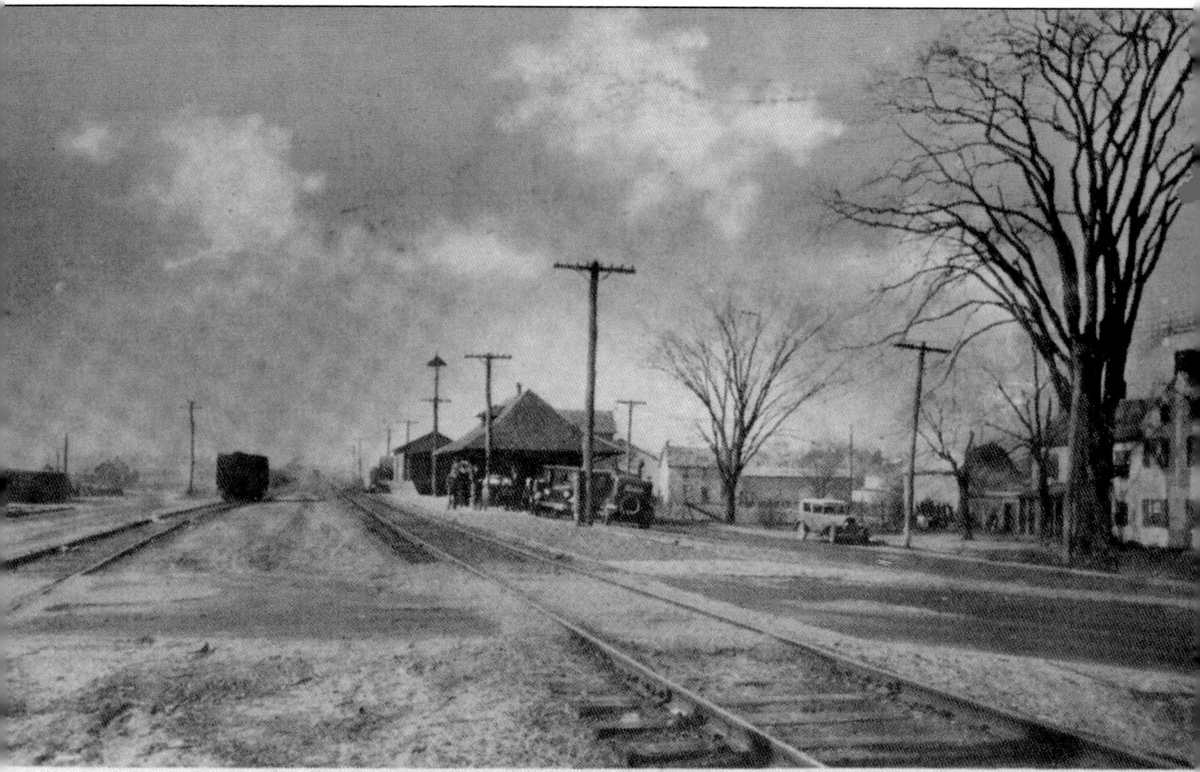

P. B. & W. Railroad Station, Federalsburg, Md.

Railroad Trade. During the early 20th century, Federalsburg was situated on the Seaford and Cambridge branch of the Pennsylvania Railroad; this became part of the Philadelphia, Baltimore, and Washington line around 1916. Two passenger and mail trains made connections daily, except on Sunday, close in time with trains at Seaford going northbound. The routes reversed in the evening. Federalsburg had the benefit of the Rural Free Delivery service, a great convenience that allowed the farmers to send and receive mail regularly, even in the coldest and busiest seasons. Other local trains included the Baltimore, Chesapeake, and Atlantic, and the Queen Anne Railroads. The fruit and produce shipped from here daily by market car service arrived in Baltimore, Philadelphia, and New York in time to sell in the market the following morning. Products from the grain mills and canning houses, strawberries, and eggs were some of the items shipped in large quantity to these large city markets. Many goods received by merchants and businessmen arrived over the Pennsylvania Railroad as well. The steamer ships, which carried some goods to and from the town, ceased to operate because they could not compete with the load capacity, delivery time, nor the cost of shipping goods by rail. (From the Charles S. Long collection.)

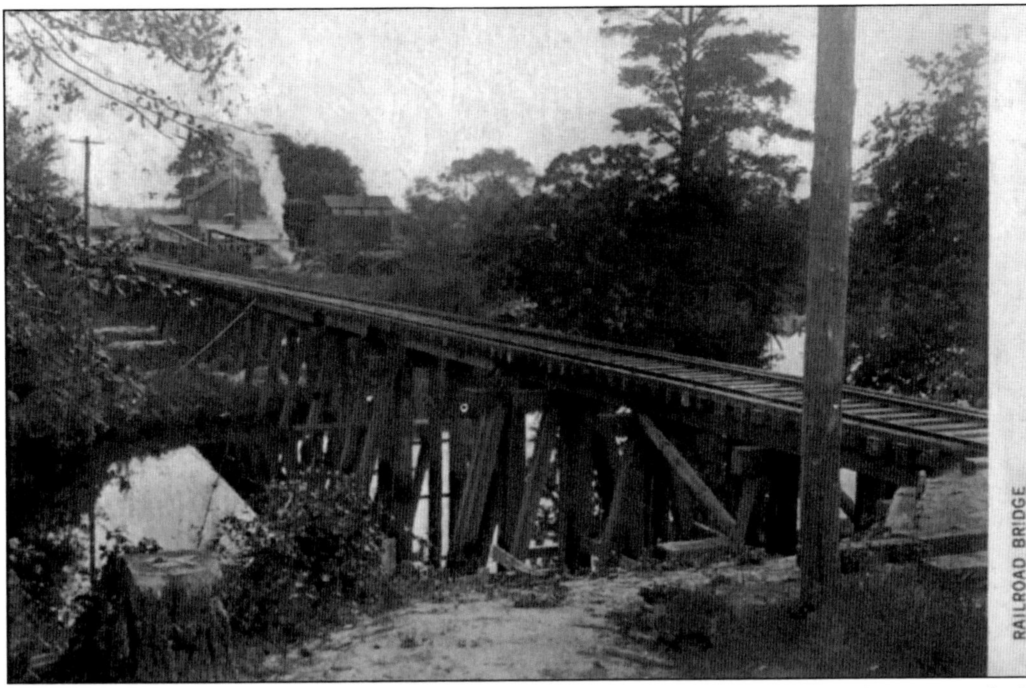

RAILROAD BRIDGE. The first railroad bridge crossing the river was an open-trestle structure built on piling in the late 1860s. This allowed water to run freely under it in time of flood or high water. When it became necessary to replace it in 1905, according to Ellenor Merriken, "the railroad company in some way managed to change the river into a creek. The North West Fork of the Nanticoke River suddenly became the Marshy Hope Creek. The reason might have been that a river calls for a draw in a bridge, a creek does not. This no doubt eliminated the necessity of having to build a draw. Trainloads of dirt were hauled in and dumped on both sides, narrowing the river at this point." (Top postcard from the William F. Gray Jr. collection; bottom postcard from the R. Allan Gorsuch collection.)

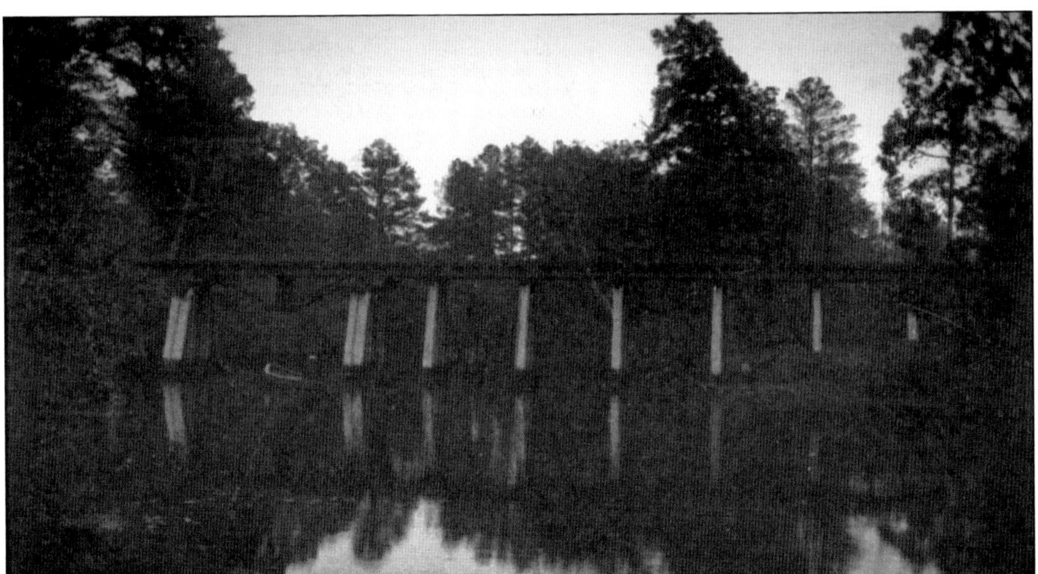

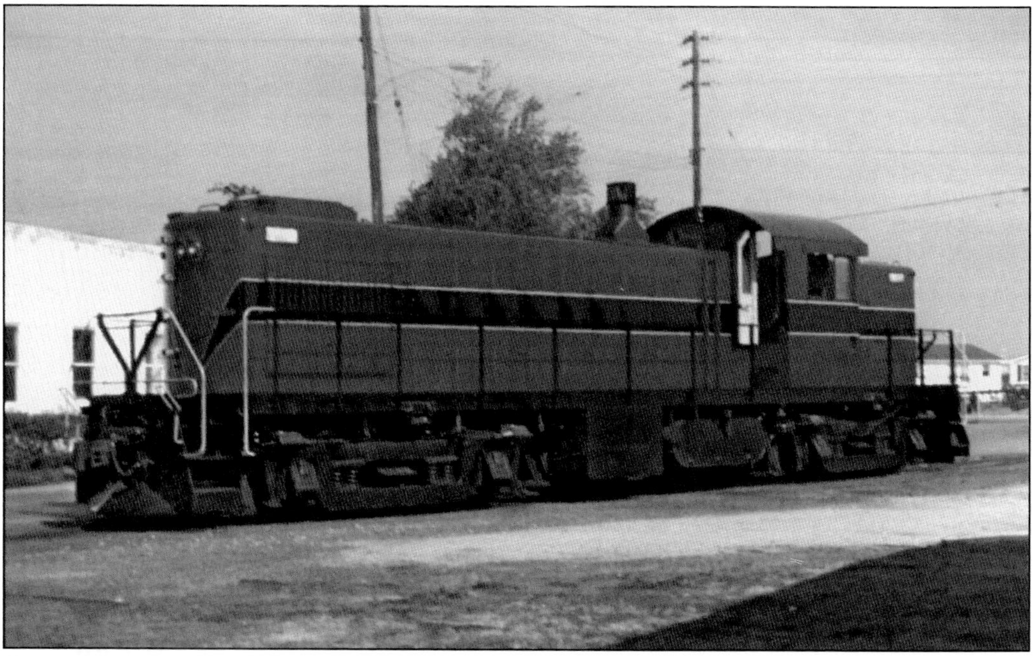

ALCO RS-1 NO. 20. This is a postcard which shows the Alco RS-1 No. 20, assigned to local freight service on the Maryland & Delaware Railroad which travels today between Seaford, Delaware and Cambridge, Maryland. (From the Scott Freeman collection and copied courtesy of Audio-Visual Designs, Herkimer, New York.)

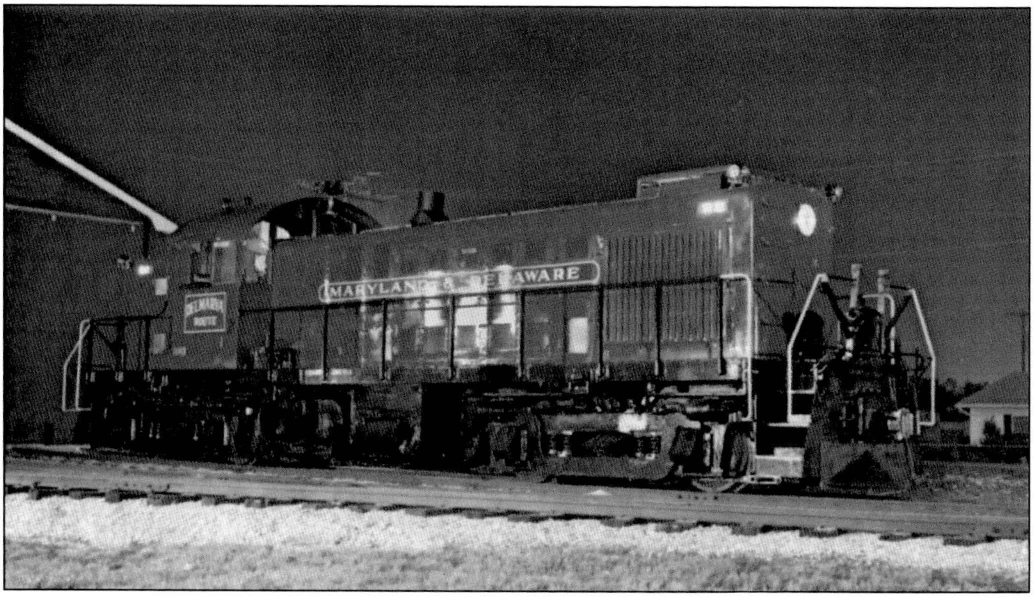

MARYLAND AND DELAWARE RAILROAD. Newly overhauled and repainted, this is the Alco-built RS-1 locomotive seen at the Maryland & Delaware Railroad's headquarters in Federalsburg, Maryland on June 6, 1979. The Maryland & Delaware provides freight service on three lines on the Delmarva Peninsula with these 1,000-horsepower locomotives. (From the Scott Freeman collection and copied courtesy of Audio-Visual Designs, Herkimer, New York.)

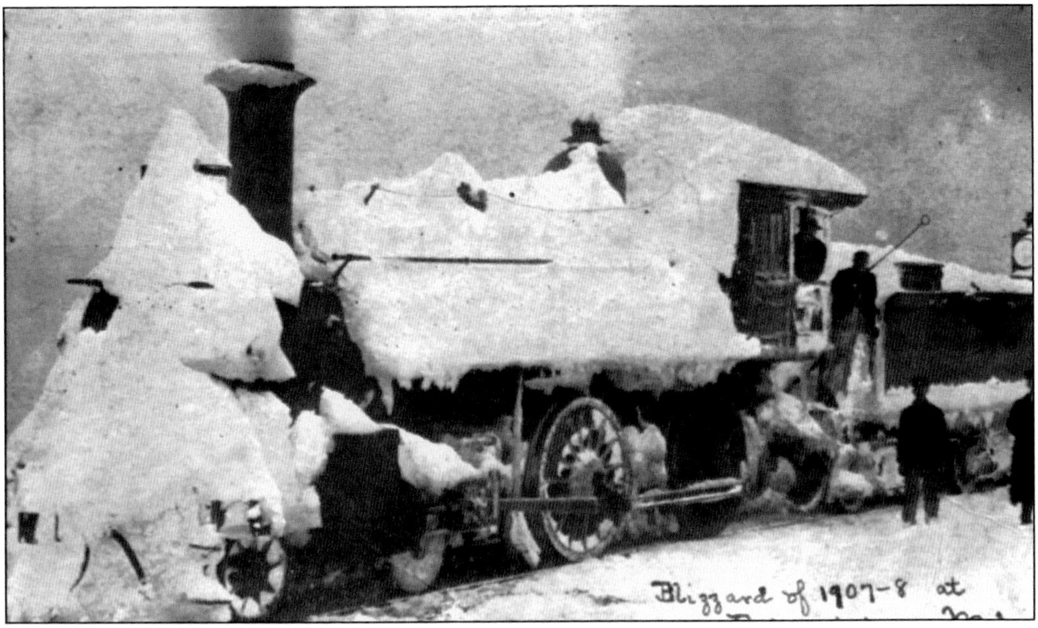

BLIZZARD OF 1907–1908 AT FEDERALSBURG, MARYLAND. It doesn't look as though this train went anywhere during this storm, but it certainly made an interesting postcard! (From the R. Allan Gorsuch collection.)

POSTCARD. This postcard shows a cancellation mark from the Seaford and Cambridge Railroad Post Office dated April 25, 1910 and sent from the Federalsburg railroad station. The sender was visiting a Mrs. Messenger at the time the message was sent. (From the Danny Phillips collection.)

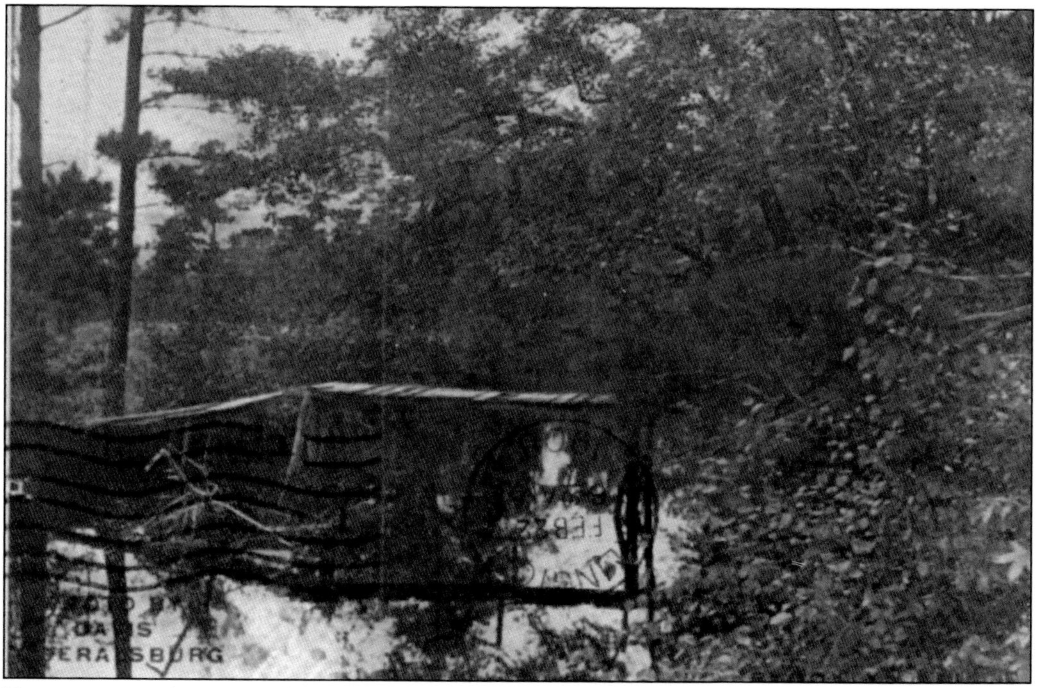

FOOTBRIDGE. The postmark on this postcard indicates it was mailed in 1909. The sender's message (see below) referred to this photo as the Brooklyn Bridge, which is believed to have been a small footbridge over the Marshy Hope Creek extending the small community of Brooklyn to Old Denton Road behind Zion Methodist Church or the Idlewild Mill. It was most certainly washed away during one of the many floods. (From the Charles S. Long collection.)

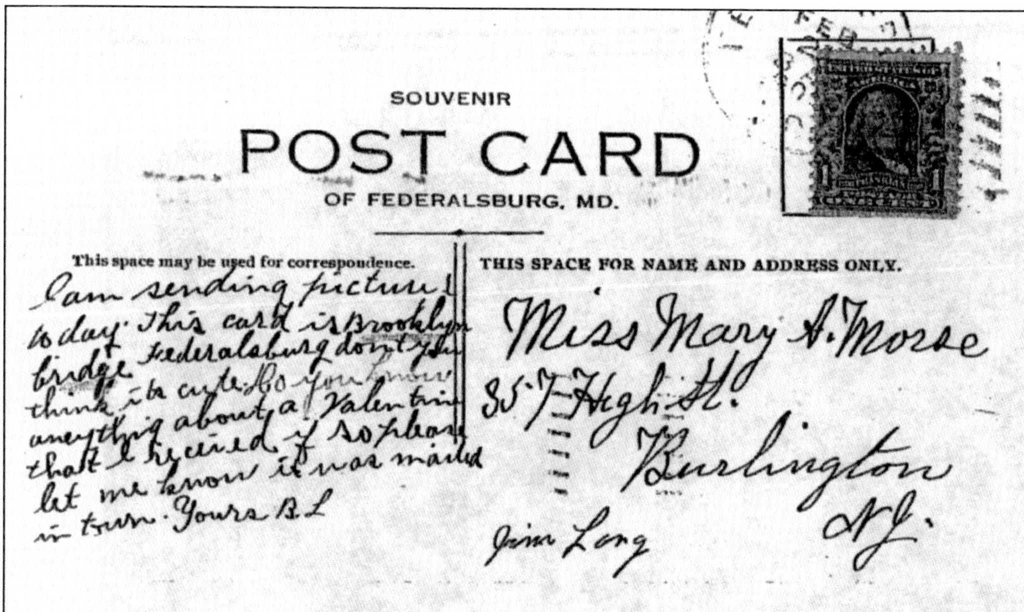

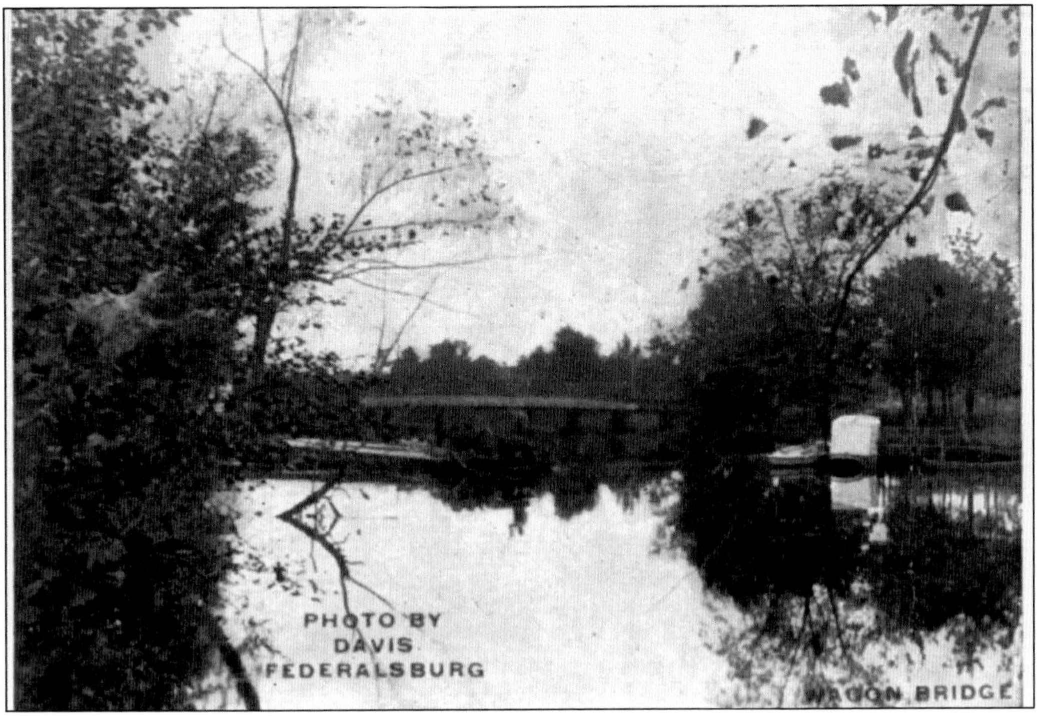

WAGON BRIDGE. The first bridge across the river in Federalsburg was built around 1750 and was called the Wagon Bridge. When this bridge washed out in the early 1800s, Eccleston Brown, then one of the prominent men of the community, and six other men were authorized to build another wooden bridge in the same place. (Both from the Charles S. Long collection.)

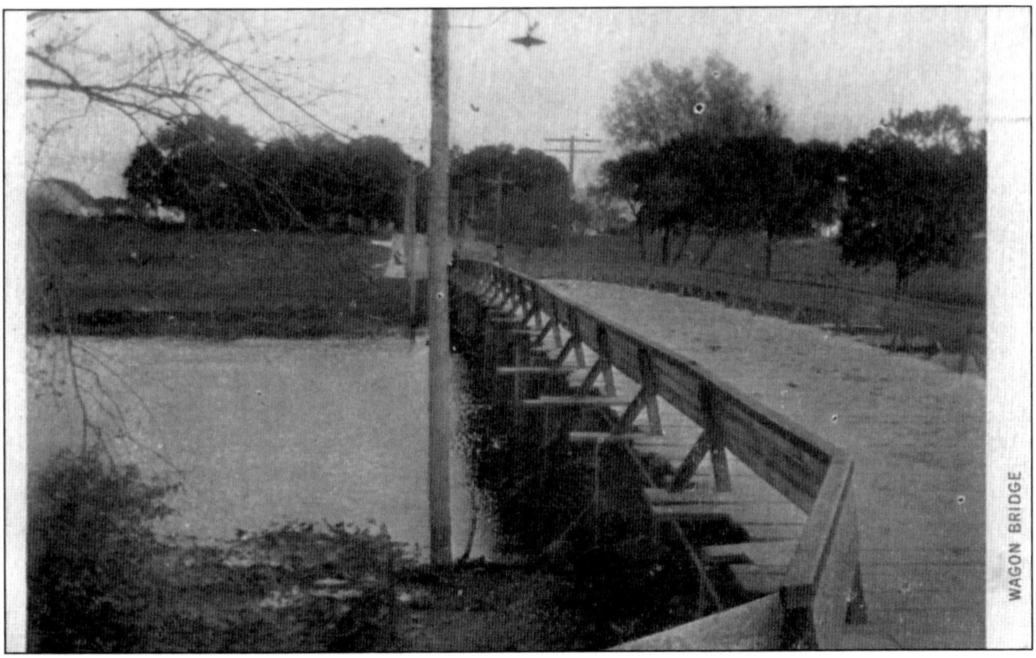

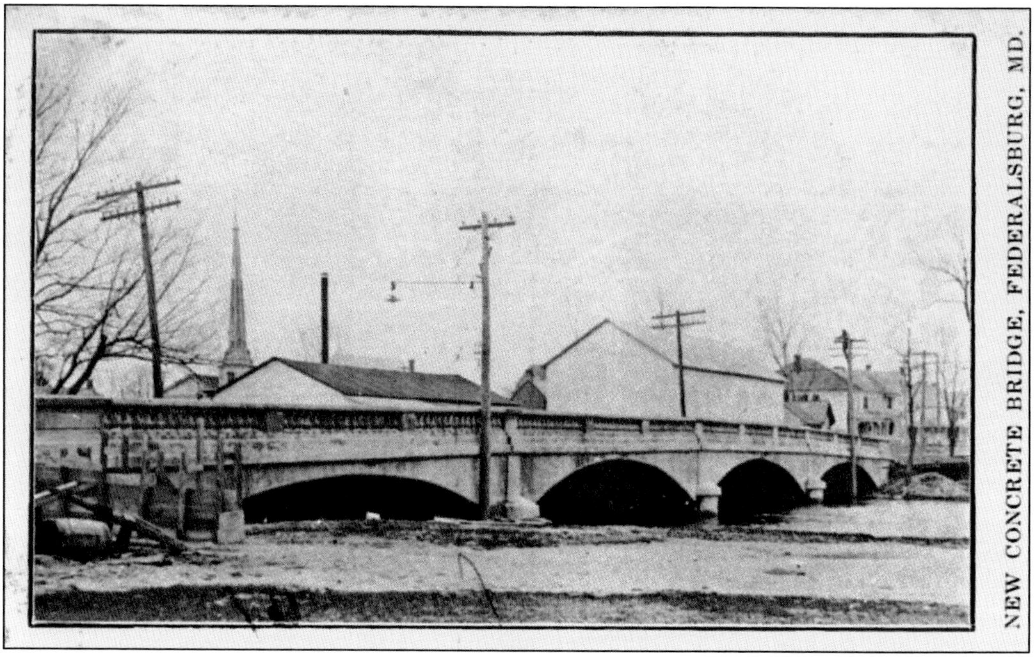

EAST CENTRAL AVENUE BRIDGE. The wooden bridge lasted until 1911 when Edward E. Goslin, then state senator from Caroline County and a resident of Federalsburg, convinced the Maryland Roads Department to take over the road leading up to and including the bridge, and on up to the center of town. This clever maneuver on Mr. Goslin's part made the state liable for the construction and upkeep of the bridge. (Top postcard from the Danny Phillips collection; bottom postcard from the Francis A. "Sonny" Callahan collection.)

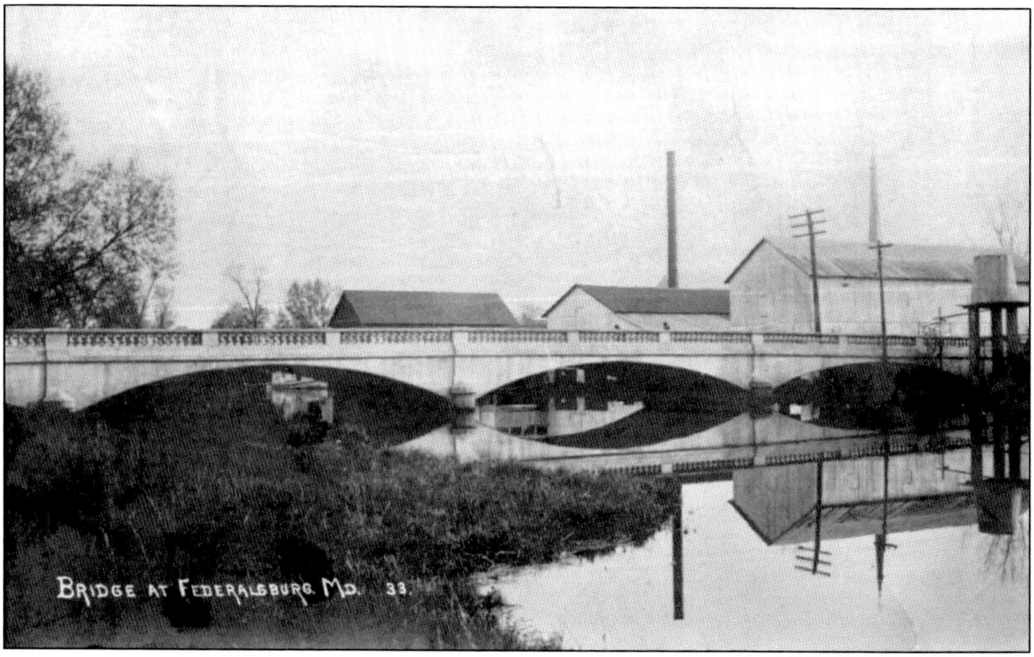

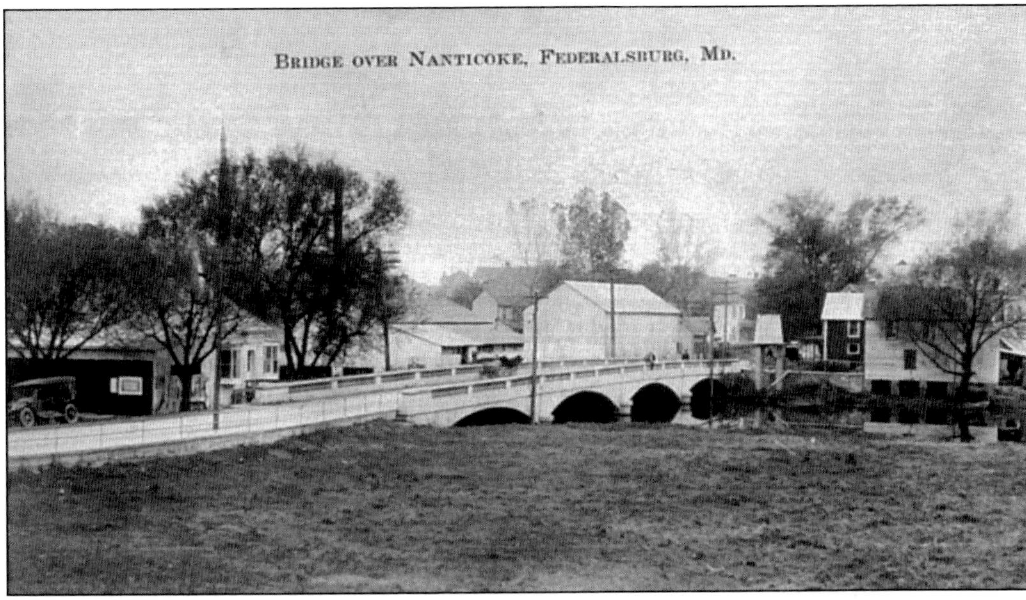

EAST CENTRAL AVENUE BRIDGE LOOKING WEST. Looking from the hill on East Central Avenue and facing west toward the downtown business area, you can see Zaffere's Bakery on the left side of the postcard image. Behind it, just over the trees is the Christ Church steeple, a landmark in many town photos. The building on the right side of the postcard shows the wooden firehouse that was replaced by a brick structure in 1927. (From the Laurence G. Claggett collection.)

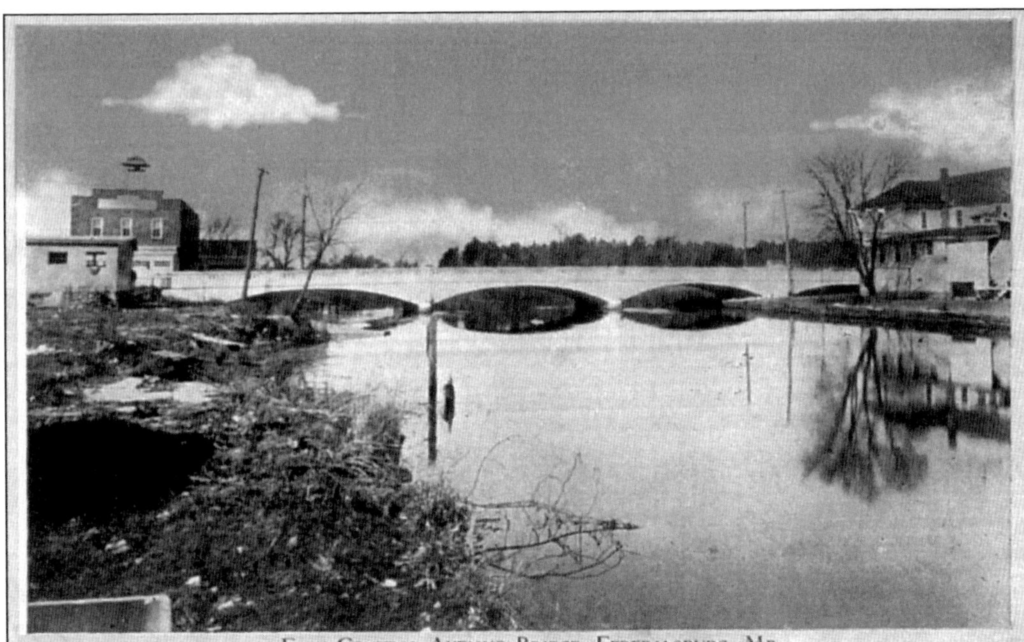

MARSHY HOPE CREEK LOOKING NORTH. This view of the concrete bridge faces north. The brick firehouse is shown to the left and Zaffere's Bakery is to the right of the bridge. (From the Laurence G. Claggett collection.)

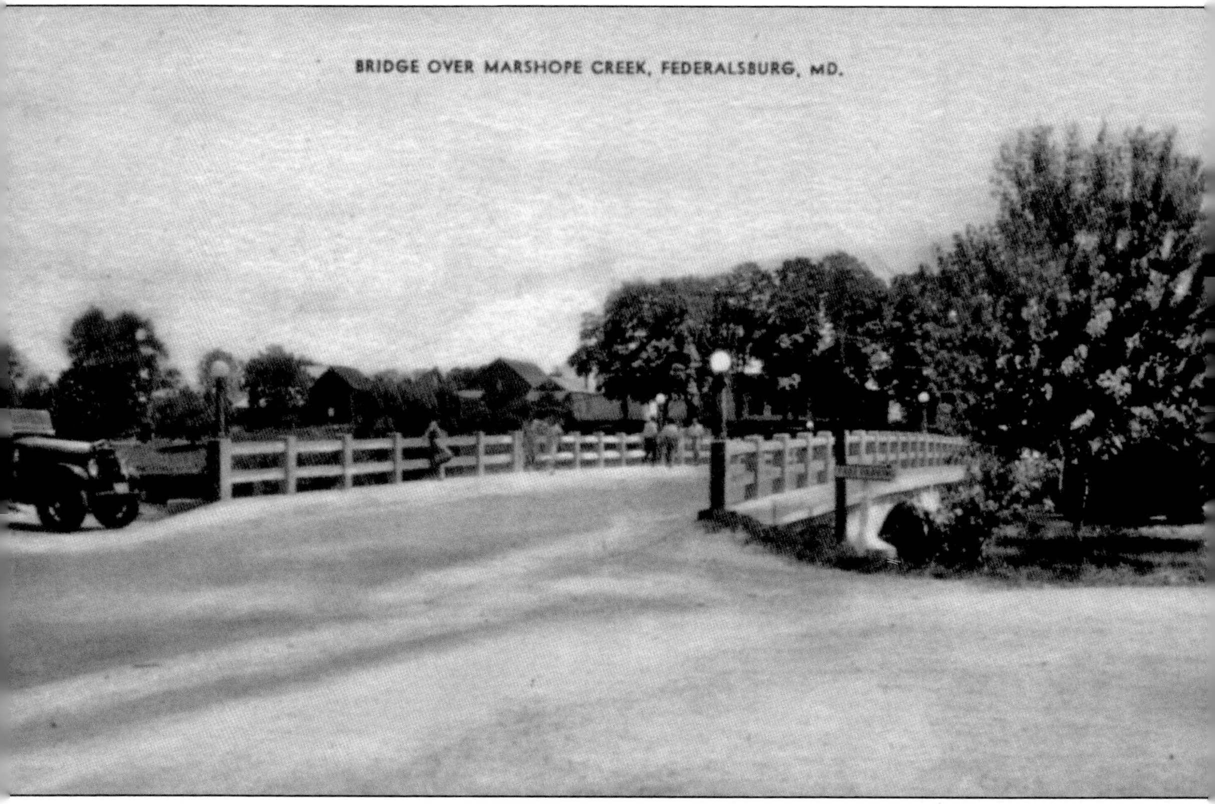

East Central Avenue Bridge Looking east. This fine concrete span succeeded the old wooden structure from which this town took one of its earliest names, "The Bridge," in the days when few bridges existed on the Delmarva Peninsula. The concrete was mixed with a hoe by hand and hauled in a wheelbarrow by Mr. Will Cleavers. The fancy railing constructed in 1911 has since been replaced with a new straight railing. Note the spelling on the cover as "Marshope" Creek. (From the Danny Phillips collection.)

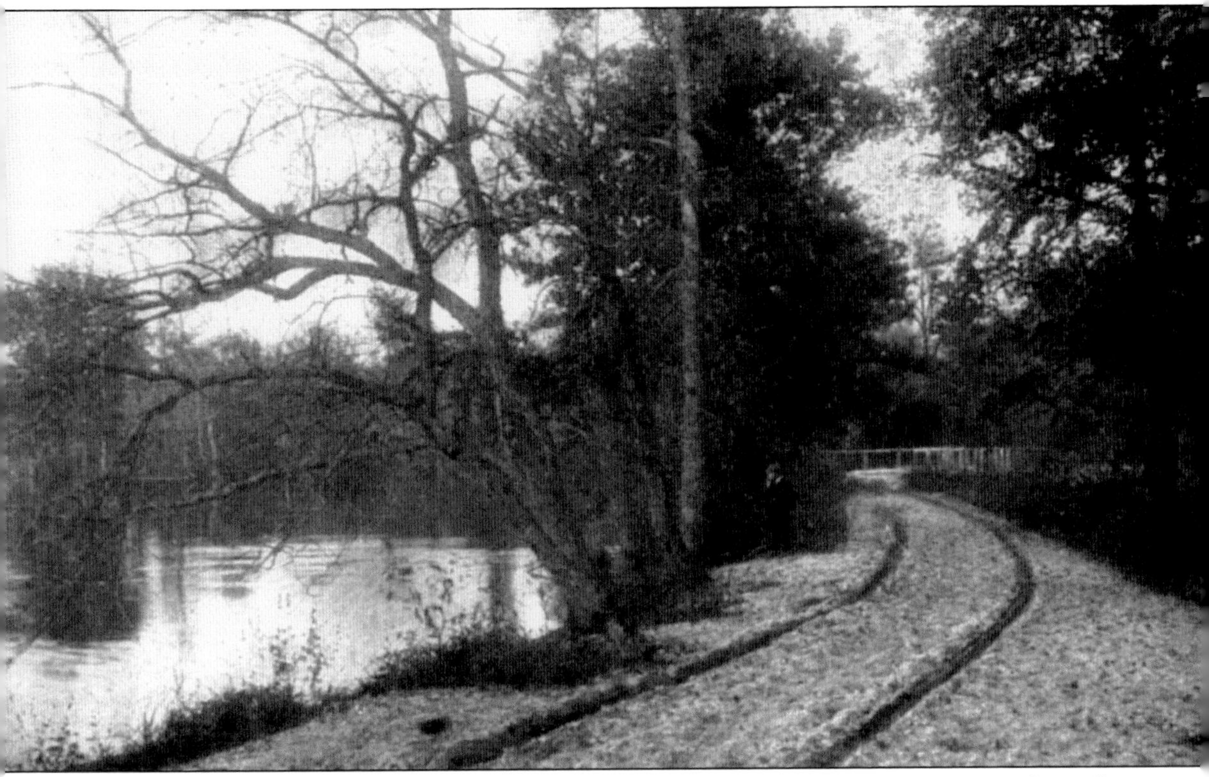

Dam Roads. Many dams across the Marshy Hope Creek held back water to power the mills along the river. They also served as a roadbed for crossing the creek and nearly all roads lead from one mill to the next one. Several wooden bridges were built over dams, including one at Faulkner's Branch at the north approach to Idlewild. All of the wooden bridges were demolished by excessive flood waters and washed away during the big flood of 1935. (From the Danny Phillips collection.)

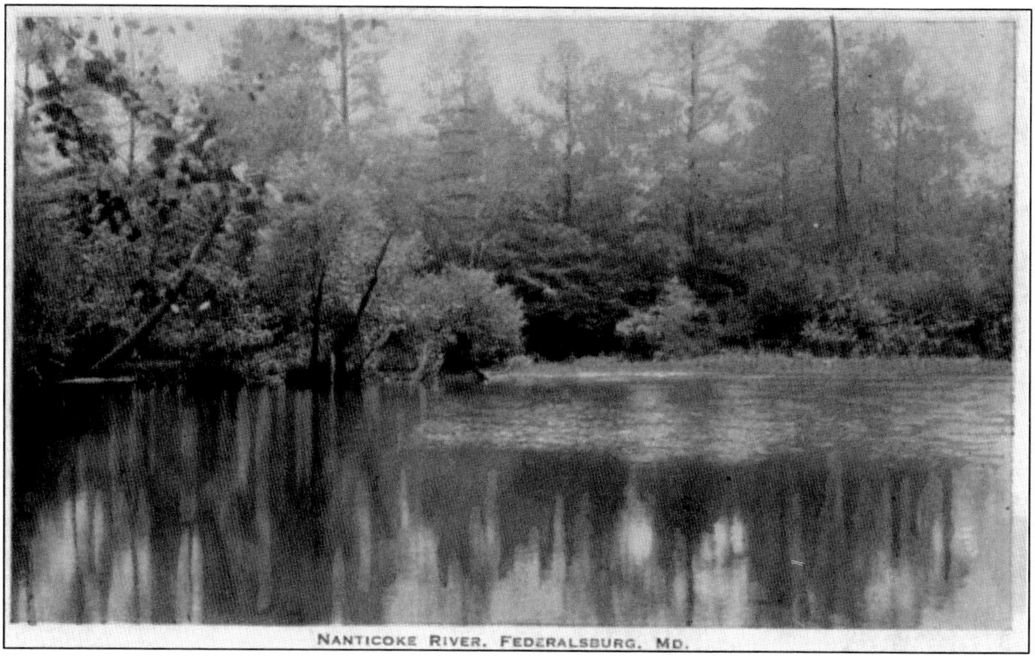

NANTICOKE RIVER. The northwest fork of the great Nanticoke River, with its clear sparkling water and high green banks, winds its way through the town 20 miles below where it joins the Chesapeake Bay. It does not have the deep water advantages of the lower part of the river, but the channel has been deepened and widened and dredged so as to protect the town from flooding, which has caused considerable damage to property throughout the town in the past. In earlier years, work boats plied the water carrying produce, wood, lumber, and other goods to the mouth of the river or on to other ports. (Both from the Danny Phillips collection.)

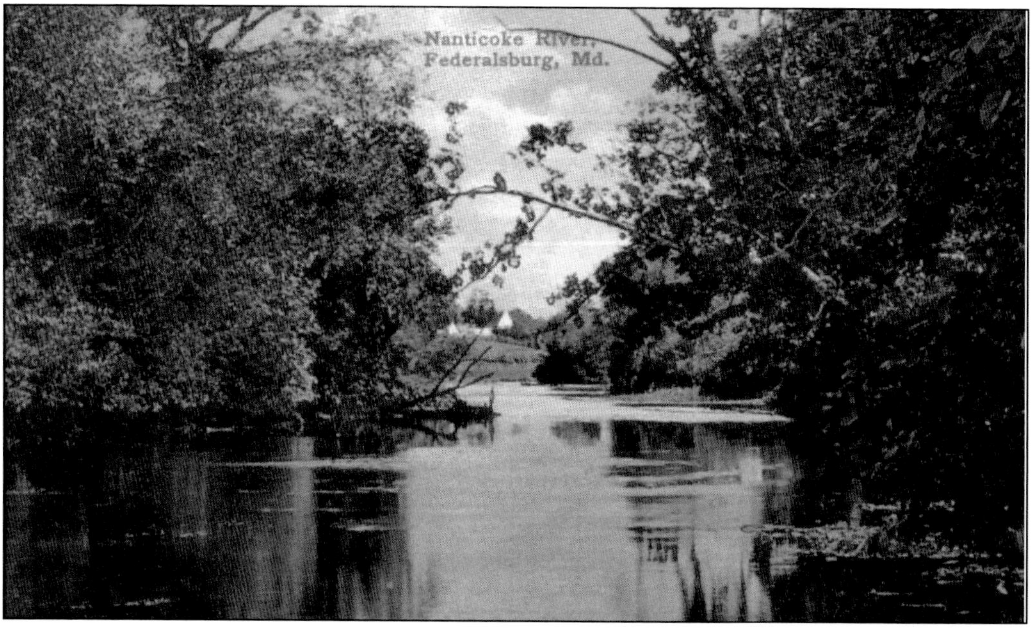

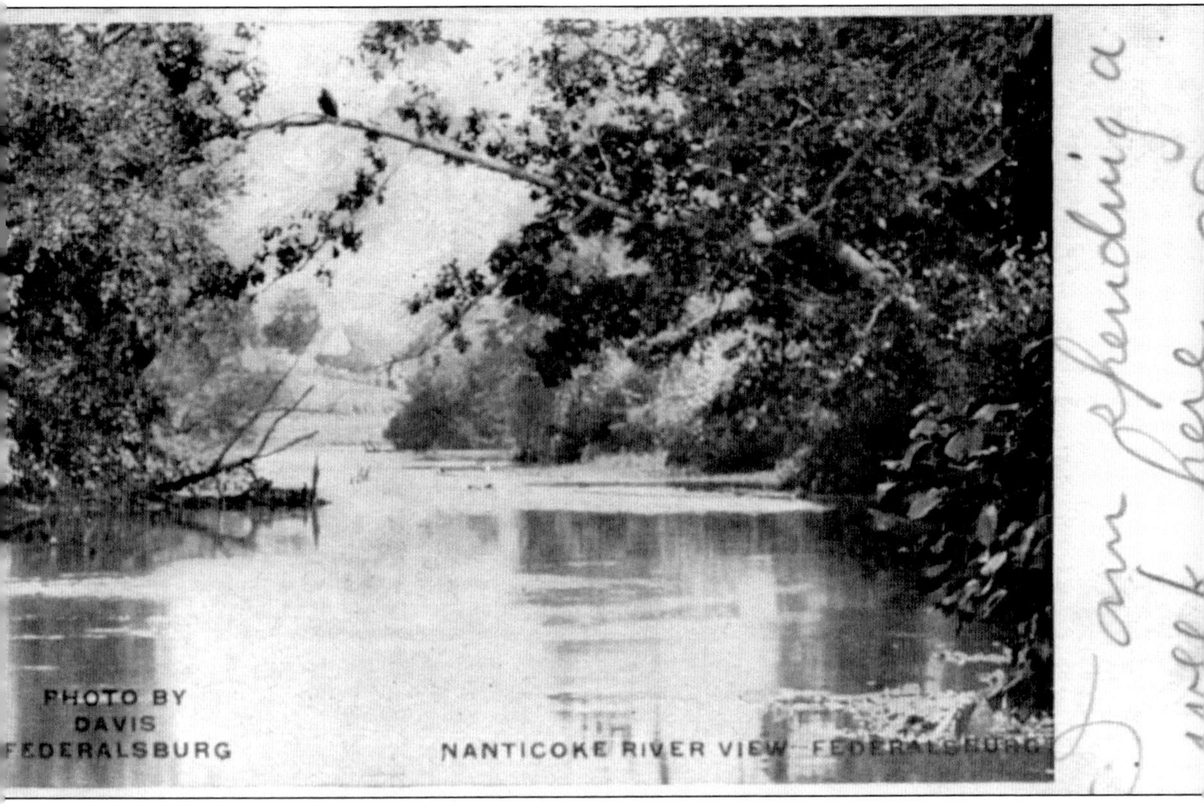

SUMMER IN FEDERALSBURG. For a summer vacation, one could not find a more desirable place than Federalsburg where one could take their line and rod and sit on the shady banks of the stream or, with a light boat, enjoy a ride on its placid waters. Hunters and anglers revel in this locality for its upland game shooting and the ducking and fishing which the nearby bay and its estuaries abundantly afford. (From the Charles S. Long collection.)

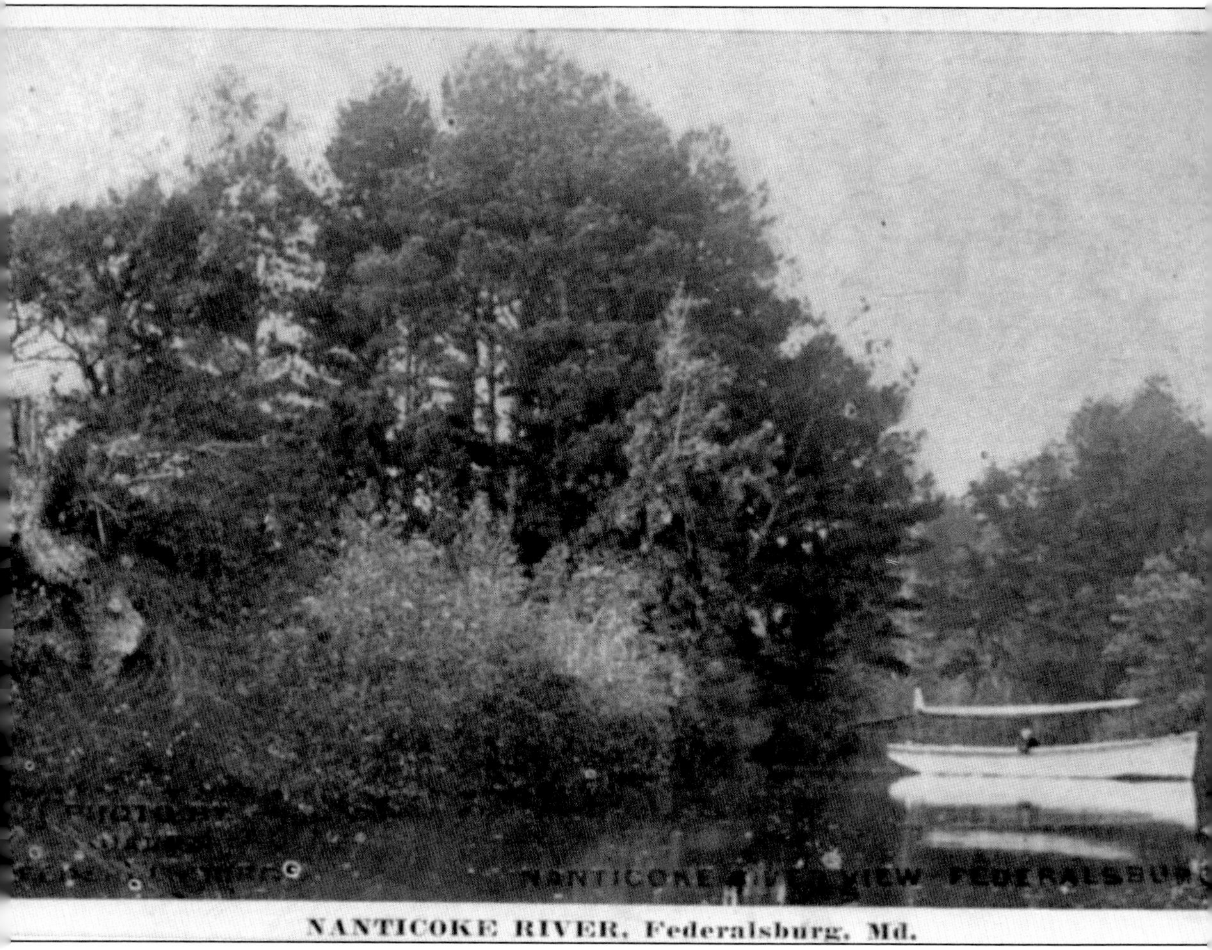

MARSHY HOPE CREEK. Marshy Hope Creek is considered the headwaters of the North West Fork of the Nanticoke River. Early settlers built their homes along the river, which provided the only mode of transportation to distant places. As it winds its way through lush countryside and dense forest, the scenic river has also been a principal source of food and healthful recreation. Fishing, as well as hunting within the surrounding woods, has long been a favorite pastime. And boating, whether by small craft or excursion, have offered wonderful opportunities for recreational enjoyment. (From the Danny Phillips collection.)

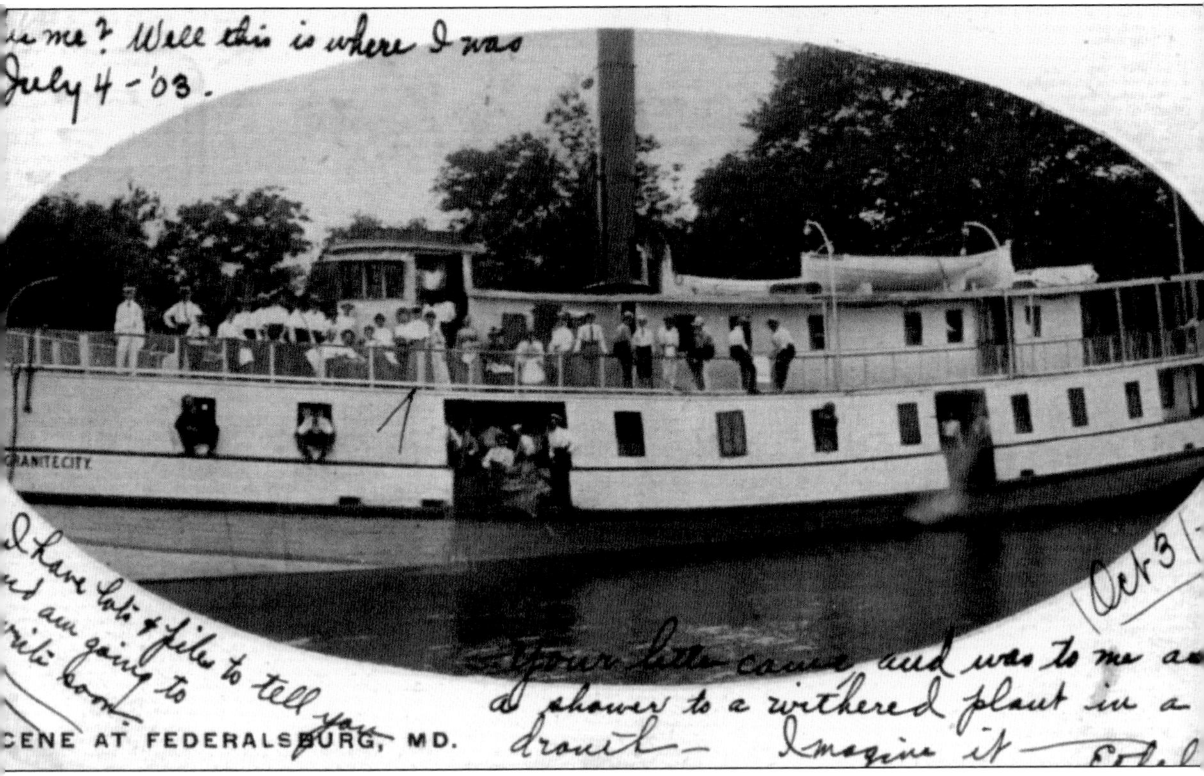

STEAMER. The steamer *Granite City* took local residents, like mayor Thomas H. Chambers, on excursions down the Nanticoke River and Chesapeake Bay. One such trip took place over the Fourth of July weekend in 1903 when the steamer carried a load of about 40 people from outside Federalsburg and the immediate vicinity to Old Point Comfort and the surrounding towns of Norfolk, Hampton, and Newport News, Virginia. In 1906, the steamer made regular trips between Cambridge and Baltimore, leaving Cambridge after the arrival of the evening train, and returning the following night, so passengers could take the morning train from Cambridge. For a while, the steamer was used as a freight hauler on the but by the end of 1906 this halted. The *Granite City* could only make three trips a week and, because it was limited in the amount it could carry, it only stopped at two or three places along the river to load cargo. The merchants and farmers needed more shipping capacity and pickups every day, so they resorted to the rail lines. The railroad offered such low freight rates that the *Granite City* could no longer compete. (From the Charles S. Long collection.)

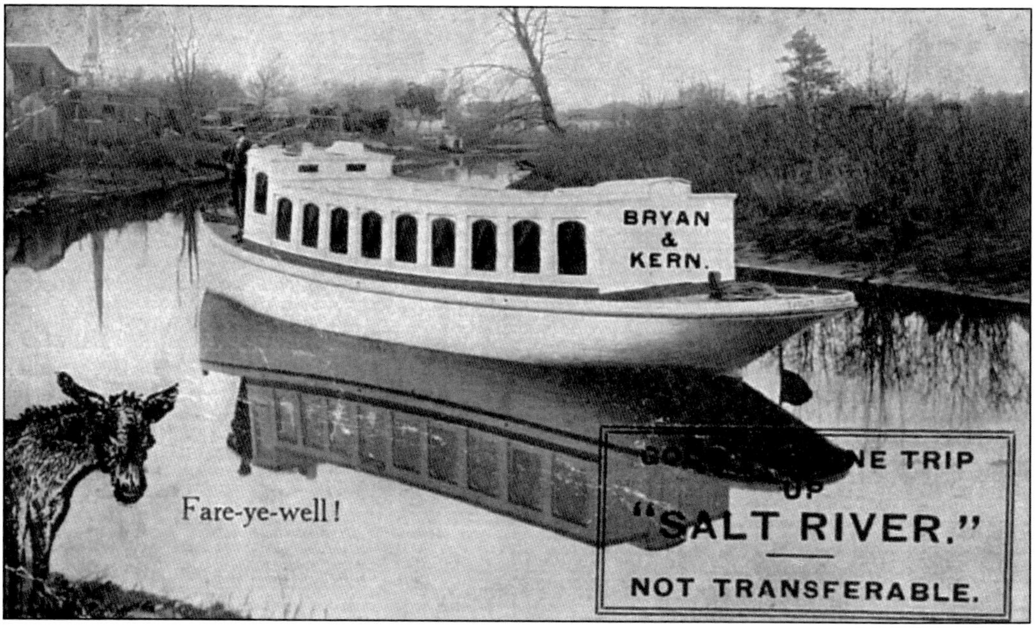

Scenic Boat Tours. The boat in the top image, taken around 1904, was owned by Will Davis, a town merchant, and piloted by John Coulbourne of Federalsburg. Mr. Davis had the print put on postcards and distributed them to his friends; the card offered a "coupon" for a trip down the river. The bottom image shows a different boat. These scenic tours were a favorite Sunday recreation for locals and tourists in the early 1900s. Notice the Christ Church steeple, which is prominent on the left side of the top postcard. (Top postcard from the Laurence G. Claggett collection; bottom postcard from the William F. Gray Jr. collection.)

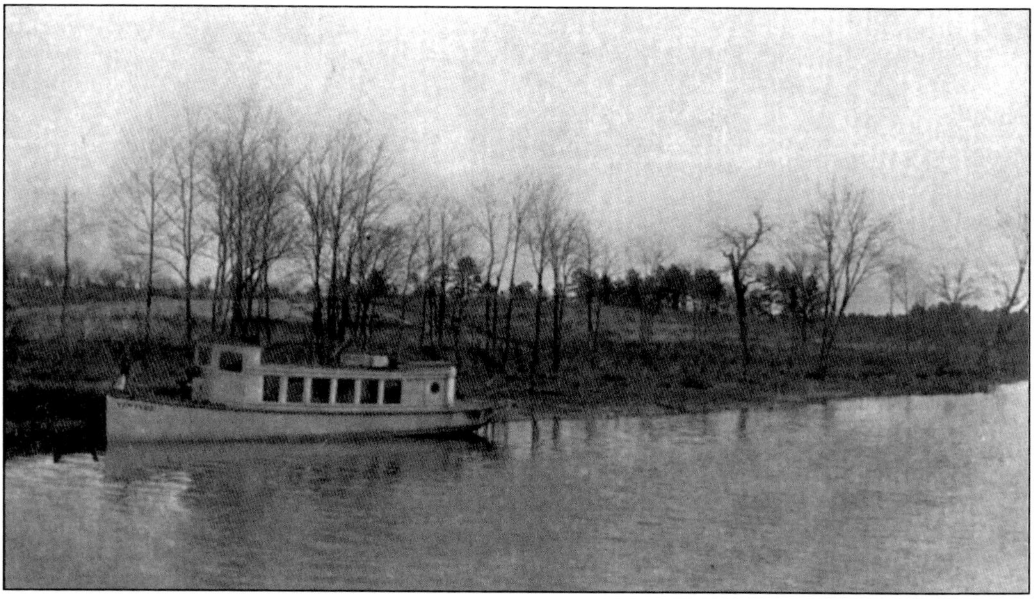

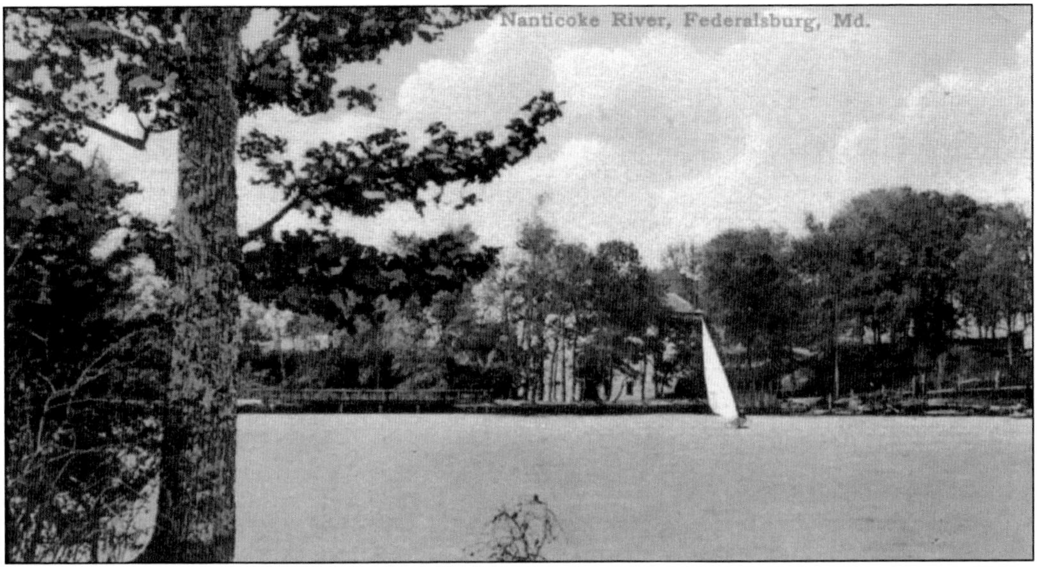

IDLEWILD LAKE. A small dam on the Nanticoke River in Federalsburg provided water power to turn the old water-wheel at a grist mill. As time went on, additional power was needed and the dam was raised and extended across the river to the other side, thus backing up enough water to form a lake. The dam was made of dirt, with heavy hewed timbers for frame-work on the two flood-gates, these being about 150 feet apart in midstream. The gates had to be opened and closed by hand. When finished, it backed up enough water to create a beautiful body of water and was named Idlewild Lake. It covered a basin of approximately 200 acres and was considered one of the beauty spots of the Eastern Shore, providing a constant source of pleasure for people interested in boating and fishing. Sweepings from the grist mill were thrown overboard and into the river every day, which attracted all kinds of fish. Fish went up stream in the spring to spawn, especially herring, and after the dam was built up, they accumulated below it in such quantity that people with dip-nets could stand and dip them up by the hundreds of bushels. (Top postcard from the Danny Phillips collection; bottom postcard from the Mary Holt collection.)

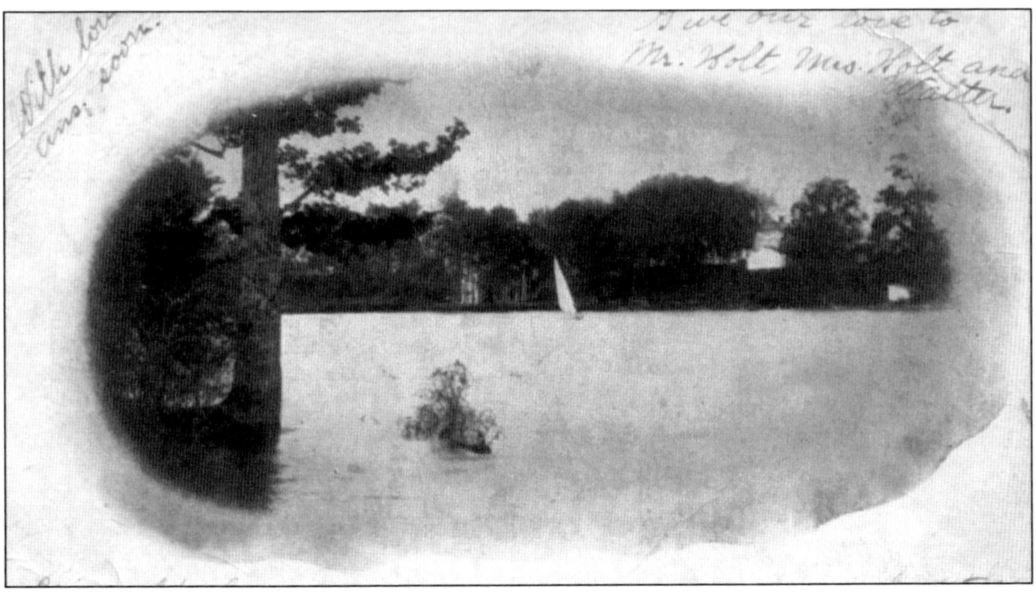

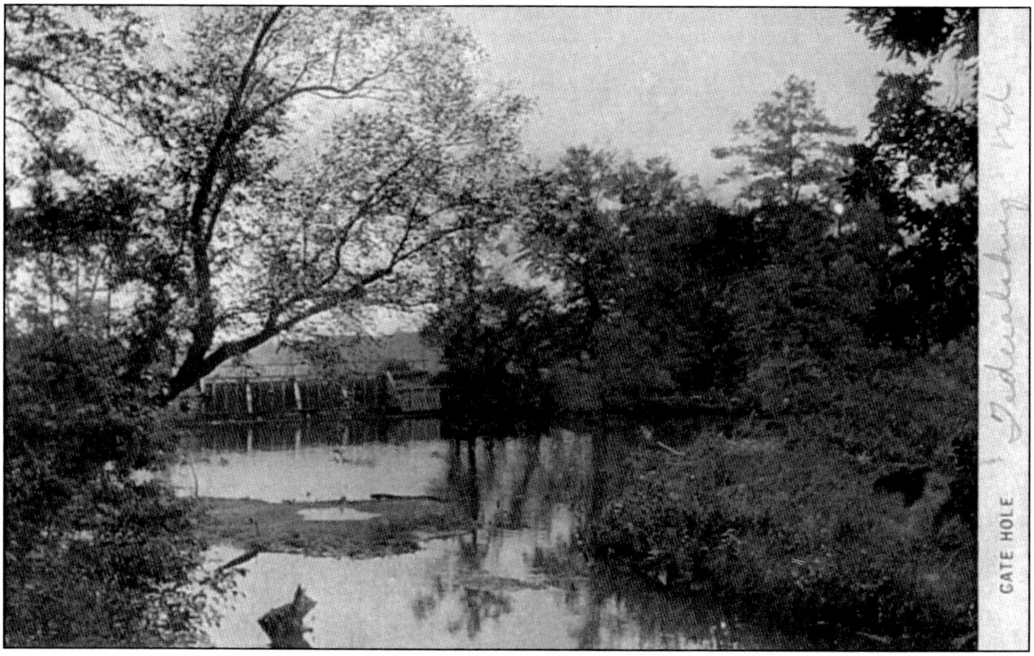

Idlewild. Behind the Idlewild Mill and below the dam was a great place for fishing and swimming. When the dam was improved, heavy-hewed timbers provided the frame-work for two flood gates which were about 150 feet apart in midstream. These gates had to be opened by hand. Eventually, the old swimming hole became known as the "Gate Hole." After the flood of 1935, the Inland Game and Fish Commission bought the property and put a fence all around it barring fishing and swimming. In 1952, several groups were able to open the lower end of the dam once again for fishing. (Both from the Laurence G. Claggett collection.)

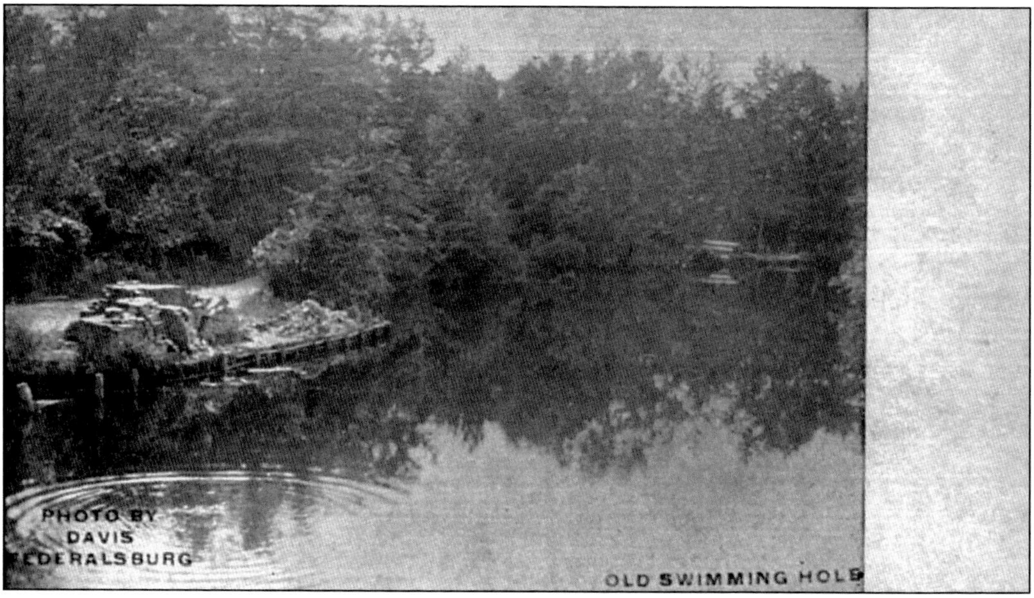

Old Swimming Hole. Ellenor Merriken wrote the following in her book entitled *Herring Hill*: "There is more to the lure of a fishing hole than the fish. For many, both old and young, it's the relaxation they need, the solitude one finds only in such a natural habitat. There is real contentment in just sitting and listening to the quiet ripple of the stream, the chatter of birds, the rustling of leaves, and watching a glorious sunset on summer evenings. In winter, another picture, reflecting the sun as it sets briefly behind charcoal etchings of bare-limbed trees and the cold clean whiteness of it all, is music for the soul." Today, this area is part of the 3,000+ acre Idlewild Wildlife Management Area, managed by the State of Maryland Department of Natural Resources. (Both from the Danny Phillips collection.)

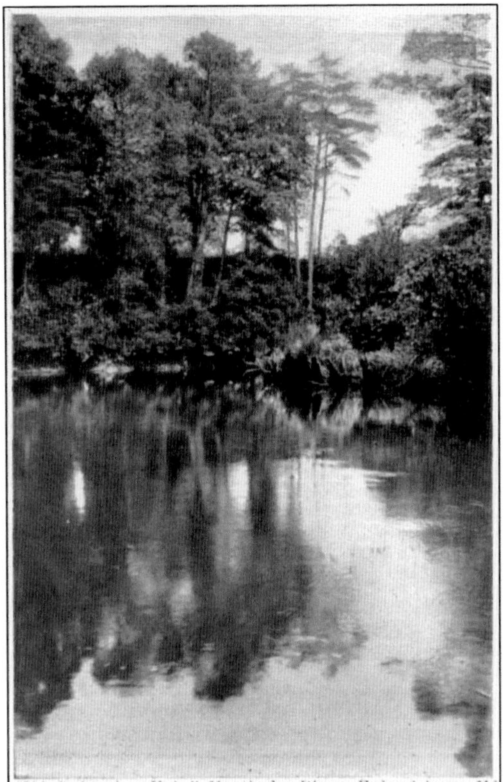

"Old Swimming Hole," Nanticoke River, Federalsburg, Md

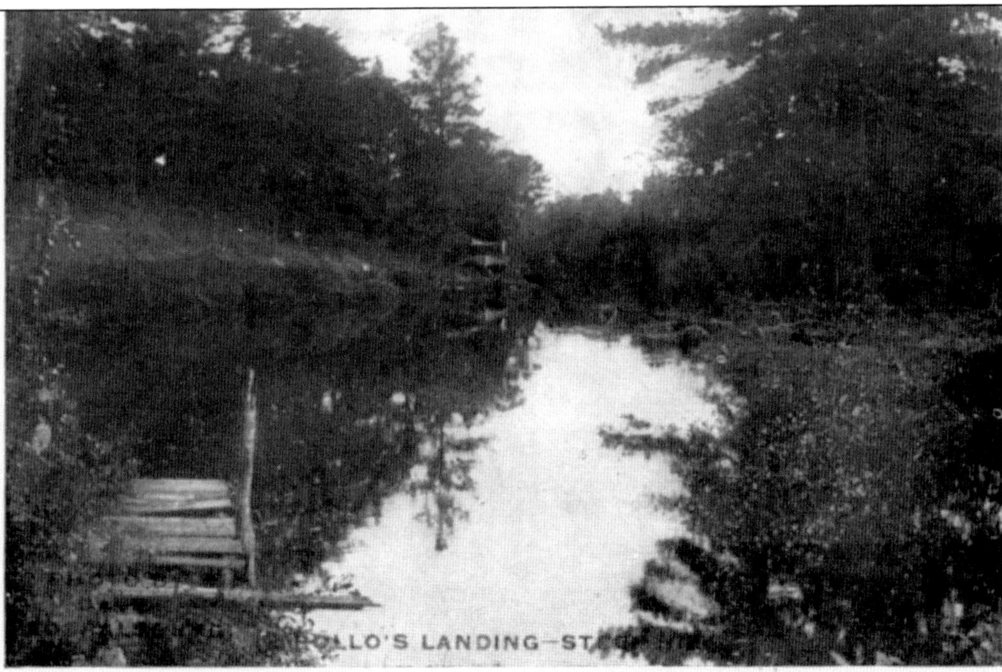

OLD SWIMMING HOLE, Federalsburg, Md.

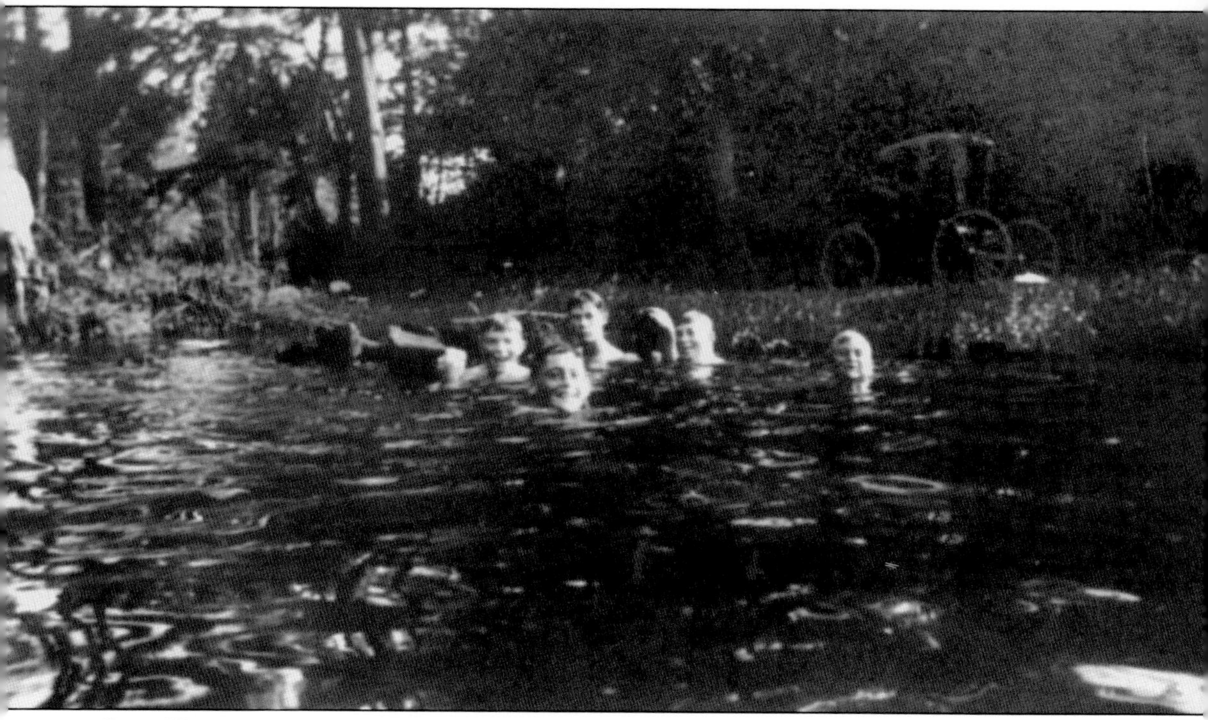

GATE HOLE AROUND 1915. When the flood-gates were put into operation, the old fishing hole gradually became known as the gate hole. John Brown purchased the mill in 1858 and later built up the dam with two more feet of dirt on top of the existing dam, which increased the size of the lake once again. Idlewild Mill ceased all operation in 1915 when it was destroyed by fire. During the flood of 1935, the dam broke and it has never been rebuilt. The lake is gone now, and while one can still navigate a small boat on the creek and fish in the waters, nothing compares to the grandeur of days past. Aside from the great fishing, the "Gate Hole" was known as the local swimming hole. The second boy on the left was Henry B. Messenger and the third from the left was Robert "Bob" Holt. Both of these boys grew up to become prominent businessmen of the town. (From the Mary Holt collection.)

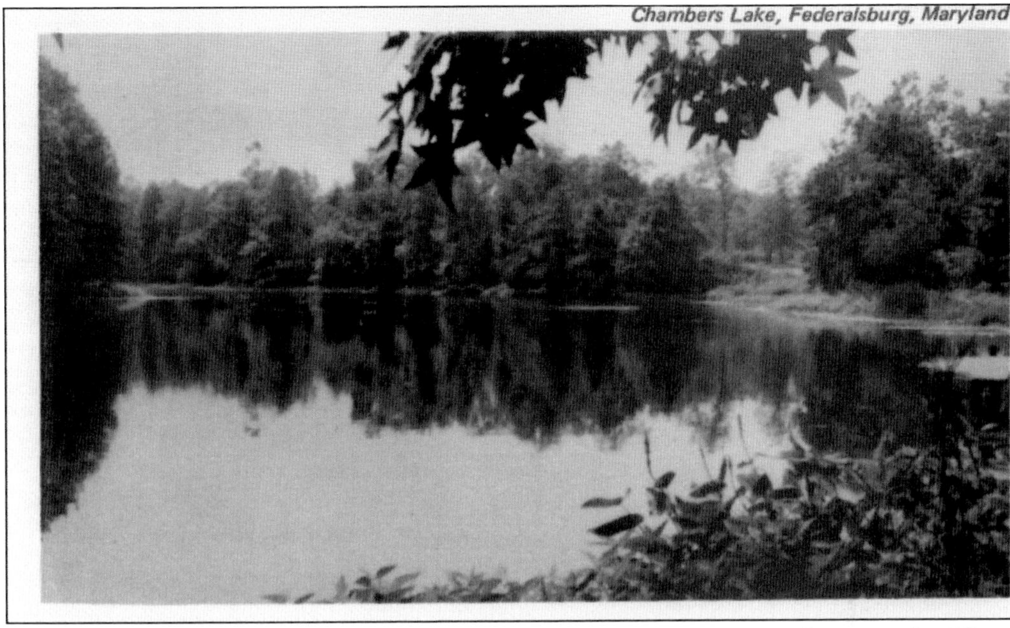

CHAMBERS LAKE. Land for Chambers Park and Lake was given to the town by Thomas H. Chambers, who served for over 30 years as Federalsburg's mayor. He wanted to leave something lasting for the community in memory of his wife, Ada Elliott Chambers. The Federal Government provided $15,000 to transform the area into a recreation center. The lake was created with Civilian Conservation Corps labor in the 1930s as a WPA Project under Roosevelt's New Deal, and was a great source of pleasure to adults and children, many of whom took swimming and safety lessons provided by the Red Cross. Each year, local people and businesses worked to dredge the lake and install a new sandy base. The lake, which opened in 1938, continued operating as a swimming hole until the mid-1960s. The area included a pier, a diving board, a lifeguard stand, bath houses, a concession stand, and benches. When winters were cold and the lake was covered with a thick layer of ice, many would meet at the site for ice skating. (Top postcard from the Archie Palamaras collection; bottom postcard from the Danny Phillips collection.)

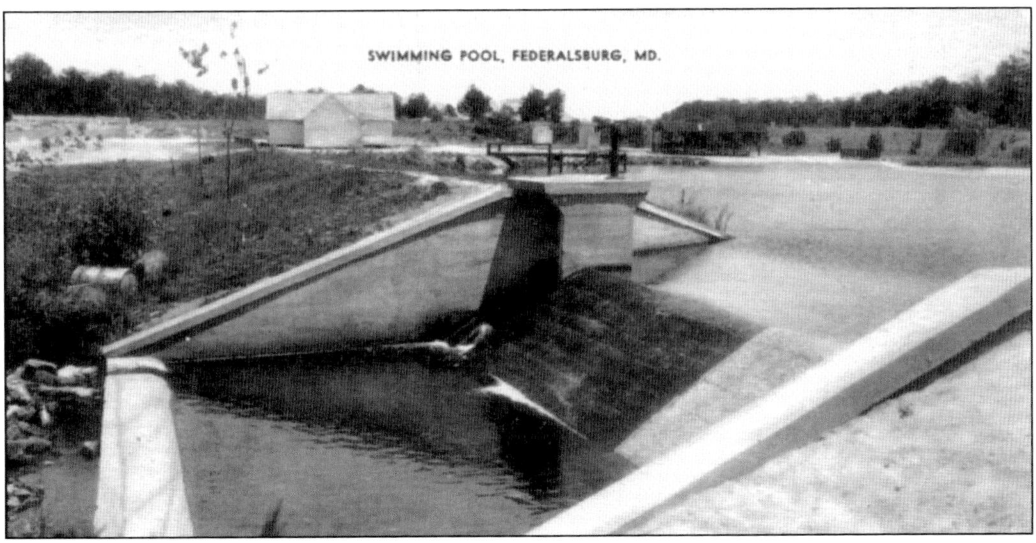

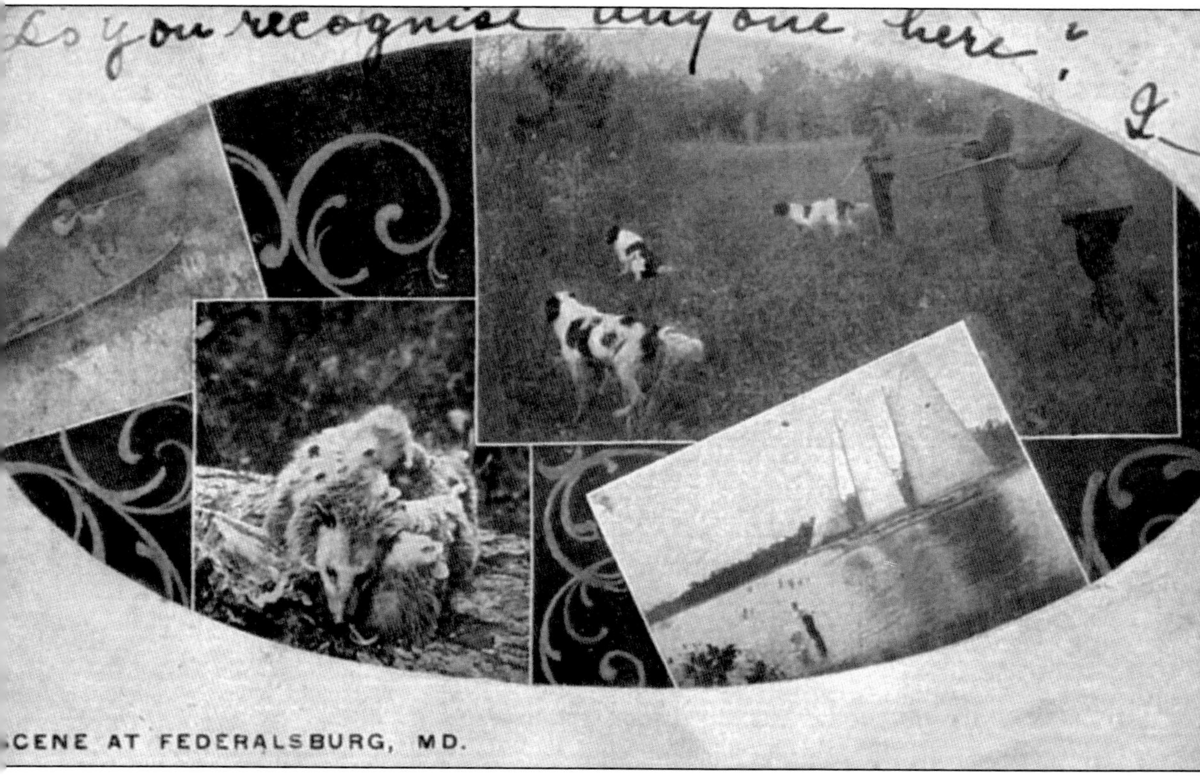

FEDERALSBURG RECREATION. This postcard, *c.* 1932, was made as a collage of some of the outdoor sports enjoyed in this area—hunting, fishing, and boating. (From the Laurence G. Claggett collection.)

Four

Schools and Churches

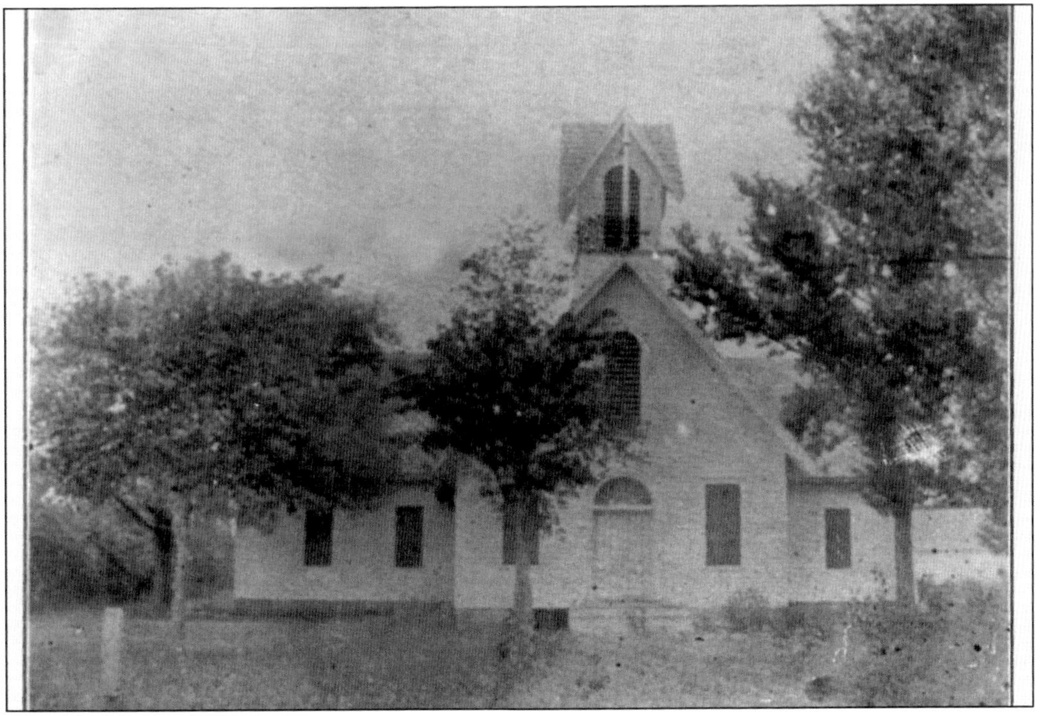

Federalsburg High School. Federalsburg's first official school, known as the Academy, was a four-room frame building with no modern conveniences. The faculty in 1904 consisted of a principal and three assistants. There were 168 pupils, 17 in high school and 151 in the elementary grades. At this time, several small houses around town were also used for educational purposes. (From the Federalsburg Historical Society, Inc. Collection.)

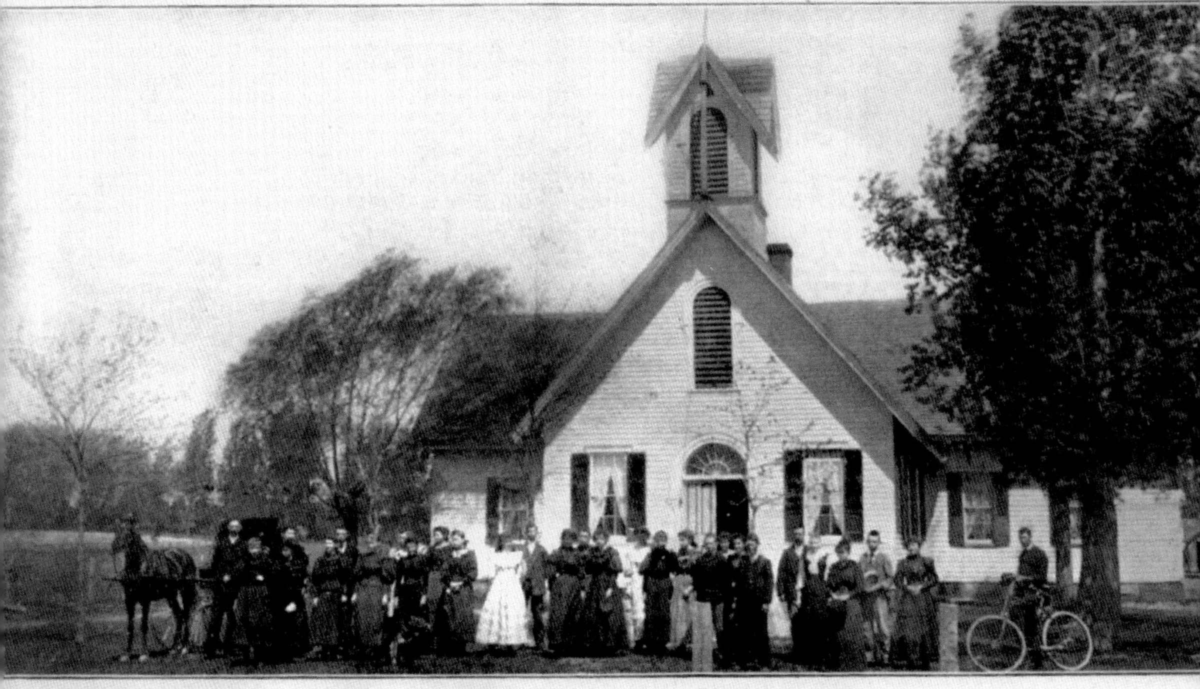

FEDERALSBURG ACADEMY—FOUR ROOMS

FEDERALSBURG ACADEMY/HIGH SCHOOL. Through the untiring efforts of Hon. Edward E. Goslin, president of the board of trustees, the 1904 session of the General Assembly passed a bill providing for an annual state appropriation of $500 for Federalsburg. The county school board ordered the Federalsburg High School established and the regular state high school course of study was pursued. Along with the advantage of offering an accredited high school education came the desire for families to settle in Federalsburg. This building was used until the new school opened in 1914. The old school was used in later years as a blacksmith shop and was subsequently destroyed by fire.

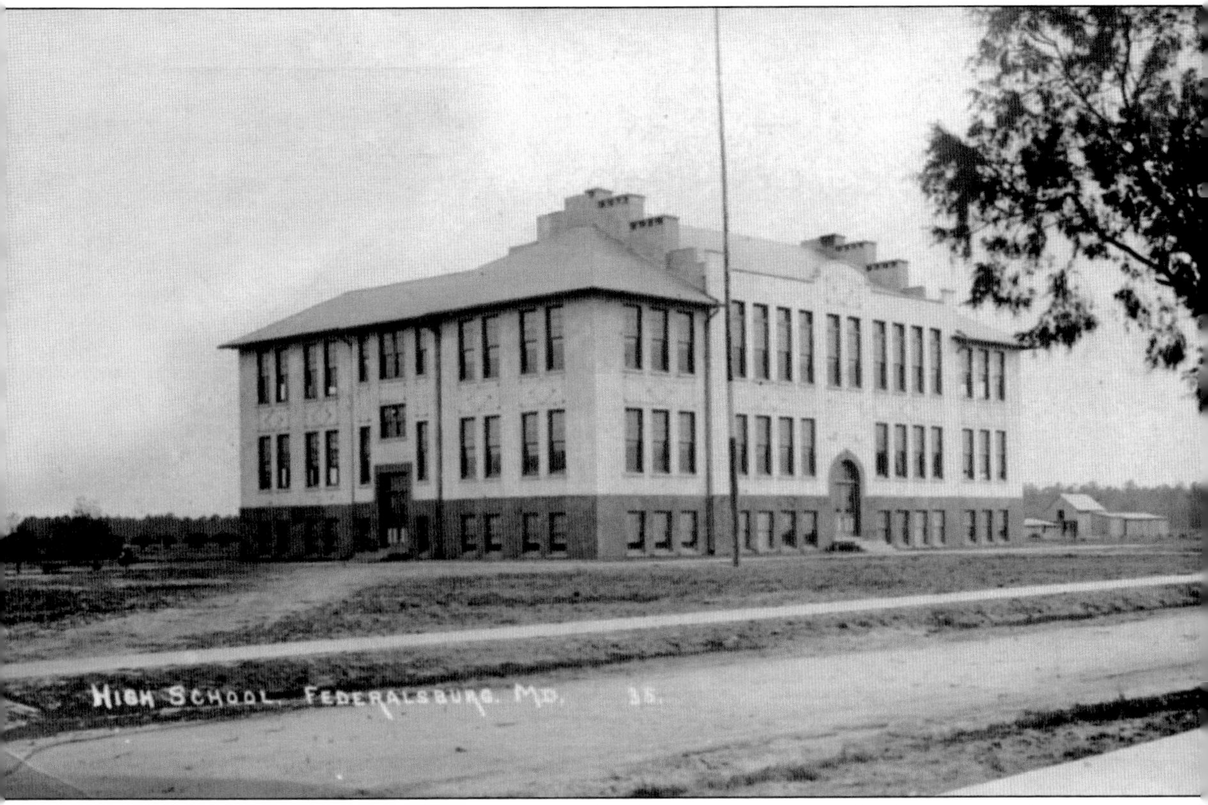

FEDERALSBURG SCHOOL. The Federalsburg School was constructed of hollow tile and stucco with an asbestos roof. It was lighted by electricity, heated with an oil heating plant, and water was supplied by the Town Water System. It contained 18 classrooms, an auditorium, a cafeteria, a shop, and some auxiliary rooms. There were numerous sports fields and playground equipment (swings, seesaws, etc.) made by the Industrial Arts Department. In 1932, there were 18 faculty members (9 in high school and 9 in the elementary grades) and the school included instruction in music, industrial arts, household arts, and commercial branches, besides the usual subjects. There were 11 grades, with an enrollment of 525 children (175 in high school and 350 in elementary school). Six busses transported over 200 of these children from the surrounding community daily. (From the Danny Phillips collection.)

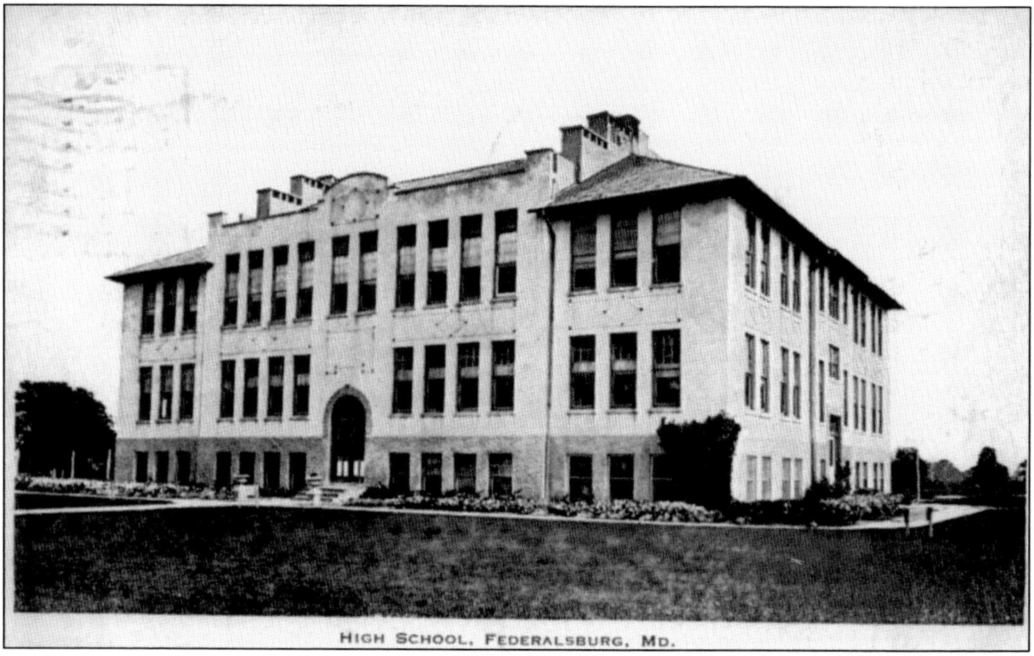

FEDERALSBURG SCHOOL. The Federalsburg School was built in 1914 and was in operation until the mid-1950s. Through 1950 only 11 grades were required for graduation. The first class that completed 12 grades was graduated from this school in 1951. After the completion of a new brick school building, the Federalsburg School was completely demolished. The last class to graduate from the Federalsburg High School was the class of 1961. Then the high school was moved to the new Colonel Richardson High School at American Corner. (From the Danny Phillips collection.)

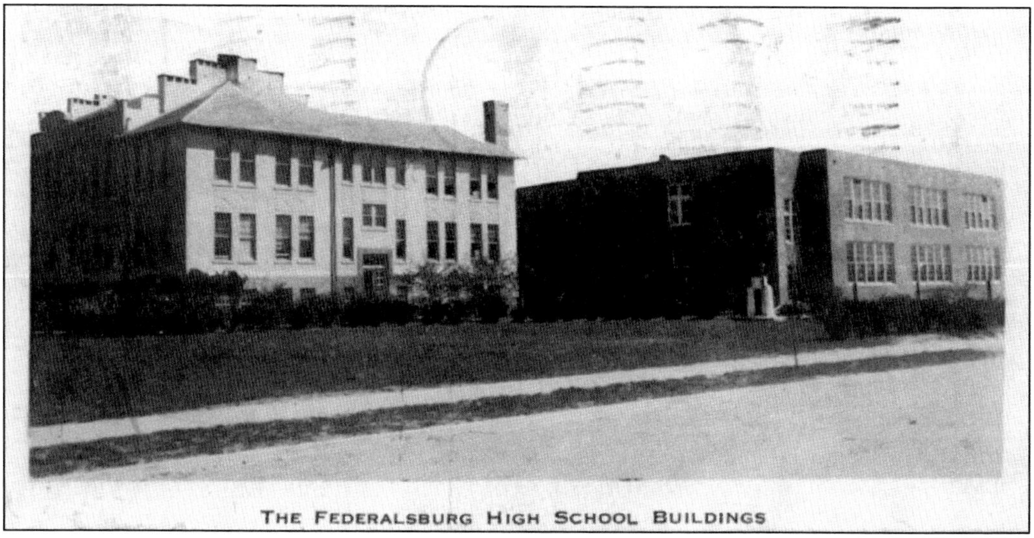

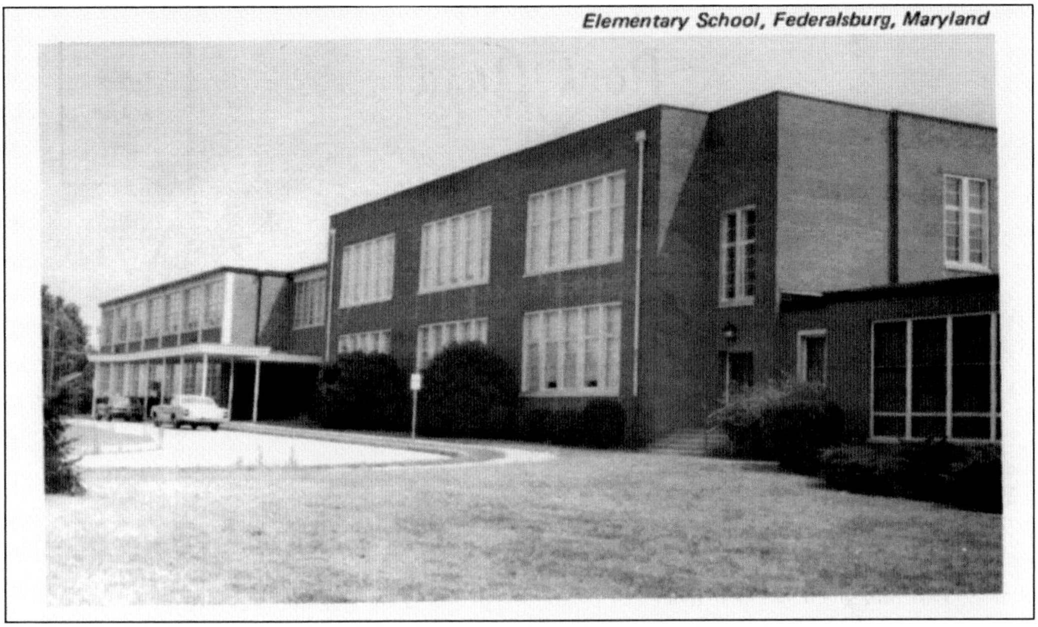

Federalsburg Elementary and Colonel Richardson School. In 1962, the Federalsburg High School and the Preston High School moved to the newly consolidated Colonel Richardson High School at American Corner; the first class graduated from Colonel Richardson High School that same year. Later, a new high school was built at the Colonel Richardson location and the Federalsburg Middle School, along with the Preston Middle School, was moved to the former high school building. The photo below shows the building when it was Colonel Richardson High School, but is now the Colonel Richardson Middle School. The new high school sits a short distance to the left of this building. (Top postcard from the Danny Phillips collection; bottom postcard from the Federalsburg Historical Society collection.)

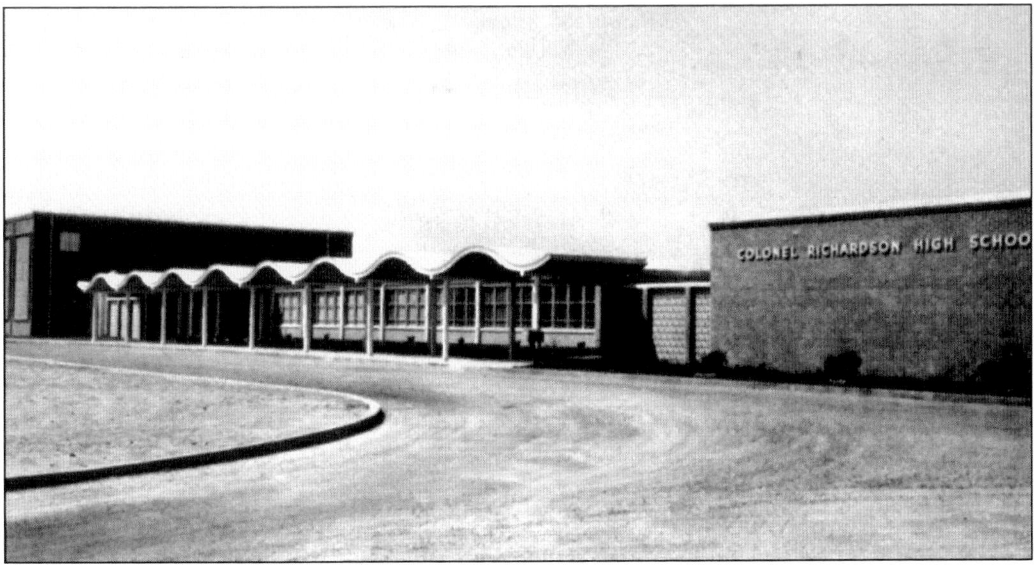

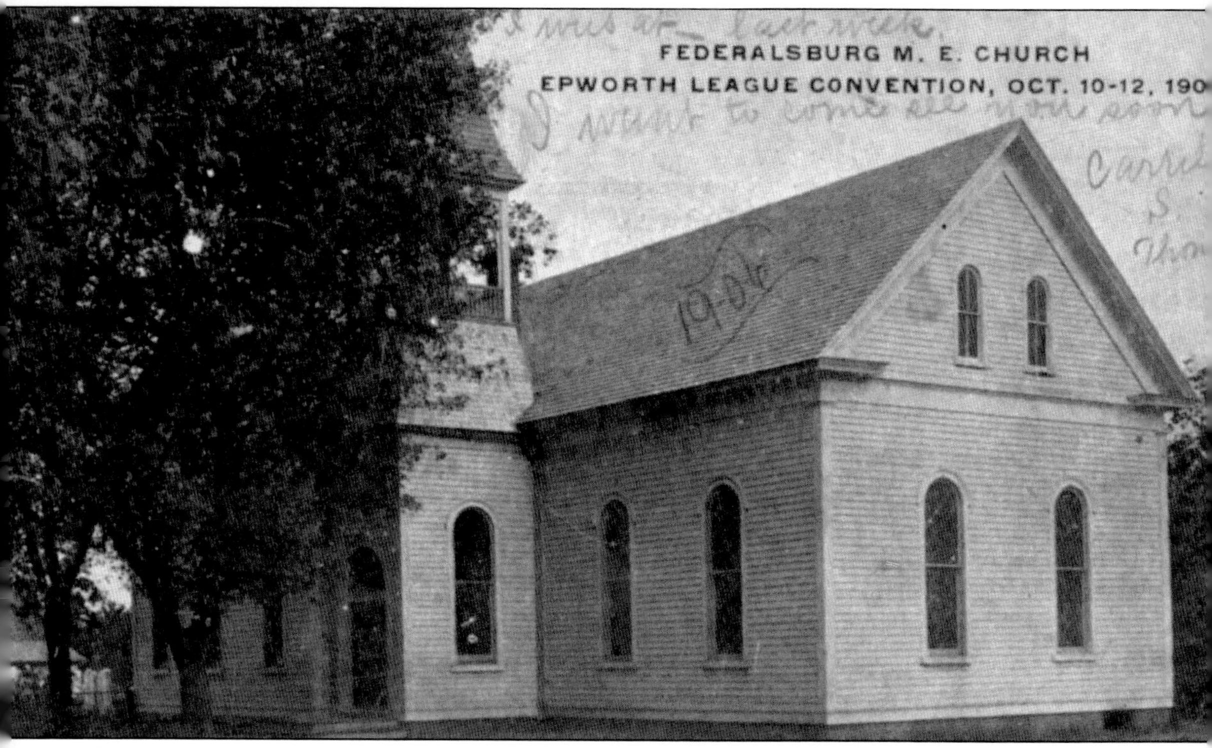

UNION M.E. CHURCH. The first church building at this site had been erected around 1815 in the middle of the present cemetery. This was moved about a hundred yards south and on the east side of Main Street when the new church was erected in 1850. Around 1885, improvements included taking the first bell in back of the church and added the steeple where the bell was swung. (From the Danny Phillips collection.)

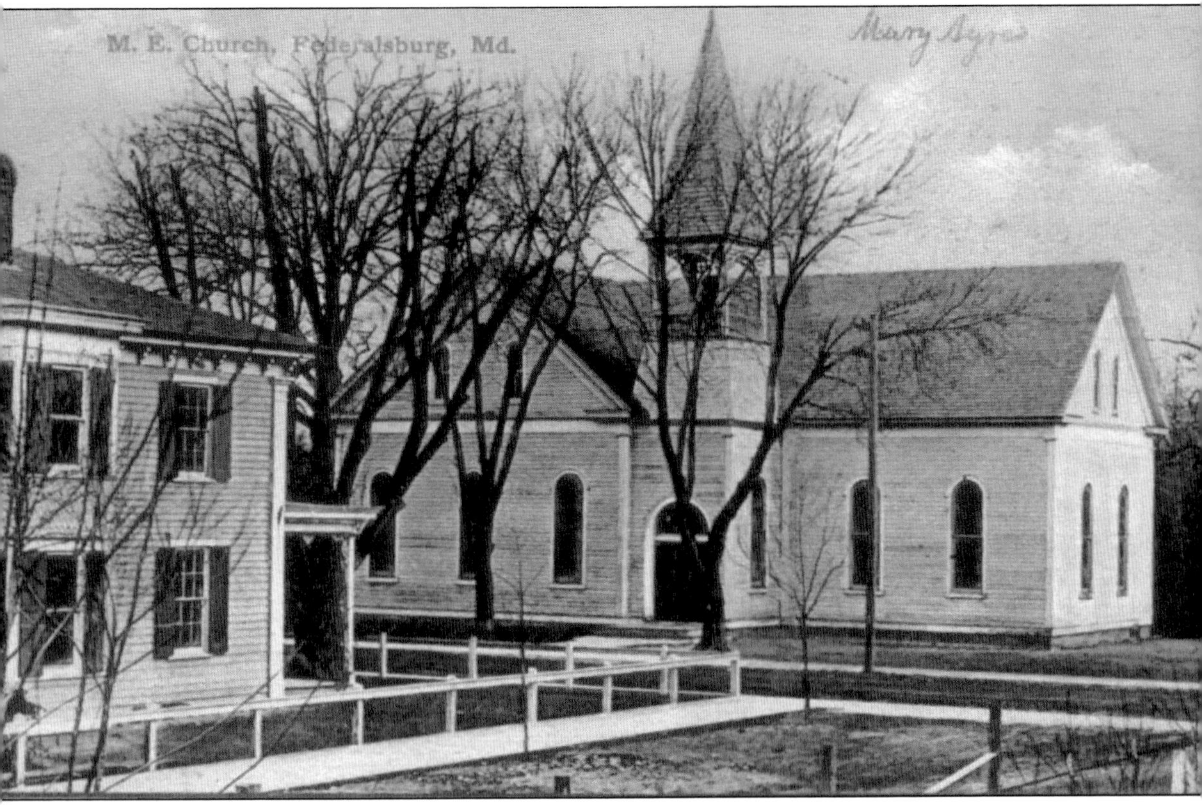

Union M.E. Church. In 1901, the pastor, Rev. Thomas S. Holt, led an effort to replace the roof, refinish the auditorium, purchased a new Mason and Hammond organ, added a Sunday school unit, and shifted the bell tower and entrance. Other repairs were made and completed in 1912, such as painting and varnishing the building, inside and out. (From the Danny Phillips collection.)

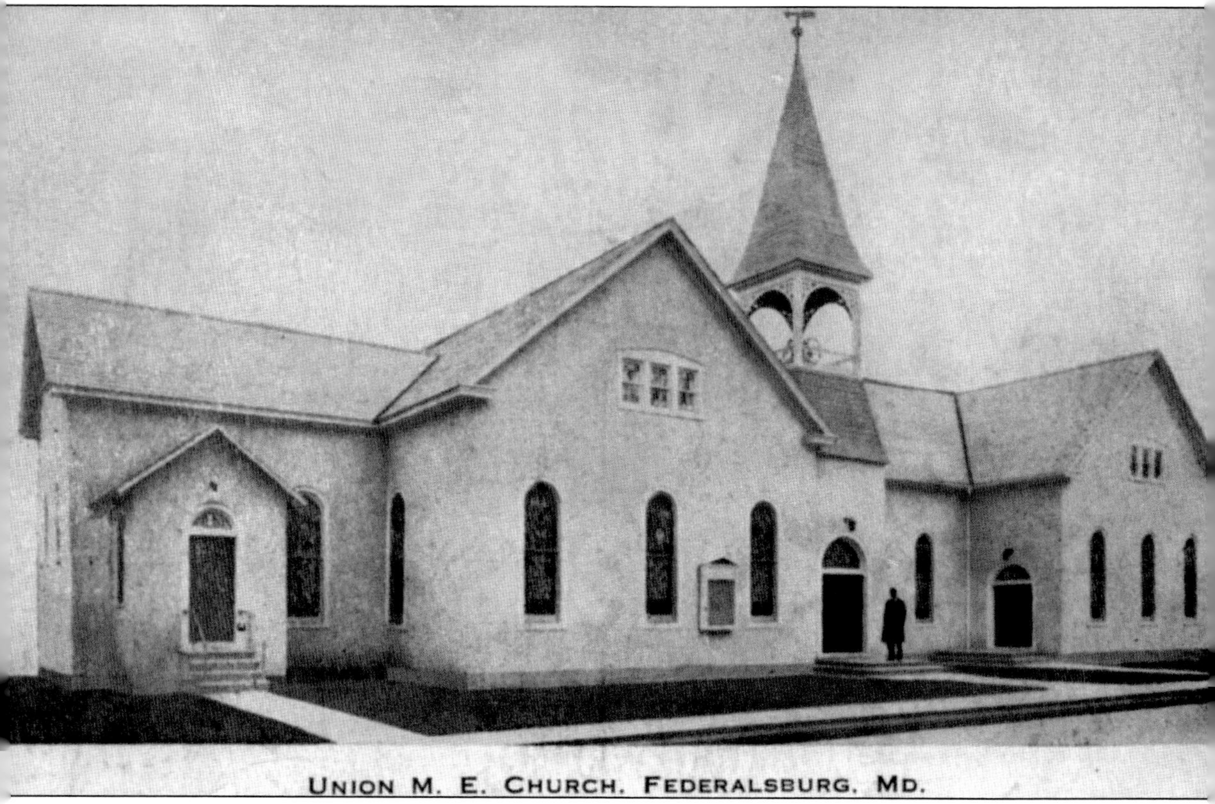

MODERNIZATION. The greatest undertaking to modernize Union Methodist Episcopal Church resulted in a complete overhaul of the old building and the erection of a new social and educational unit. The outside walls were stuccoed and many improvements to the church and Sunday school departments were accomplished. These improvements were dedicated in 1930. About the time the debt was paid for the improvements the church had an unexpected setback. The town suffered the great flood of 1935 and the auditorium had five feet of water in it. There was considerable damage to floors, seats, organ, furnace, and hymn books and other supplies. Members forgot their own troubles caused by the flood and made the necessary repairs and replacements to the church. (From the R. Allan Gorsuch collection.)

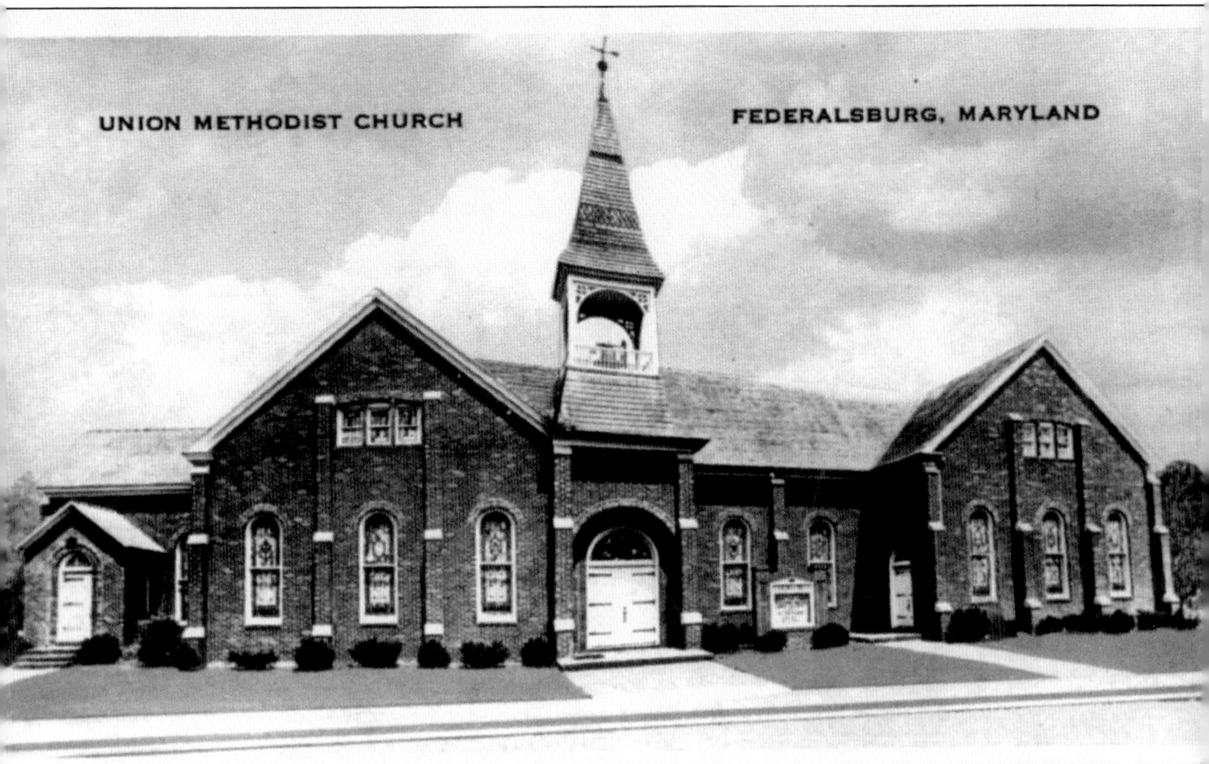

Renovations. In 1948, the late mayor Thomas H. Chambers had constructed and presented to the church the chapel on the south side of the sanctuary in memory of his wife, Ada Elliott Chambers. At this time brick veneer was added to the outside of the entire structure. Ground was broken in 1970 for the addition of the Educational Building (not shown in the postcard, but it is located on the right side of this church) and Fellowship Hall, office and library, and these too were finished with brick. This building was occupied in the fall of 1971. The year 1983 saw the beginning of an extensive renovation of the sanctuary during the pastorate of Rev. David Baker. At this time, the front entrance was relocated and the old steeple was taken down and replaced with the present steeple in a different location on the roof. On March 18, 1984, a celebration of re-entry was held to mark the renovation of Union Methodist Church. (From the Danny Phillips collection.)

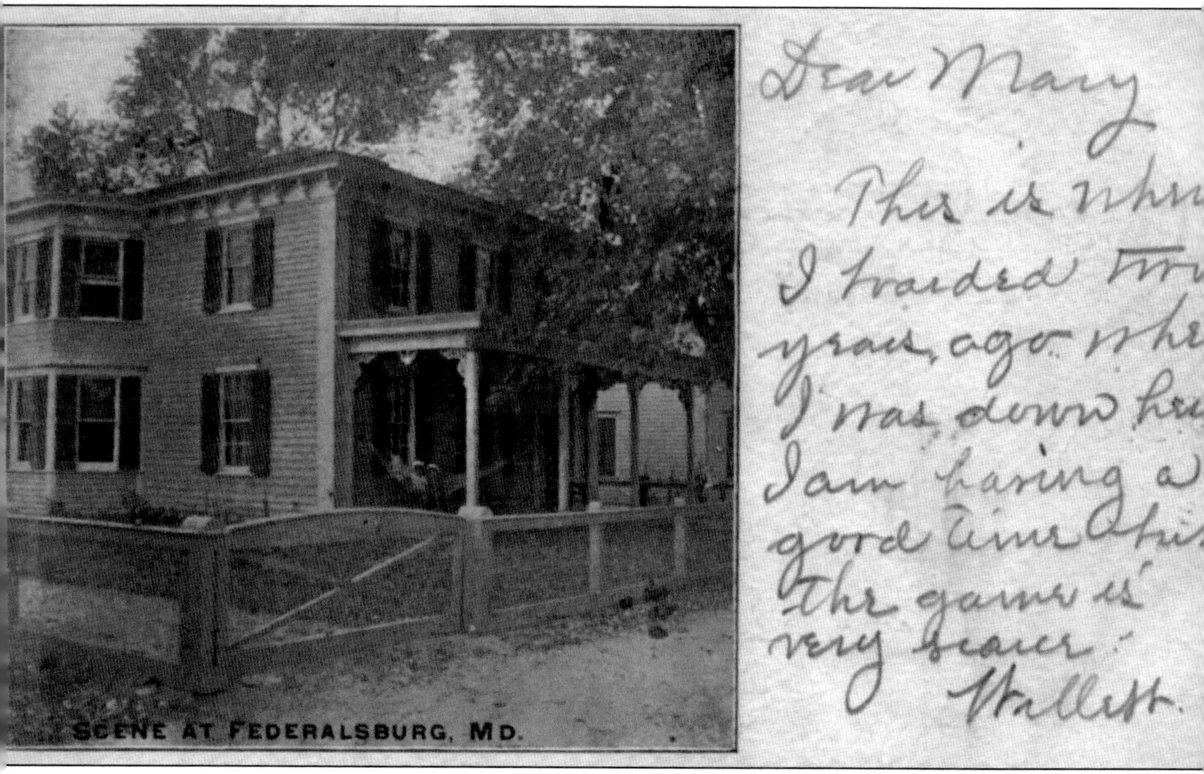

OLD UNION PARSONAGE. The "Old Parsonage" was deeded to the Parsonage Trustees of Union Methodist Episcopal Church by John F. Elliott and wife and John W. Brown and wife on June 4, 1872. It sat on the lot directly across from the church, now used as a parking lot. It served until 1948 when the property at 206 West Central Avenue was acquired. At that time, the old parsonage was converted to Sunday school rooms, an office, and an apartment for the custodians. In 1975, a new Educational Building having been added to the church, the old parsonage was sold to H. Torbert Williamson, who moved the building to Charles Street and carefully restored it. Since then it has served as his residence. (From the Danny Phillips collection.)

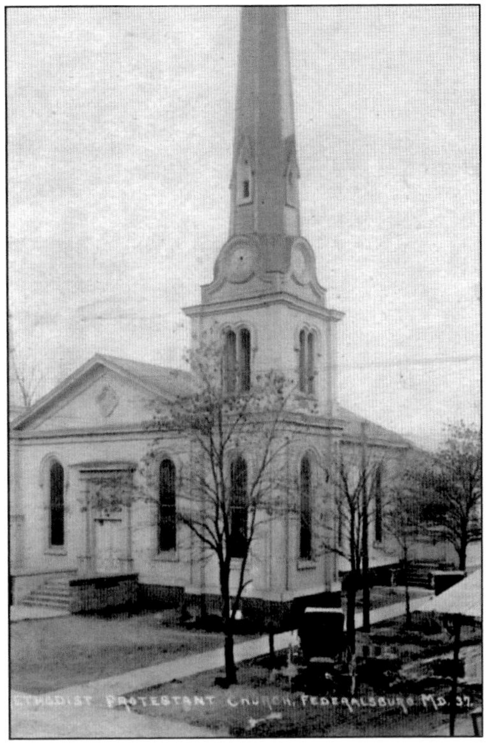

CHRIST UNITED METHODIST CHURCH. In 1902, a group of citizens formed a Methodist Protestant church in Federalsburg and bought the recently abandoned Presbyterian Church. This white church, with high-arched stained glass windows, included a handsome spire, which gracefully ascended 150 feet. Unfortunately, this spire was destroyed by fire around 1931 and was never rebuilt to its original height. Rev. H.F. Wright was the first pastor and it was during his pastorate that many improvements were made, including the erection of a parsonage on Academy Avenue. Later improvements included the addition of upper stories for Sunday School classes and the cellar converted into an attractive dining room with a large seating capacity. (Top postcard from the Danny Phillips collection; bottom postcard from the Laurence G. Claggett collection.)

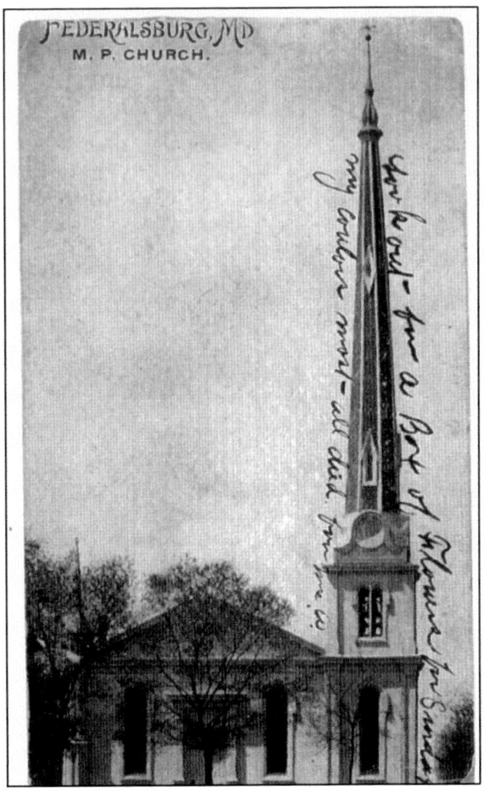

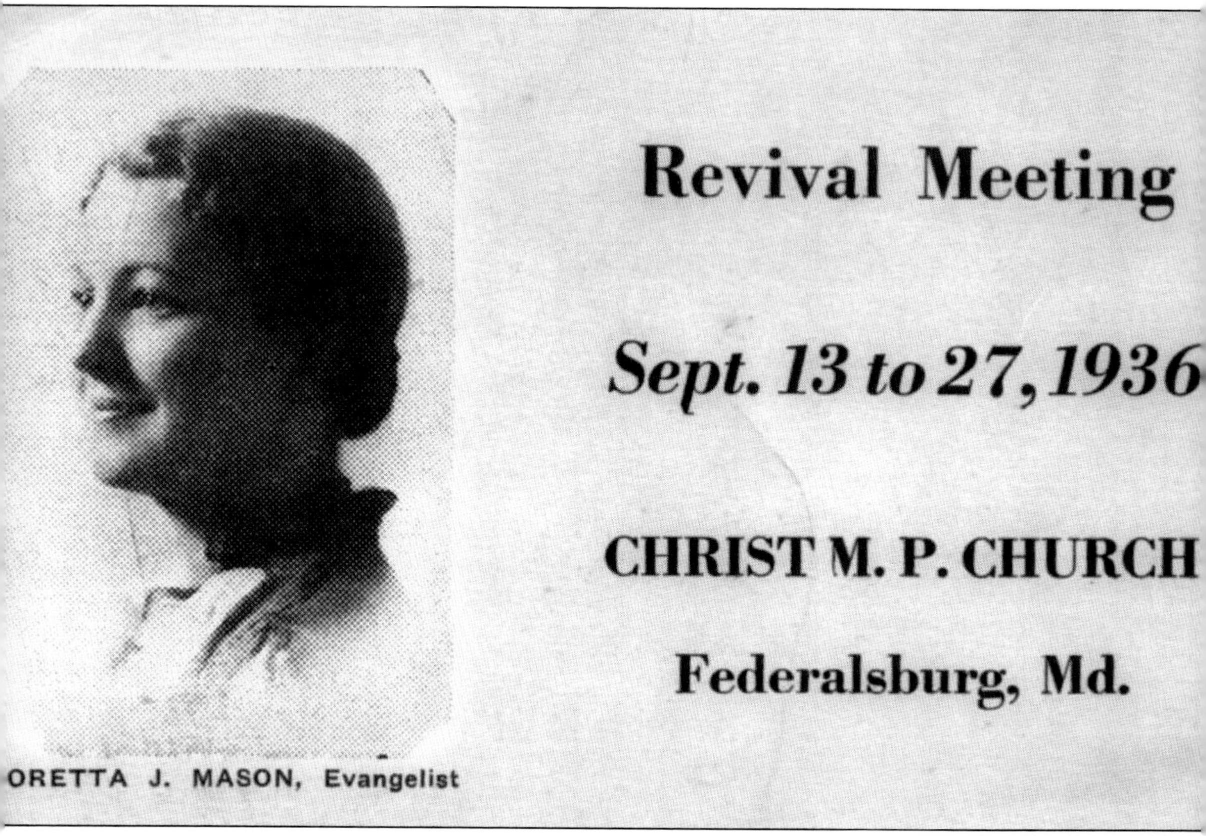

REVIVALS. Revival meetings were popular on the Eastern Shore of Maryland. Miss Coretta J. Mason was an evangelist who traveled around the Delmarva Peninsula in the 1950s and 1960s. People recollect that she was an attractive woman who was always dressed in white. (From the Danny Phillips collection.)

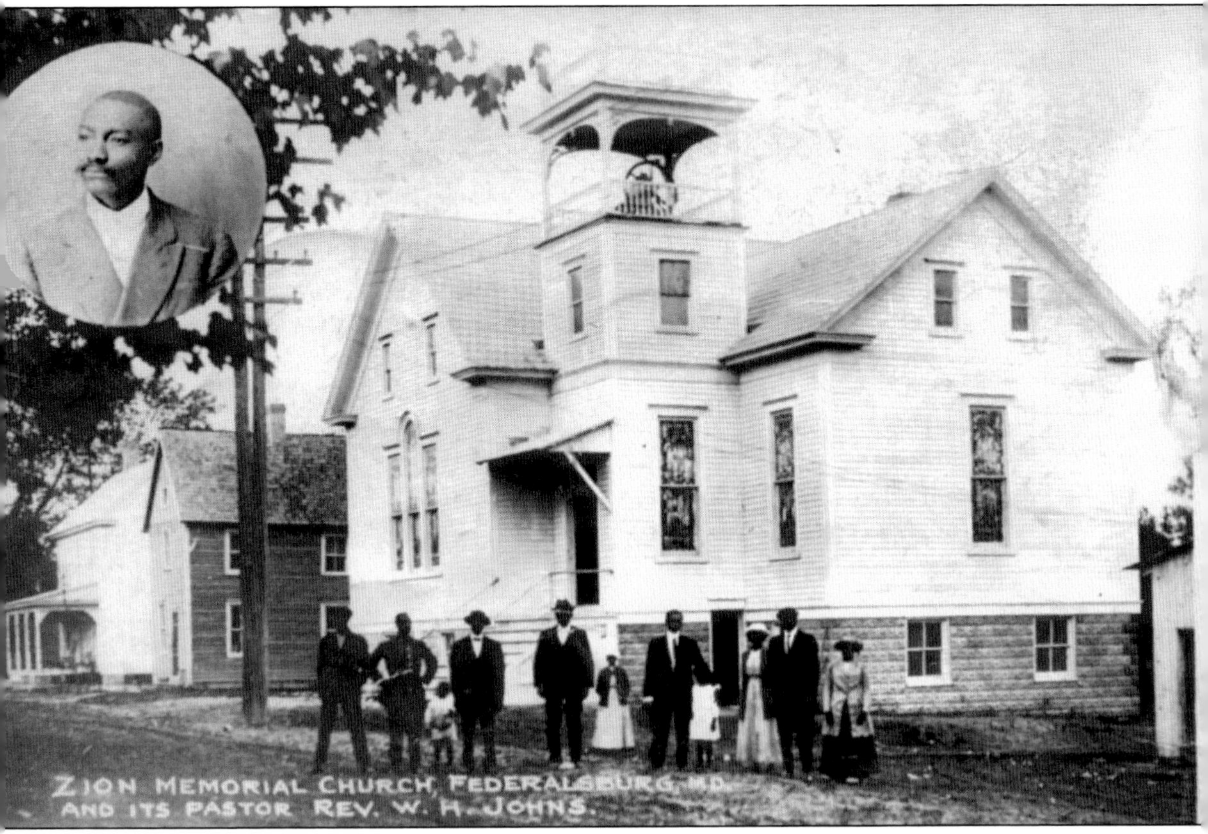

ZION UNITED METHODIST CHURCH. The black citizens of Federalsburg founded their own church in 1848 and called it Zion Memorial Episcopal Church. It was rebuilt from 1873 to 1886 on top of the hill on Old Nichols Road (now called Laurel Grove Road) where the old cemetery still remains. In 1913, a new building was built by the Rev. William Johns (inset photo) and his parishioners on Old Denton Road next to Marshyhope Creek. This beautiful building was erected at a cost of $5,800. In 1993, the church officially became known as Zion United Methodist Church. (From the Francis "Sonny" Callahan collection.)

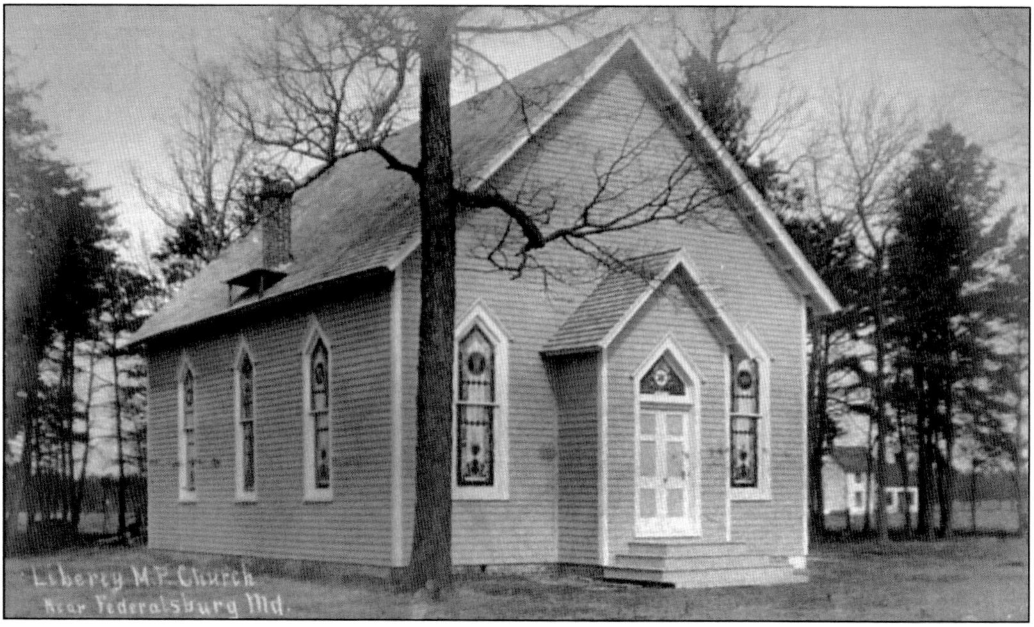

LIBERTY CHURCH. Liberty Road derives its name from the first Liberty Church, which was built in 1848. Its location was the present home of Mrs. Levi Saunders, the first home on one's left after turning onto Wright Road from Liberty Road. This plot was a part of the Charles Wright farm. Some years later ground was donated for a new church about a quarter mile further out and on the left side of Liberty Road. Here a new church (as seen in the postcard) was built and is still used for religious services. The original church was moved to what is now the Crawford farm (first farm on the left after crossing Tanyard Branch) and was used as a farm building. (From the Laurence G. Claggett collection.)

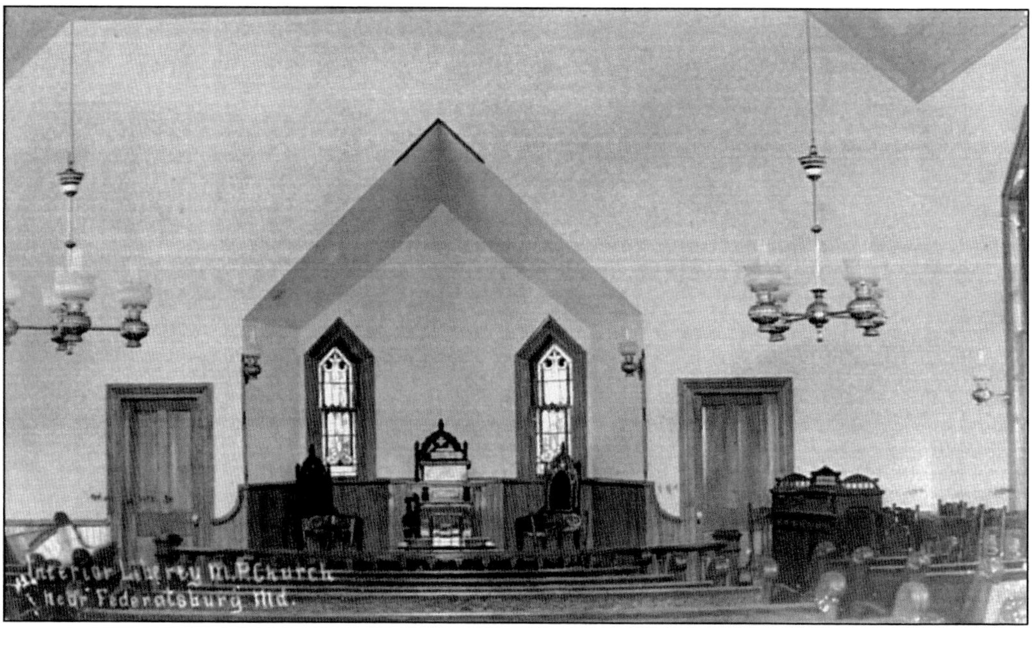

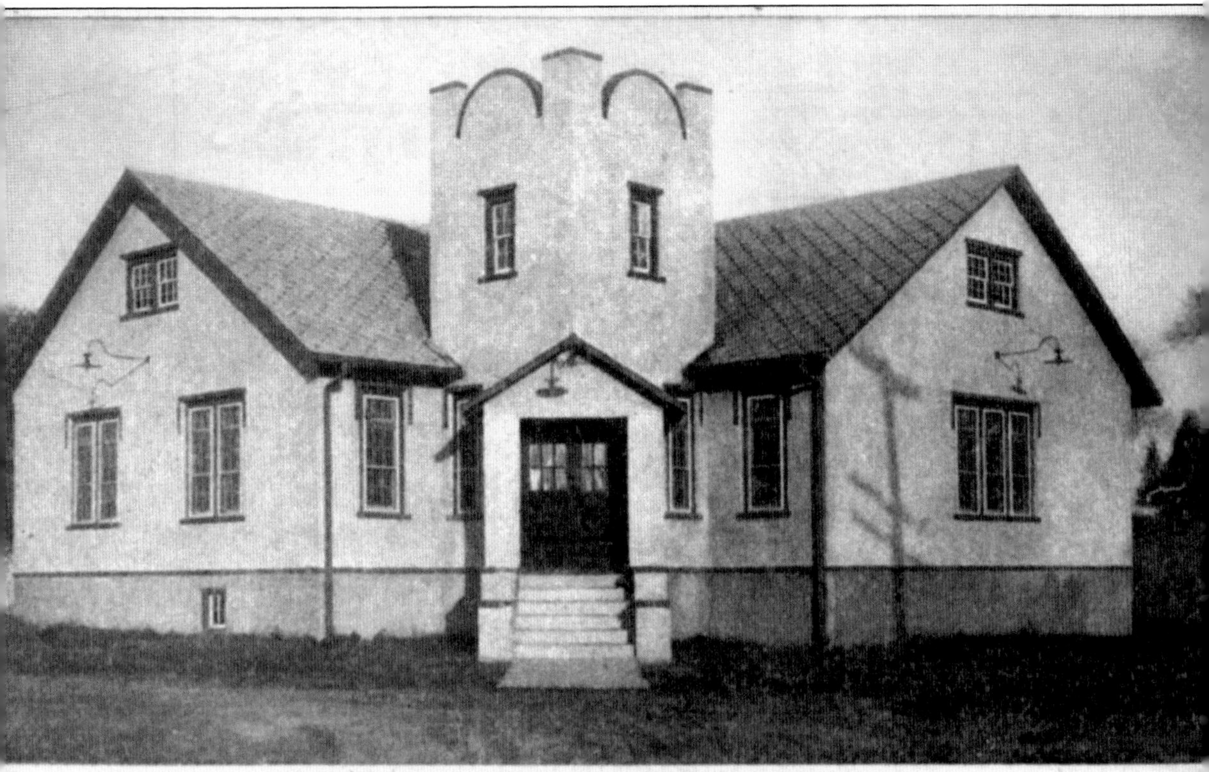

The Church of God, Federalsburg, Maryland

First Church of God. The congregation of the First Church of God in Federalsburg had its beginning in 1895 when W.J. Henry, one of the pioneer ministers of this movement, conducted services a few miles outside of Federalsburg on the Preston road. Later the old Quaker Meeting House was secured as a place of worship, until the Little Brown Church was built in 1896. In 1925, a stone building in Federalsburg was erected at a cost of about $12,000. In 1934 a basement was put under the building and was divided into individual classrooms. (From the Danny Phillips collection.)

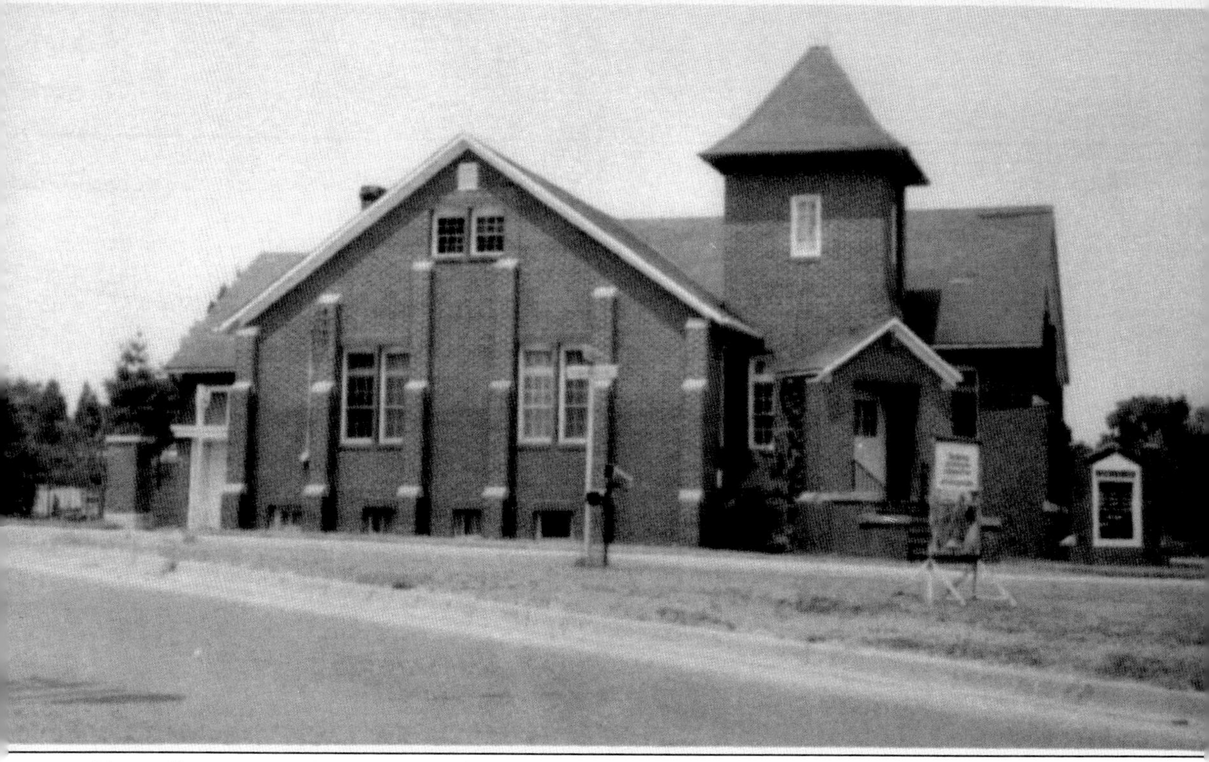

FIRST CHURCH OF GOD. In 1947 the exterior of the building was covered with red brick, which enhanced its attractiveness. In 1952, another remodeling took place which included an addition which housed the chancel, choir loft, baptistery, and two classrooms on the ground floor, and a large classroom in the basement. A stained glass window depicting Christ at prayer is located above the baptistery. (From the Danny Phillips collection.)

Five

Postcards of Interest

Postcard Regulations. The comment on the back of this card read, "Private Mailing Card, Authorized by Act of Congress of May 19, 1898." On December 4, 1901, the United States government granted the used of the words "Post Card" on one side with a black-and-white photograph on the other side. In the United States, writing was not permitted on the address side until 1907; there were no divided backs. Until this time, messages were written on the photograph side and the printers often left white space for this purpose. This helps sometimes to date the age of the postcard. Many of the local postcards were printed at J.W. Stowell Printing Co. and many of the photographs were taken by Davis Photo House, both of Federalsburg. (From the Mary Holt Collection.)

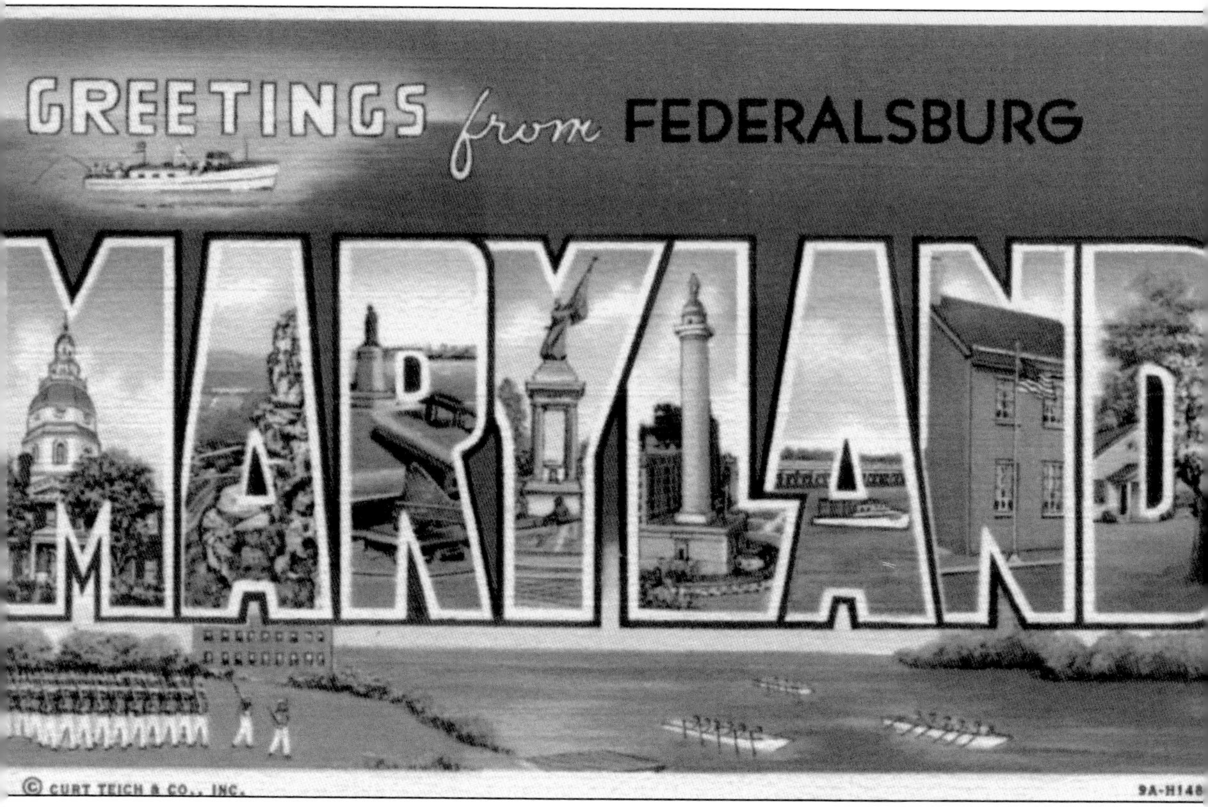

GREETINGS FROM FEDERALSBURG, MARYLAND. Sometimes, the postcard had a generic greeting such as the one above, which shows scenes recognizable throughout Maryland. The lower photos could depict scenes of Federalsburg, but it is unknown. (From the Charles S. Long Collection.)

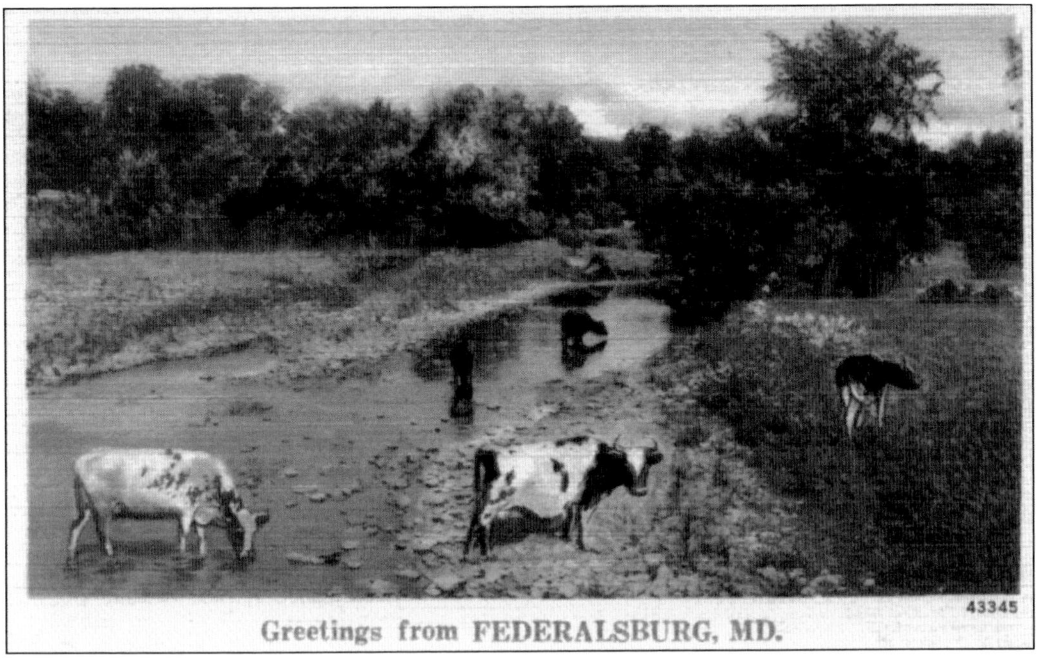

FEDERALSBURG POSTCARDS. Federalsburg is situated in Caroline County, Maryland, coined as the "Green Garden County." The above greeting could be from Federalsburg and looks similar to the photo below, which shows the banks of the Nanticoke River. The above color postcard was made during the Linen Era (1930 to 1945) when the printing was done on a linen-type paper stock with very bright and vivid colors. (Both postcards from the Charles S. Long collection.)

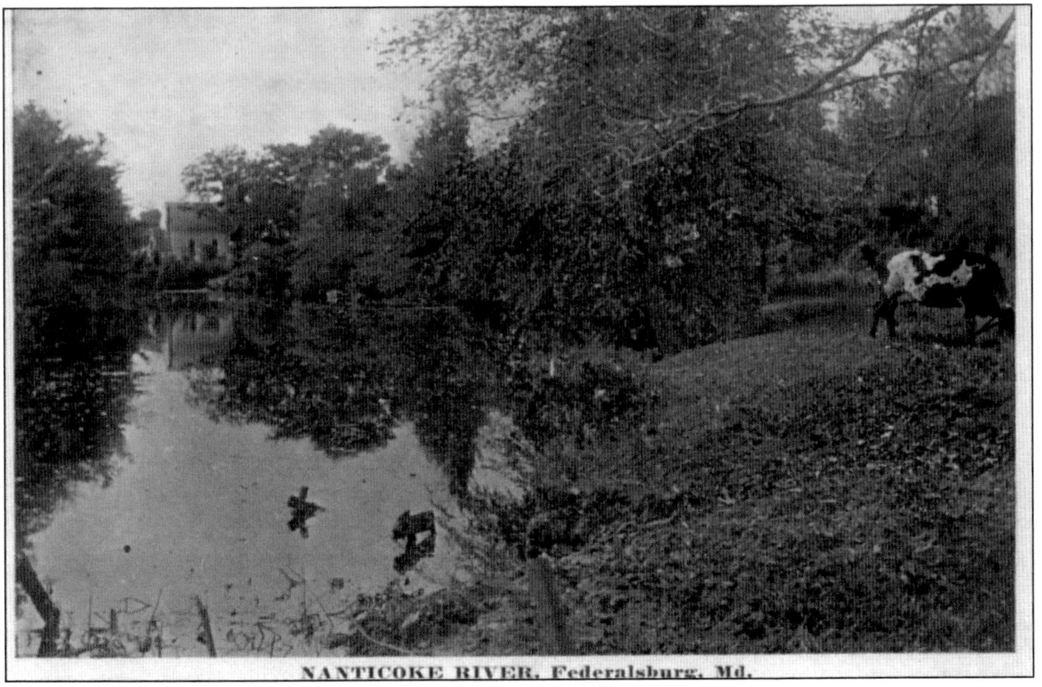

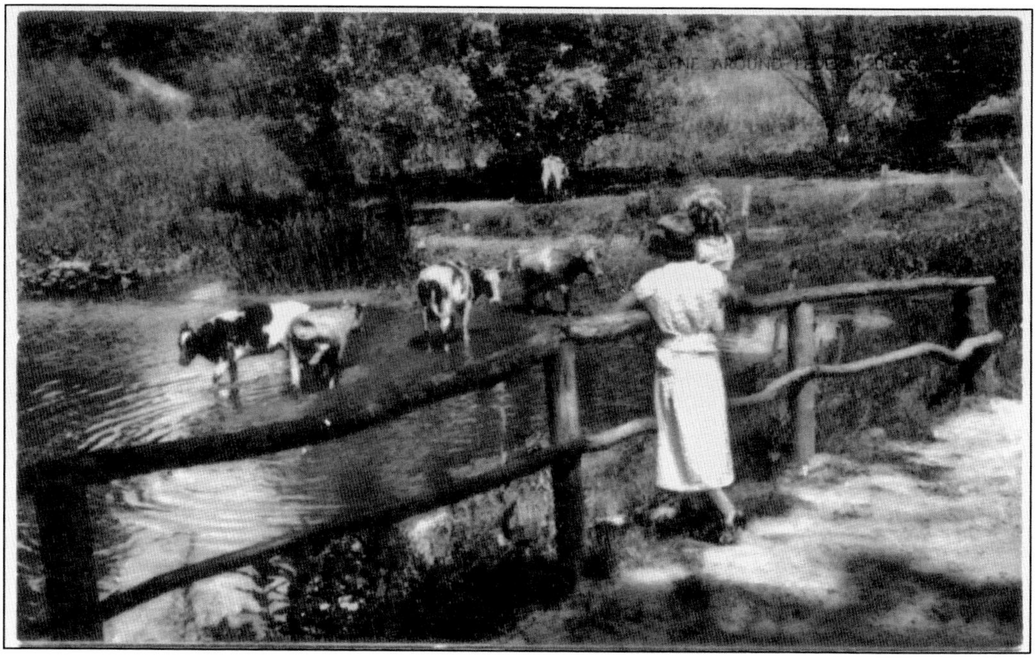

Rural Federalsburg. These are two more postcards from Federalsburg depicting the rural landscape. There were several dairies and milk routes around Federalsburg, including F.P. Glime's Dairy, Noble Dairy Co., and Cloverdale Farm Dairy. These have all ceased operation today, although agriculture is still a large part of our rural way of life. (Both postcards from the Danny Phillips collection.)

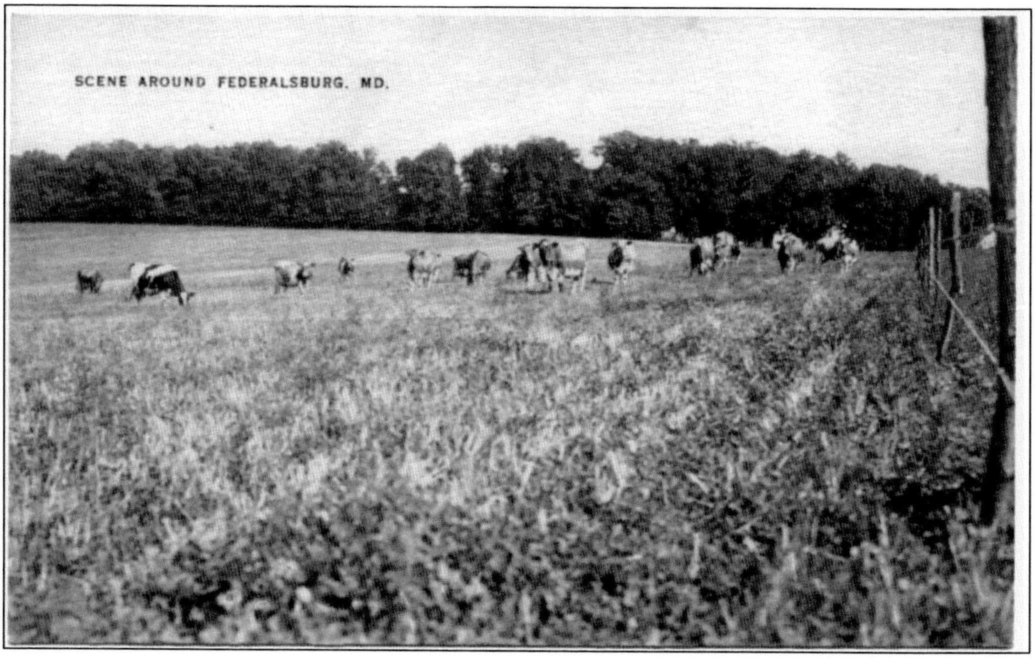

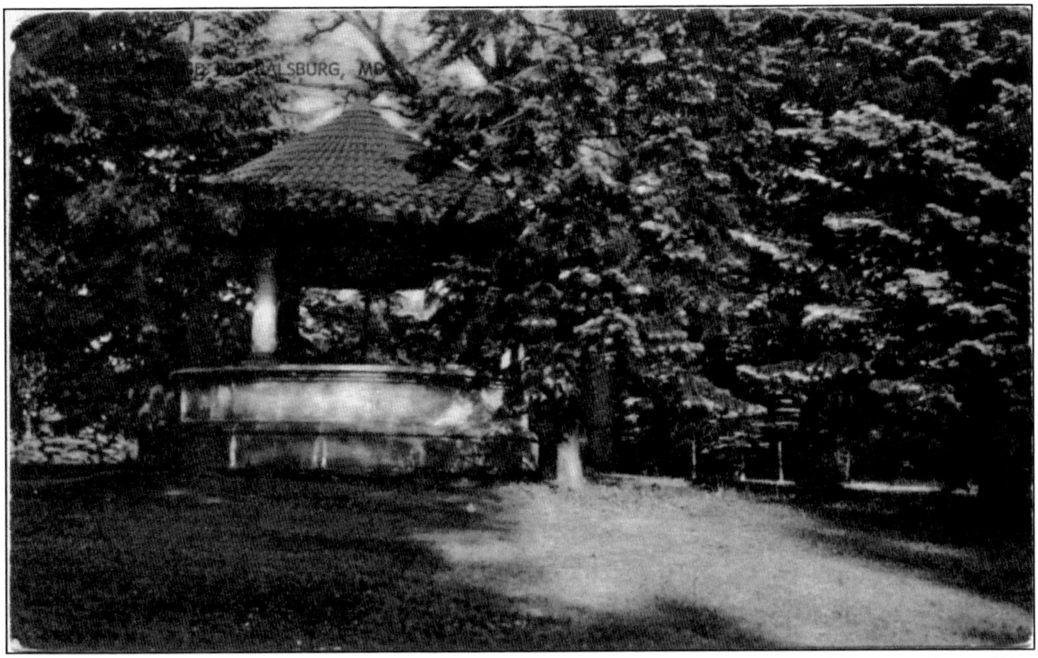

Unidentified Scene. It is unclear what this illustrates in Federalsburg. Hopefully, a reader will be able to identify this for us. (From the Danny Phillips Collection.)

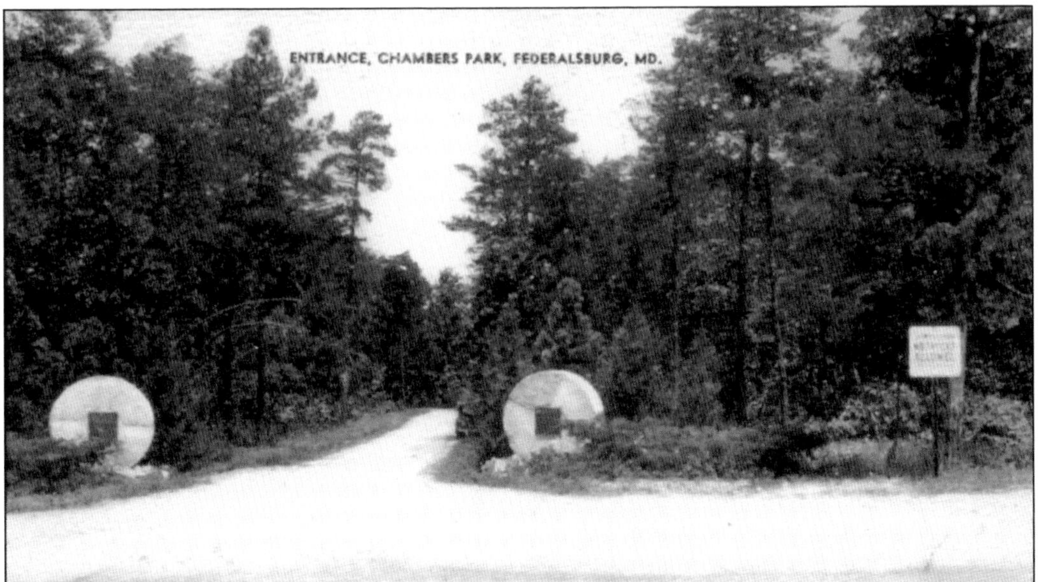

Chambers Park Entrance. Grist mills have been a large part of Federalsburg's past and these grindstones are used to welcome visitors to the entrance of Chambers Park, which is located off Liberty Road. The bronze plaques affixed to these stones read, "Ada Elliott Chamber Memorial Park 1938" as the park is a living memorial to Mr. Chambers and his wife. Mr. Chambers served as the mayor of Federalsburg for over 30 years before relinquishing the office to Mr. Clinton Poole. The municipal park developed into a shady spot of natural beauty and relaxation and is still in use today. (From the Danny Phillips collection.)

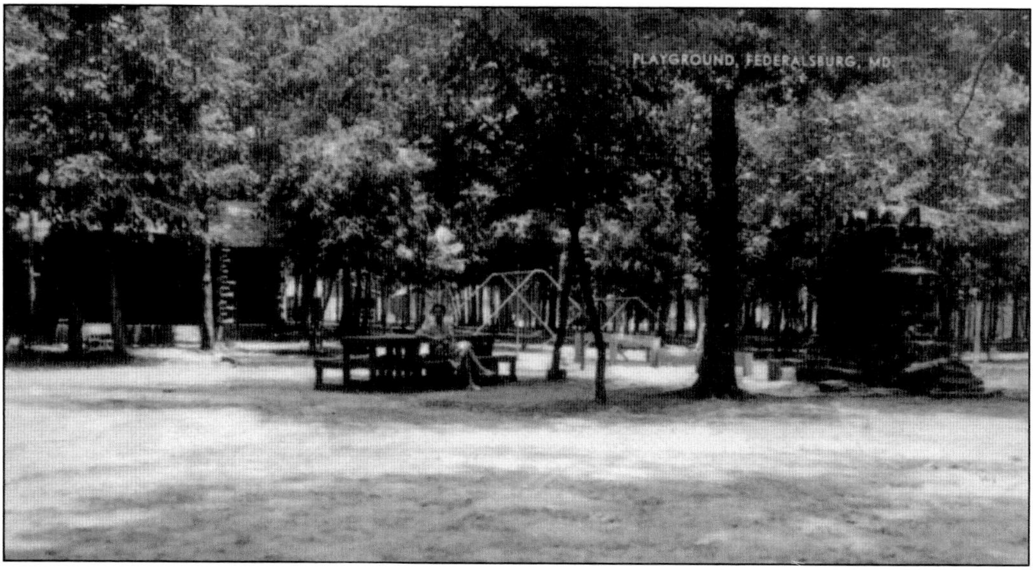

LOG CABIN. In 1937, the Log Cabin was dedicated and provided the scene for hundreds of gatherings. Boy Scouts, Girl Scouts, and 4-H clubs used it extensively, and it served as a popular place for children's birthday parties. Unfortunately, the Log Cabin is not open to the public today. Behind the Log Cabin is a large outdoor fireplace for grilling, tables and benches for picnics and gatherings, and numerous pieces of playground equipment modernized a few years ago. (From the Danny Phillips collection.)

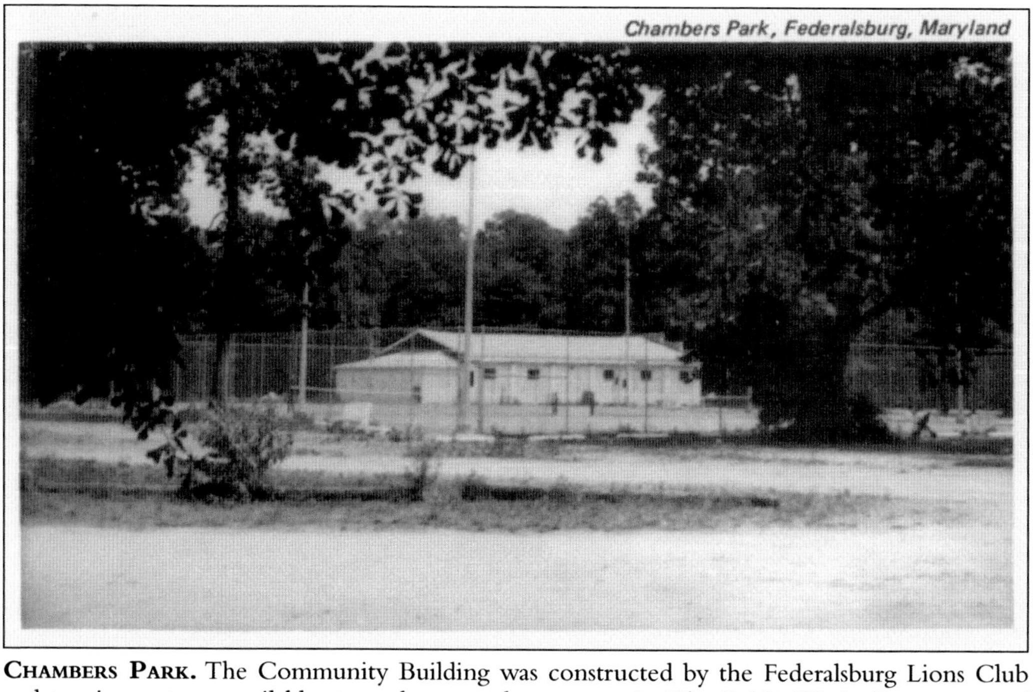

CHAMBERS PARK. The Community Building was constructed by the Federalsburg Lions Club and tennis courts are available at no charge to the community. The Public Works Department of the town maintains the park and all of its facilities. (From the Danny Phillips collection.)

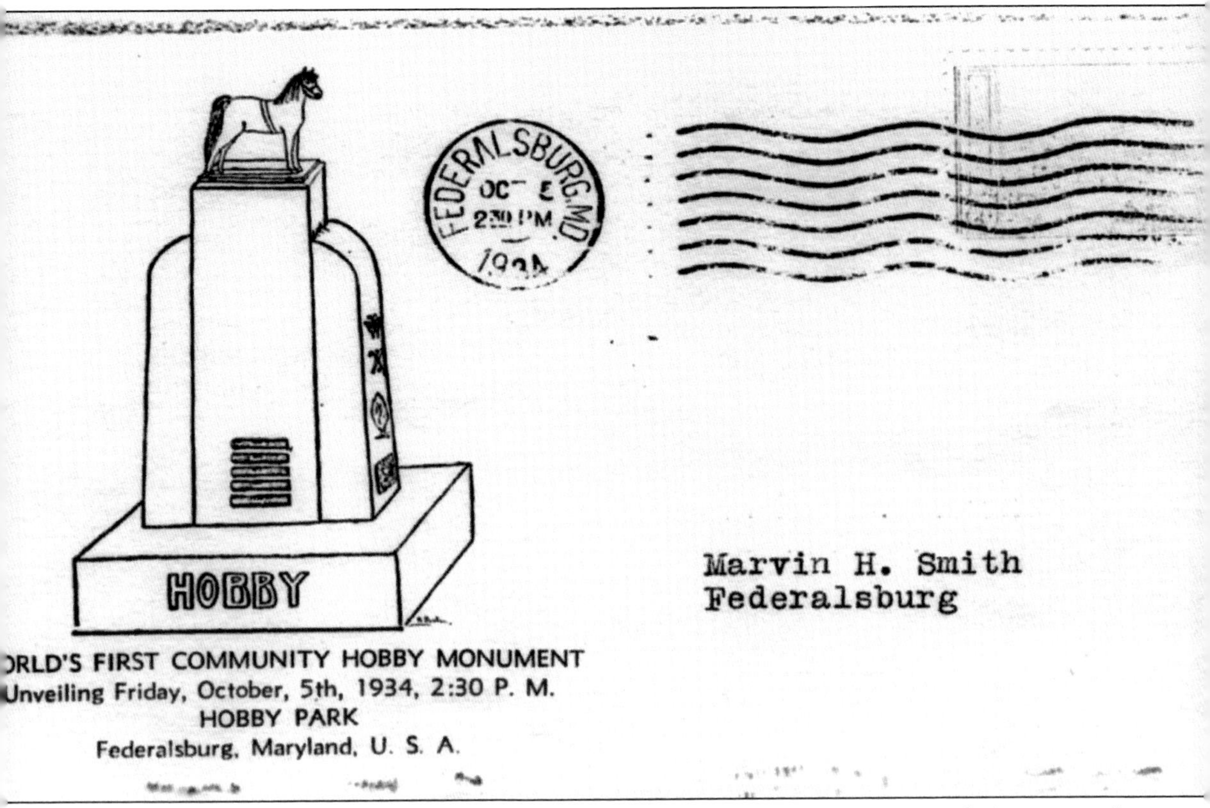

CACHET. This is not a postcard but what is known as a cachet, a commemorative design stamped on an envelope that marks a postal or philatelic event. It was issued as an outgrowth of the Hobby Fairs, which took place in Federalsburg from December of 1930 until the last one in 1937. The largest one was celebrated on October 5, 1934 when the Hobby Monument was dedicated by Albert C. Ritchie, who was governor of Maryland at that time. The cachet shows the image of the Hobby Monument, which is located today behind Federalsburg Elementary School. With prior arrangements, your name and address could appear on the envelope and on the date of the issue you would receive the post office cancellation for that date. This envelope was addressed to Marvin H. Smith, who was judged the grand-prize winner in 1932 for his stamp collection exhibit. One of Federalsburg's outstanding and historically knowledgable citizens, Judge Marvin H. Smith served on the Maryland Court of Appeals from May 1968 to August 1986. (From the Federalsburg Historical Society collection.)

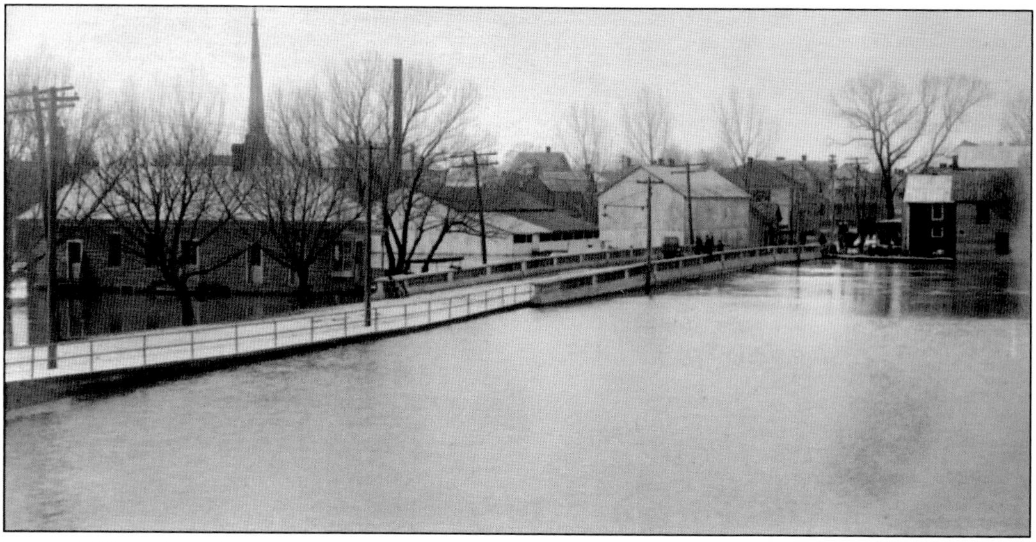

FLOOD! There have been numerous floods that caused damage in Federalsburg. The memorable ones were on September 23–24, 1876; May 30–June 1, 1889; August 13–14, 1919; August 23, 1933; September 4–6, 1935; August 1958; August 1967; February 1979; and September 16, 1999 (Hurricane Floyd). Most floods were caused by heavy rains. The greatest flood of record was caused by a hurricane that traveled up from the Florida Keys and headed out to sea through Maryland. It occurred in 1935 when the flood peak at Federalsburg reached a stage of 17.4 feet—five feet higher than any previous flood of record. A letter from the Chief of Engineers of the U.S. Army dated June 7, 1938 lists that 222 dwellings, 60 business establishments, 8 industries, and 4 churches in Federalsburg incurred damages. This photo is believed to have been taken during the 1919 flood where residents are looking at the rising waters of the Marshy Hope Creek from the East Central Avenue bridge. (From the R. Allan Gorsuch collection.)

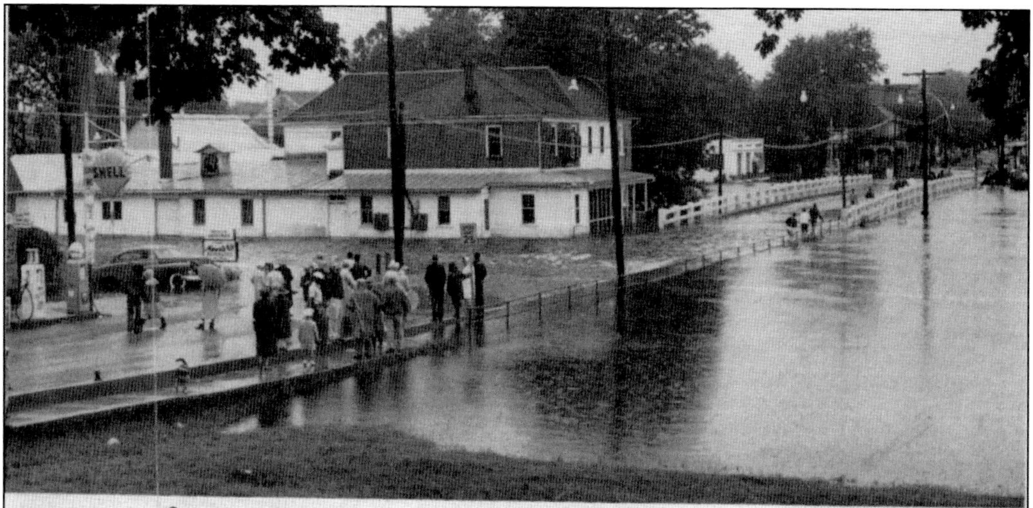

Spectators gather east of bridge as flood waters continue to rise.

FLOOD OF AUGUST 1958. This August 1958 photo shows a view of East Central Avenue looking west over the Marshy Hope Bridge, which is completely covered in water. Excessive rains caused a piece some 30 feet long and 15 feet wide to separate from the Smithville Dam, which spilled a head of water down on Federalsburg. (From the Charles S. Long collection.)

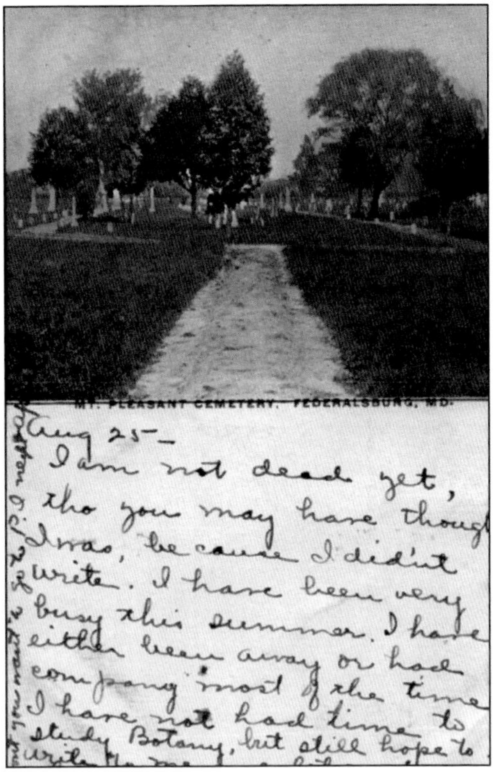

Mt. Pleasant Cemetery. On March 10, 1877, a deed was signed giving land to the Presbyterian Church of Federalsburg by the Rev. Elias L. Boring for the explicit use as a cemetery. The cemetery was called Mt. Pleasant. On October 27, 1890, the Mt. Pleasant Cemetery Co. was incorporated as a private cemetery and the name was later changed to Hillcrest Cemetery. The message makes an interesting comment regarding the photo, which was taken around 1904. (From the Charles S. Long collection.)

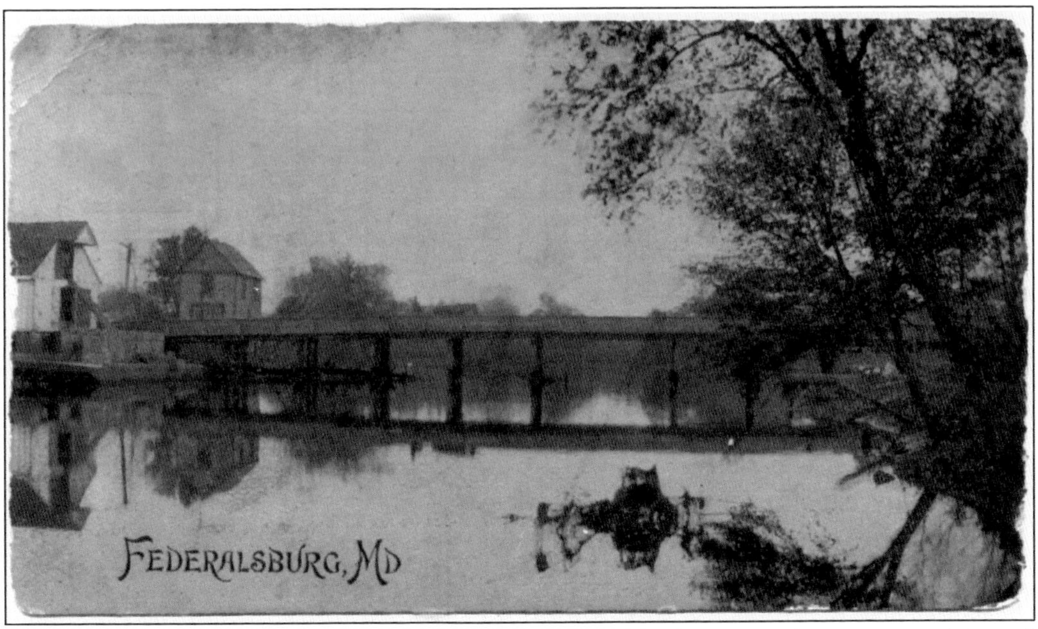

Marshy Hope Creek. The Marshy Hope Creek has lent itself to many photo opportunities and continues to do so today. This image was taken in the early 1900s after the original firehouse was built and before the old wooden bridge was replaced by the concrete bridge that remains today. (From the Charles S. Long collection.)

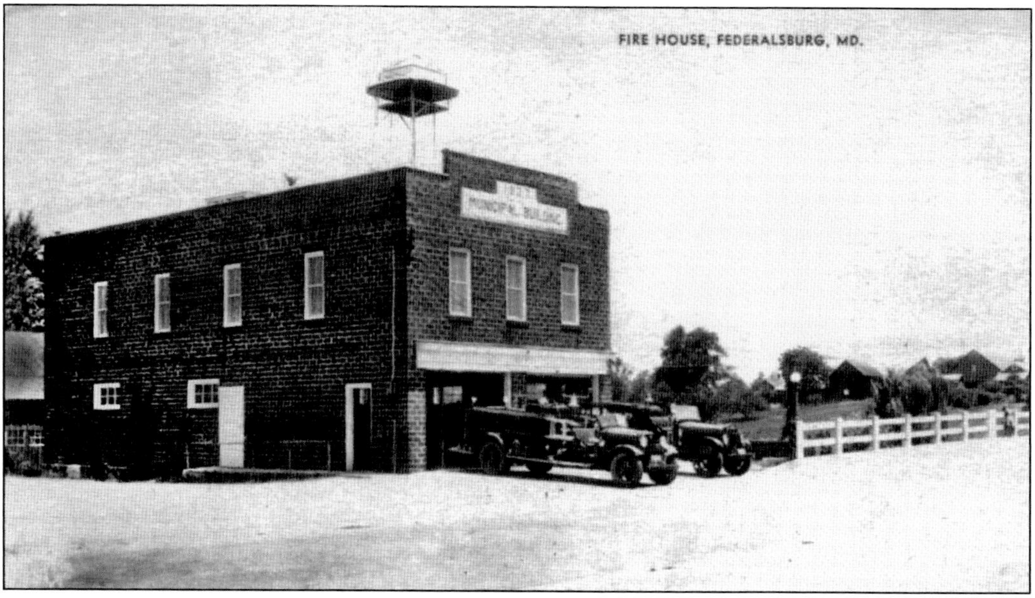

FEDERALSBURG VOLUNTEER FIRE COMPANY, INC. In 1926, a Howe Rescue Motorized Engine had been purchased and the organization officially became the Federalsburg Volunteer Fire Company, Inc. In 1927, the new brick Municipal Building was constructed on East Central Avenue, replacing the small wooden structure built in 1900 that had sheltered a chemical engine and several hundred feet of hose. (From the Danny Phillips collection.)

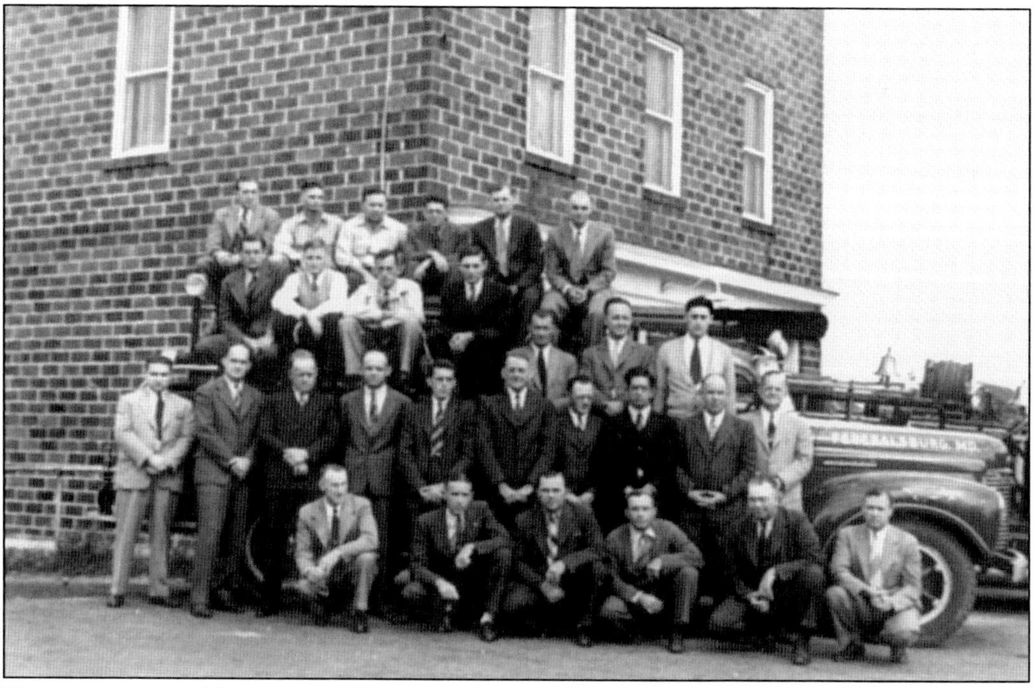

VOLUNTEER FIRE MEMBERS. In the 1920s there were 50 active volunteer members. This photo shows some of them in front of the firehouse and its two engines. First aid was provided beginning in 1934. (From the Danny Phillips collection.)

ROGERS C.B. MORTON. The Eastern Shore has produced many notable politicians, including Rogers C.B. Morton. This postcard was sent during a reelection campaign to a local resident. Notice the mailing address. Years ago, the roads outside of town were not referred to by names, but by rural route numbers. In 1962, Rogers C.B. Morton, who ran a cattle-finishing operation in Easton, ran for the Fifth District (which included Federalsburg) seat in the House of Representatives and won. He served on many congressional committees and in 1969 he gave up all of his committee seats to sit on the powerful Ways and Means Committee. In November 1970, he resigned his congressional seat to take the position of Secretary of the Interior under the Nixon Administration. Later he served a short term as Secretary of Commerce. Morton retired from public life in 1977 and returned to Pres'quile, his home in Easton. He died at his home in 1979. (From the Carlene Schmick collection.)

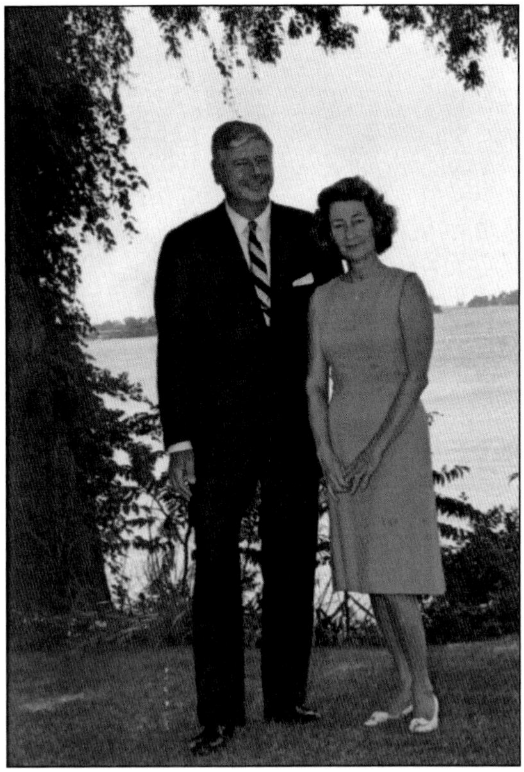

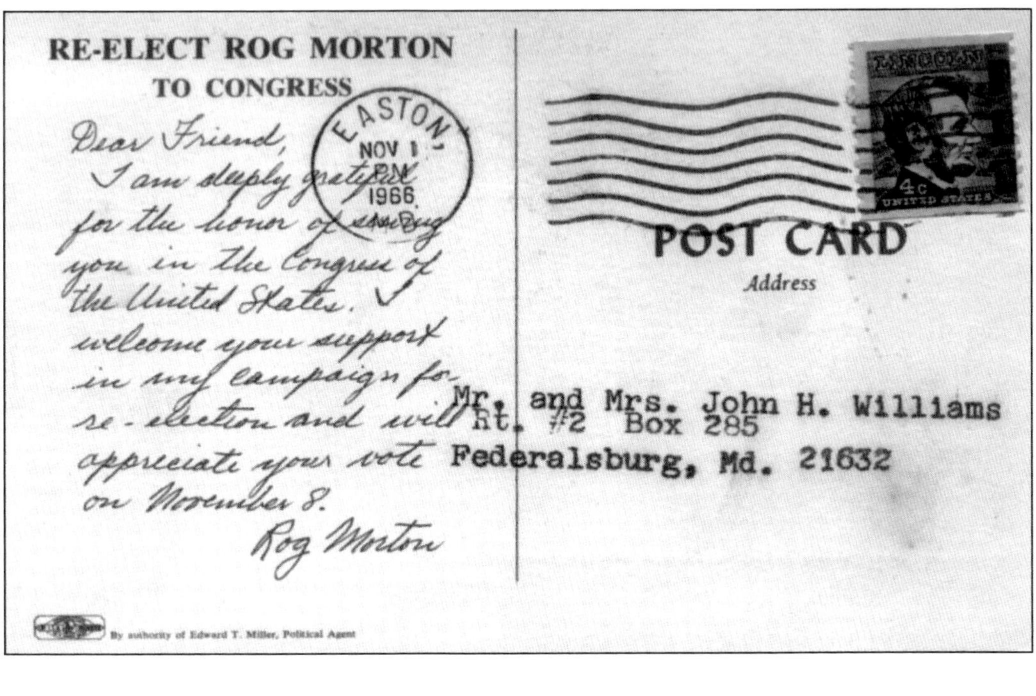

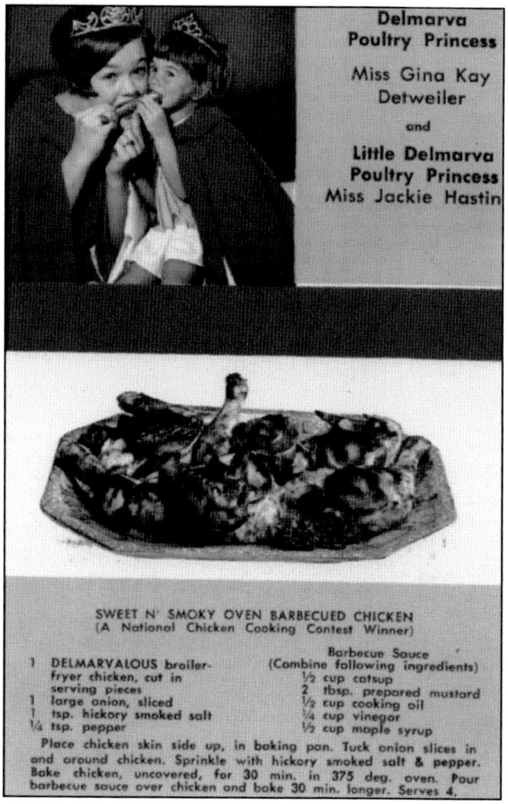

Delmarva Poultry Princess and Little Miss Delmarva. This postcard was distributed at various locations throughout the Eastern Shore promoting the poultry industry. Pictured is 17-year old Gina Kay Detweiler, daughter of Mr. and Mrs. Robert S. Detweiler of Federalsburg. She was crowned Delmarva Poultry Princess at the 20th Annual Delmarva Chicken Festival held June 21, 1967 in Dover, Delaware. Little Miss Delmarva was three-year-old Jacqueline Dawn Hastings, daughter of Mr. and Mrs. John H. Hastings of Laurel, Delaware. Miss Detweiler later wed Dufferin R. McConnell, owner of M&M Refrigeration, located in what was formerly the local chicken processing plant in Federalsburg. They have two daughters, Leslie ofVirginia Beach, Virginia, and Molly of Baltimore, Maryland. (From the Robert S. Detweiler collection.)

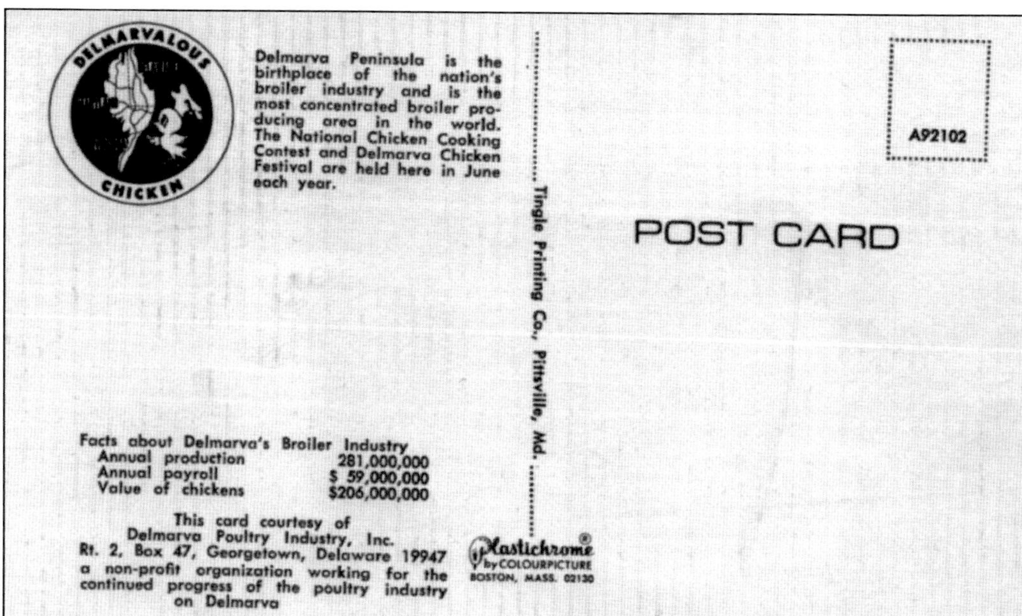

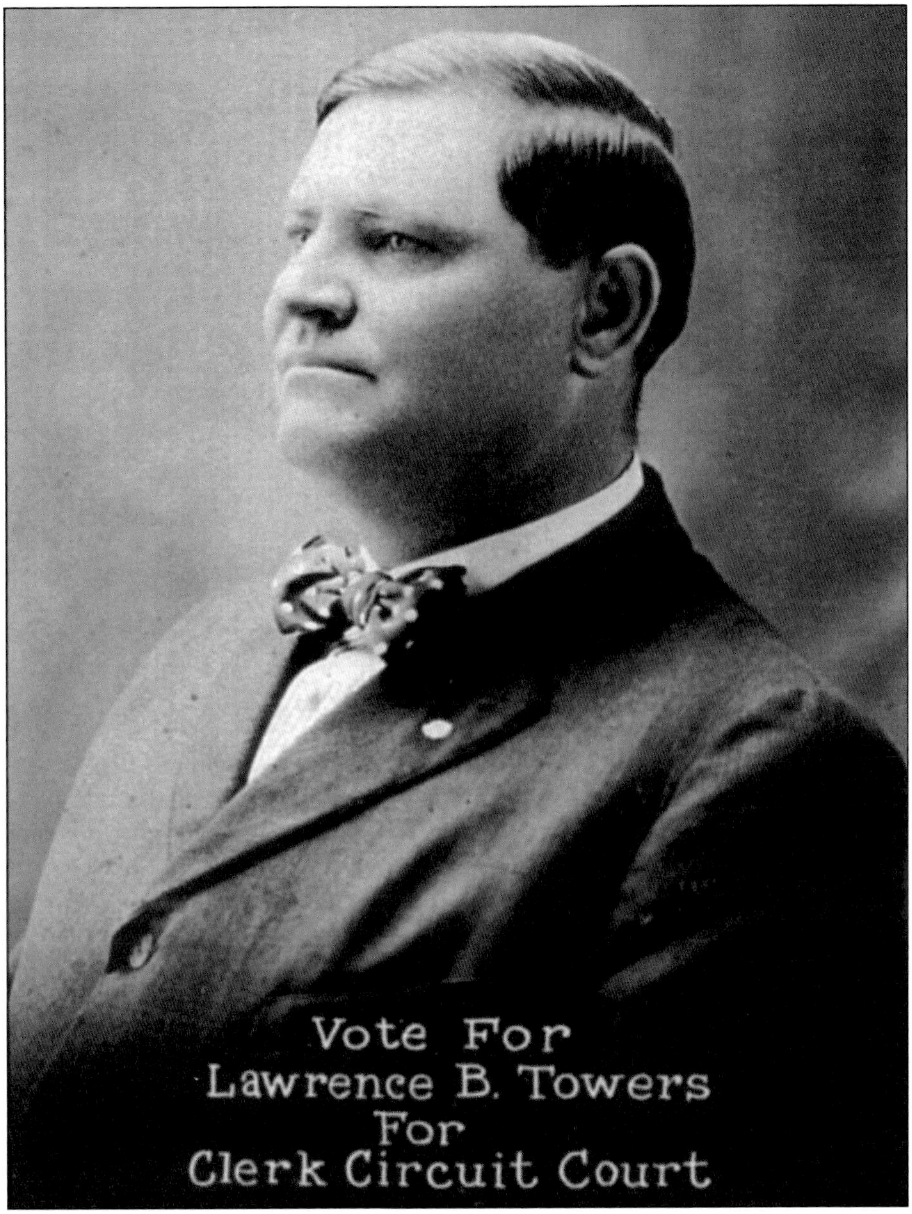

LAWRENCE B. TOWERS. This was an early campaign postcard for Lawrence B Towers of Denton to a Federalsburg resident. Contrary to the text, his obituary in February 1934 read, "He was prominent in Republican party politics, serving as chairman of the Caroline County Republican Committee for years, and also serving as a member of the State Committee. He was Clerk of the Circuit Court for Caroline county for six years, 1915–1921, and was elected to the State Senate in 1921 when he defeated M. Bates Stephens, the Democratic candidate. Thereafter, he was frequently discussed as a possible candidate for Congress or the Governorship. In 1926 he opposed Representative T. Alan Goldsborough, but was defeated. He was one of the electors in 1928 when Hoover was elected President of the United States and in 1931 was appointed Collector of the Port of Baltimore, which post he resigned last year [sic]." (From the Danny Phillips collection.)

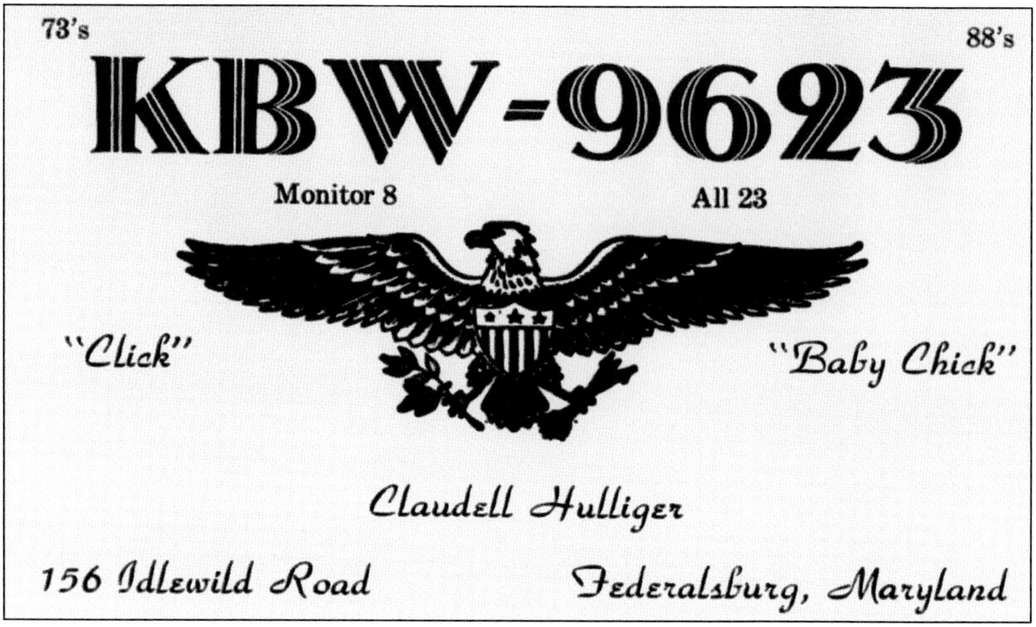

FOR CLAUDELL HULLIGER. This postcard was sent to other ham radio operators with the call numbers for Claudell Hulliger. (From the Danny Phillips collection.)

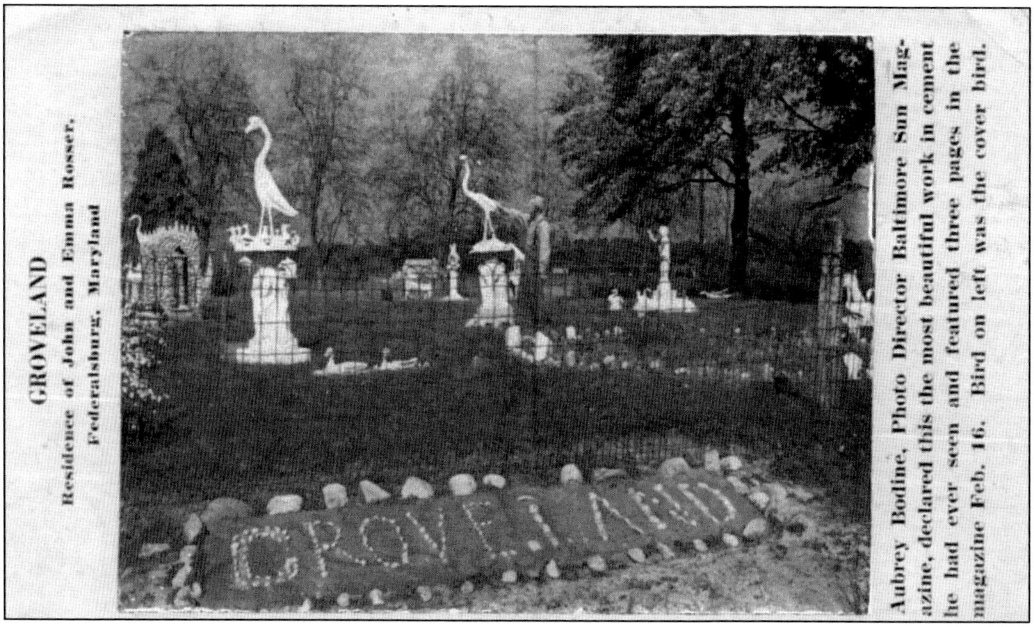

AUBREY BODINE AND JOHN ROSSER. Aubrey Bodine, a renowned photographer for the *Baltimore Sun* Magazine, did the supplement described on the right side of the postcard in 1947. John Rosser, a retired farmer born in 1867, created beautiful cement statues for his yard. He turned to sculpturing at the age of 72. He was also described in the supplement "as an orator, poet, philosopher, evangelist, inventor and raconteur extraordinary." (From the R. Allan Gorsuch collection.)

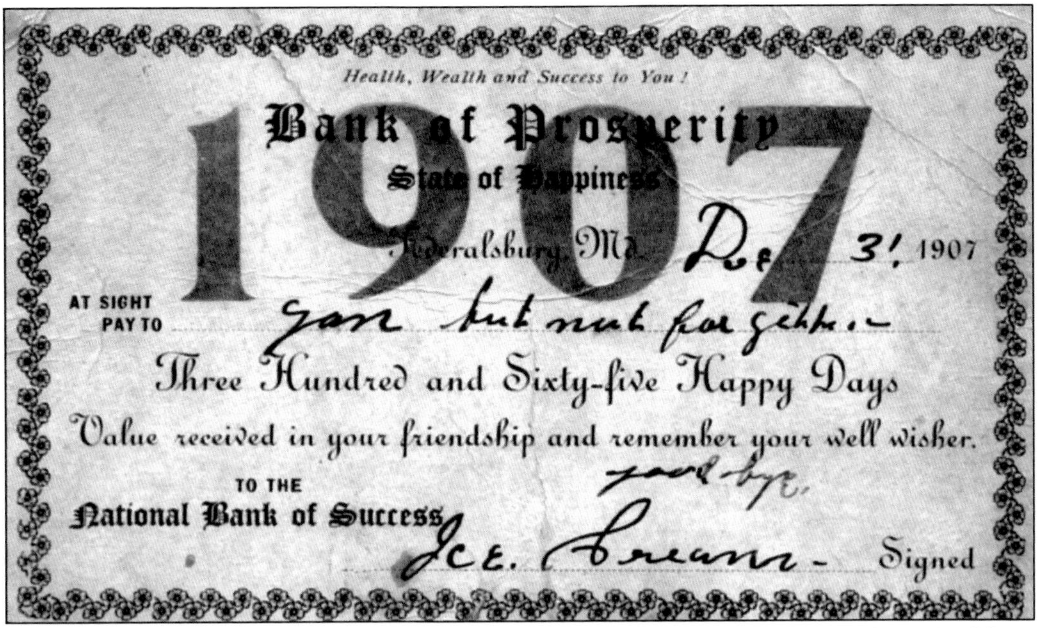

NOVELTY POSTCARDS. While we reviewed numerous novelty postcards printed with "Federalsburg MD," we liked these two particularly. We hope this collection of postcards has enlightened and entertained the reader. (From the Danny Phillips collection.)

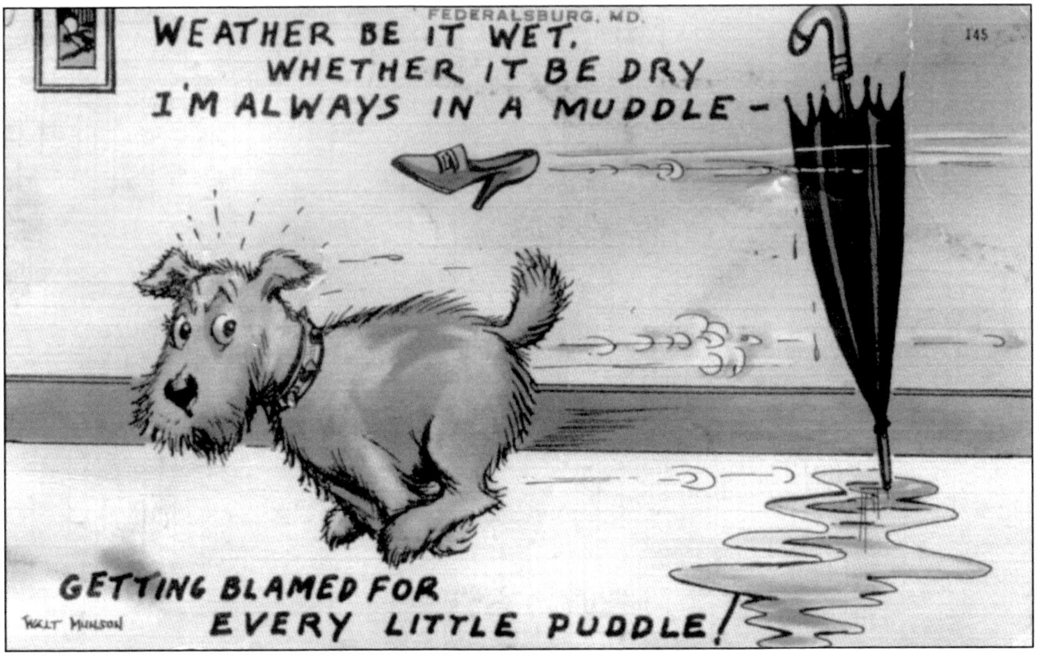

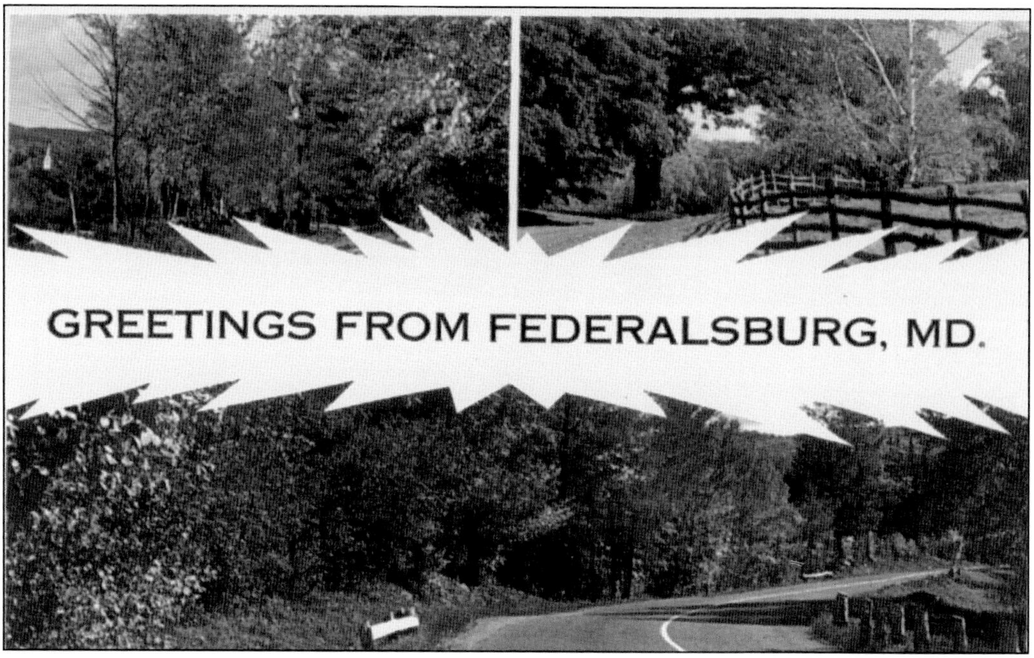

NOVELTY POSTCARDS. Here are more novelty postcards sent from Federalsburg. (From the Danny Phillips collection.)

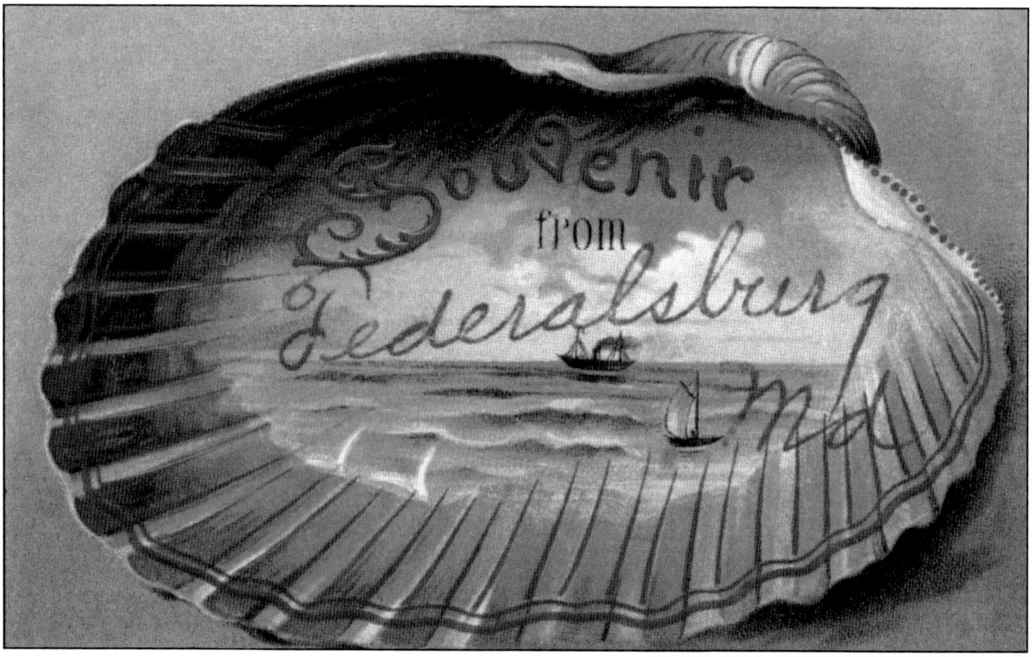

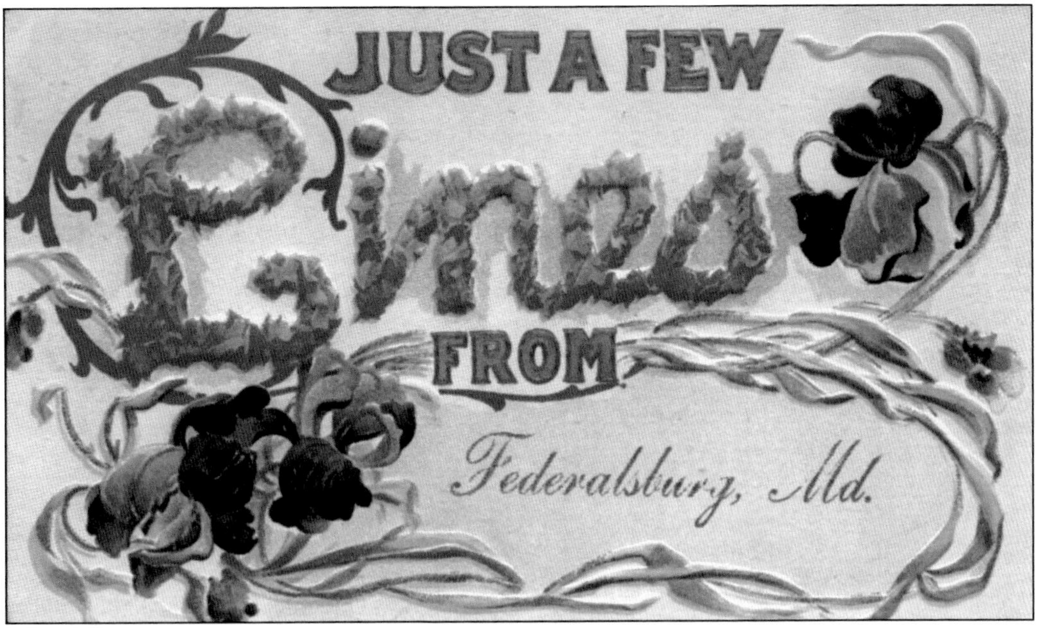

FINAL GREETINGS FROM FEDERALSBURG. (From the Danny Phillips collection.)

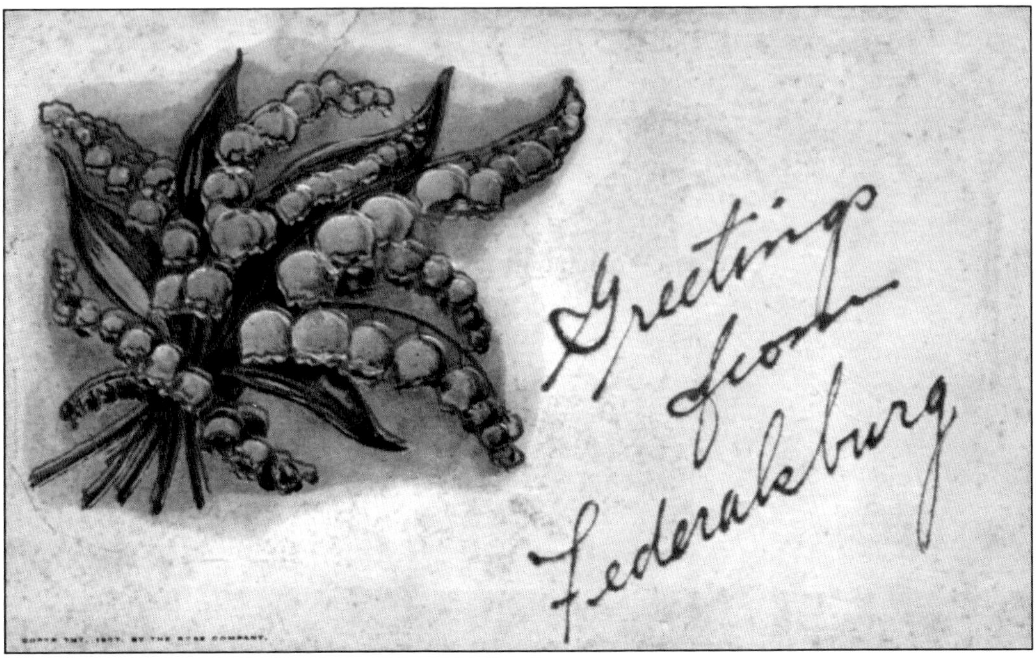

SELECTED BIBLIOGRAPHY

Charles, J. Raymond. *1932 An Historical Souvenir of Federalsburg.* Federalsburg, Maryland: J.W. Stowell Printing Co., 1932.

Davis, Noble and Kinder Families, *Davis Noble and Kinder Reunions 1930, 1935, 1940.* Federalsburg, Maryland: J.W. Stowell Printing Co., September 1941.

Employees of the Excelsior Pearl Works, Inc. *The Button Duster, Vol. I No. 1.* Federalsburg, Maryland: *The Federalsburg Times*, August 1939.

Federalsburg Improvement Company. *1804–1904 Historical Souvenir Book Federalsburg.* Federalsburg, Maryland: J.W. Stowell Printing Co., 1904.

Federalsburg Volunteer Fire Company Program. *100th Anniversary Celebration Federalsburg Vol. Fire Co. 1900–2000.* Federalsburg, Maryland: October 14, 2000.

First Church of God Program. *1895–1970 75th Anniversary of First Church of God.* Federalsburg, Maryland, 1970.

Hallman, E.C. *The History of Union Methodist Church.* Federalsburg, Maryland: Union Methodist Church, 1947.

Horsey, Eleanor. *Origins of Caroline County, Maryland From Land Plats Vol. II.* Denton, Maryland: Baker Printing Company, 1981.

Jensen, Christian E., M.D. *Lives of Caroline County Maryland Physicians 1774–1984.* Denton, Maryland: Baker Printing Company, 1986.

Material Largely Contributed by the Teachers and Children of the County. *The History of Caroline County Maryland From Its Beginning.* Federalsburg, Maryland: J.W. Stowell Printing Co., 1920.

Merriken, Ellenor R. *Herring Hill.* Denton, Maryland: Baker Printing Company, 1969.

Roth, Hal. *You Still Can't Get to Puckum.* Vienna, Maryland: Nanticoke Books, 2000.

Schmick, William G. *Tanyard Trace A History of Tanyard Branch and Liberty Road.* Federalsburg, Maryland, 1993.

Upper Shore Genealogical Society of Maryland. *Beneath These Stones, Cemeteries of Caroline County Vol. III.* Decorah, Iowa: Anundsen Publishing Co., 1985.